Sir Rawson William Rawson

Sequel to Synopsis of the Tariffs and Trade of the British Empire

Prepared, and presented to the Commercial Committee of the Imperial Federation

League

Sir Rawson William Rawson

Sequel to Synopsis of the Tariffs and Trade of the British Empire
Prepared, and presented to the Commercial Committee of the Imperial Federation League

ISBN/EAN: 9783337175443

Printed in Europe, USA, Canada, Australia, Japan

Cover: Foto ©Suzi / pixelio.de

More available books at **www.hansebooks.com**

SEQUEL TO SYNOPSIS

OF THE

TARIFFS AND TRADE

OF THE

BRITISH EMPIRE.

PREPARED, AND PRESENTED TO
THE COMMERCIAL COMMITTEE OF THE
IMPERIAL FEDERATION LEAGUE,
BY ITS CHAIRMAN,
SIR RAWSON W. RAWSON, K.C.M.G., C.B.

PRINTED BY ORDER OF THE EXECUTIVE COMMITTEE, AND
PUBLISHED AT THE OFFICE OF THE IMPERIAL FEDERATION LEAGUE,
30, *Charles Street, Berkeley Square, London, W.*

1889.

PREFACE.

As this work has assumed a form and dimensions which were not anticipated when it was commenced, the Author may be permitted to offer two or three remarks upon its completion.

He would deprecate any unfavourable criticism upon its construction, or upon the choice of periods or years made for observation, upon which improvements might have been introduced, if so large a development of the subject had been contemplated at the beginning. Especially he would claim indulgence for any disarrangement of the order of his statements caused by the interpolation of the discussion relating to the Export trade in coal.

He would point out that he has purposely abstained from putting forward opinions, though he may have sometimes indicated conclusions, bearing upon controversial points, lest they should create an imputation of bias in making the numerous calculations and comparisons, which have been prepared solely for the information and use of the Committee of the League and the public. In this he hopes he has succeeded, as the reception of the first part of the work has shown that the information contained in it has been adduced in support of exactly opposite views upon the main points which the statements were intended to elucidate.

The Author desires to express his grateful acknowledgments to Her Majesty's Secretary of State for the Colonies for having referred the first part to many of the Colonial Governments for their observations and correction of figures, in a despatch of which a copy is annexed. These have been noted in the memorandum of corrections and additions placed in the appendix.

The encouragement of the Commercial Committee of the Imperial Federation League, and the liberality of the Council of that body in undertaking the heavy expense of publication, have stimulated the Author to endeavour to make an adequate return for such generous support. To the Council the public are altogether indebted for the information contained in this work ; and it will be a disappointment if they are not eventually reimbursed their expenditure by a satisfactory addition to the members of the League, if not by the sale of the limited edition of the publication.

P.S.—The delay which has occurred in the publication of this volume has afforded an opportunity, within ten days of the close of the year, of adding the chief results of an examination of the trade of the year, 1888, compared with those for 1887, and of thus demonstrating the usefulness of the method suggested by the author.

		1887.	1888.	Percentage Increase.
Total Imports—				
Total tonnage	Milln. tons	26·0	27·1	4·2
,, value	,, £	361·0	386·0	6·8
Average value per register ton....	£	13·9	14·3	2·1
Total Exports—				
Total tonnage	Milln. tons	30·2	31·7	5·0
,, value	,, £	280·0	298·0	6·4
Average value per register ton....	£	9·3	9·4	1·0
Exports, exclusive of coal —				
Tonnage	Milln. tons	13·7	13·7	nil
Value	,, £	270·0	287·0	6·3
Average value per register ton....	£	19·8	20·9	5·5

R. W. R.

12th January, 1889.

SUMMARY OF CONTENTS.

Part III.—Trade of the United Kingdom, 1854-88.

Part III.—MARITIME TRADE OF THE UNITED KINGDOM, 1854-88.

Introductory.

It is proposed in the following pages to examine the progress of trade in the United Kingdom and in the British Empire respectively, during a series of years ending in 1886-87. In the first half of this work* a description was given of the existing tariffs in all parts of the Empire, and of their operation and financial results, with an abstract of the trade (Imports and Exports) of each part, and of the whole, of the Empire in the year 1885. The present review will extend, as regards the United Kingdom, over a period of thirty-four years, from 1854 to 1888, during which only the computed or declared values, both of Imports and Exports, have been recorded, and will be carried still further back as far as Exports are concerned. As regards the Empire the review will be less extensive, but will comprise a period of fifteen years, from 1872 to 1886, which is sufficiently long to furnish a fair view of the progress of commerce in India and the Colonies, and the means of comparison with that of the United Kingdom in the corresponding years. A chapter will be devoted to an examination of the character and nationality of the shipping employed in the commerce of the United Kingdom, and of the several British possessions at different recent periods.

Before proceeding further it is necessary to recall the observations already made† with regard to the caution to be observed in dealing with official returns of Imports and Exports, and especially in comparing the value of either in one year with that in another. Mr. Giffen has conclusively shown, in the reports already referred‡ to, that while the returns exhibit with sufficient accuracy for all practical purposes the aggregate value of merchandise imported or exported in each year, according to the current prices of the year, they do not show the volume of such merchandise, or the corresponding amount of business transacted from one year to another, because a general, or even an extensive partial rise or fall in prices will affect the aggregate value, perhaps in direct opposition to the aggregate volume of trade. The quantity, or volume, may increase, but a fall in price may cause a decrease in the aggregate value, and there will be an apparent falling off in the trade, although the contrary is the fact ; or a rise in price may counterbalance and conceal an actual decrease in the volume of trade.

* Published by the Imperial Federation League in March last.
† Part 1, pp. 39—46.   ‡ Ibid., p. 40.

B

Cap. 1.—Methods of Ascertaining the Volume of Trade, and Changes in the Prices of Imports and Exports.

§ 1.—Mr. Giffen's Method: Index Numbers.

There can of course be no direct method of accurately measuring the volume of trade, composed of such an infinite number of articles, and recorded in quantities of so many various denominations. If it were possible to bring them to a common denomination, the result would not repay the labour of computation.* But indirect methods may be found of arriving at a satisfactory process of comparing one year with another—of measuring the volume of trade, Imports and Exports separately, and of ascertaining whether changes in their aggregate value are caused by an increase or decrease in the volume of merchandise, or by a rise or fall in the prices of commodities.

Mr. Giffen has adopted, and partially applied, one method in the valuable series of Reports above referred to. These are prepared with special reference to the question of the effect of changes in price upon the aggregate value of Imports and Exports, and thence of determining what changes, if any, may have occurred in the volume of the Import and Export trades. It will help to explain the method, if some account be given of the materials which were at Mr. Giffen's command, of the use which he has made of them, and of the valuable results of which so much use has been made in the following pages.

The "Statistical Abstract" of the United Kingdom, published annually by the Board of Trade, contains two series of tables: 1°. of the quantities and declared value of the principal articles of Colonial and Foreign merchandise imported, and of the produce and manufactures of the United Kingdom exported; and 2°. of the average declared price of each of those articles, deduced from the declarations of quantities and value.

* It has been suggested that as a majority of the articles are estimated by weight, all these might be reduced to a common denomination, say tons, and that most, if not all other articles, even liquids, might be measured by weight, or their equivalent in weight, and by this means a measure of total quantity might be obtained. But independently of the trouble which such a calculation of millions of transactions would cause either to traders or officials, there could be no possible advantage in bringing into a common aggregate of weight things, e.g., so dissimilar as coals and diamonds, metal and feathers, wine and wood. If it were practicable, there might be some advantage in this method if it would indicate the tonnage of shipping to which employment is given; but a ton in weight is not a ton in bulk for shipping purposes, and while a knowledge of the total weight of all Imports and Exports would be without value, it is probable that the recorded tonnage of vessels entering and clearing with cargoes affords information quite as useful as that of the approximate aggregate bulk of all imports and exports, if it were possible to compute the latter.

The number of articles thus specified is about 120 of Imports and 70 of Exports. There has been little variation in the number of these articles during the last thirty years, but it will be instructive to examine further on those which have dropped out, and those which have been added to the category of "principal" commodities.* The proportion which the value of these articles bore to the total values at the extreme ends of the period was as follows:—

		Value of Enumerated Articles.		
In 1854.	Imports........	91·1 per cent.	Exports........	95·0 per cent.
„ 1886.	„	92·3 „	„	95·0 „

In only two years, viz., 1866-67, has the proportion of such Imports fallen below 90 per cent., and of Exports it only once fell to 94 per cent., viz., in 1871. The "principal" articles, therefore, as enumerated in the "Statistical Abstracts," fairly represent the mass of trade.

But among them is a number of which the value only is given, as the quantities cannot be stated in a convenient form, or for any useful purpose. The proportion of these has increased considerably during the period under review. Thus the proportionate value of enumerated articles of which the quantities are not stated to the total amount was—

Of Imports in 1854.......	2·5 per cent.	Of Exports........	22·5 per cent.
„ '86........	10·7 „	„	26·2 „

The proportion of the total value which was unavailable for the estimation of the change of prices according to Mr. Giffen's method was, as stated in his last report—

Of Imports in 1854........	11·9 per cent.	In 1886........	21·4 per cent.†
„ Exports „	31·1 „	„	39·0† „

From these materials Mr. Giffen has compiled a series of tables, of which the first shows the average price in each year of each principal article of which both the quantities and value are stated. These he calls "enumerated," and the rest "unenumerated."‡ In

---

* See p. 47.

† The difference between these figures and those resulting from the preceding statements, which are 18·4 and 31·2, arises from Mr. Giffen's figures belonging to a series spread over a number of years, in which it was necessary to include only articles that could be shown for the whole period.

‡ These terms, used in Mr. Giffen's tables without any qualification, and adopted by Mr. Bourne without remark, are apt to mislead, as in Customs and common parlance the term "enumerated" is applied to all the "principal" articles specified by name, whether both the quantities and value, or only the value be recorded, and the term "unenumerated" is applied to the smaller class of "all other articles" which are not enumerated or specified by name, and of which no separate record is published. But the above distinction in the use of the terms must be borne in mind. The insertion of the particle "herein," or of some equivalent, would have prevented any mistake.

his first Report, laid before Parliament in 1879,* the calculations were confined to Exports of the produce and manufactures of the United Kingdom, and to certain years, ten in number, between 1861 and 1877. In the subsequent reports† they have been extended to Imports also, and in the last two they have been carried back to 1854 for Imports, and to 1840 for Exports, and forward to 1886 for both. The number of articles embraced in the latest report was 115 of Imports, and 67 of Exports.

The second table shows the percentage proportion which the value of each "enumerated" article bears to the total value in the same years. Upon this table Mr. Giffen has based his index number, the method of obtaining which is explained in the first Report in the following terms: "I have first tried to obtain a suitable index "number for the entire articles constituting our export trade, so "far as they are separately enumerated in the Abstract, and where "quantities and values are given; and taking the prices of 1861 "as a basis, I have tried to show how much the index number has "been made to vary in certain years by changes in the price of "each constituent of the number. To get the index number my "plan has been to ascertain the percentage proportion of the value "of the exports of each enumerated article to the value of the whole "export trade in alternate years since 1861, and to add the propor- "tions for each year together" (p. 5). He has taken the prices of the articles in 1861 as the standard with which to compare the prices of the articles in other years, and the percentages which the enumerated articles in 1875 bore to the total value of the Imports and Exports in that year as the index number for the Import and Export trades respectively.

To illustrate this explanation, Table II of his series shows that the percentage proportion which the first article, alkali, contributed to the total of the year 1875 was 1·0; lower down cotton plain piece goods contributed 14·9; the total of specified articles amounted to 73·1, which is the index number of that year. The proportion of unenumerated articles amounted to 26·9 per cent.

Some readers may desire to know what an index number means. As here employed, in ascertaining fluctuations in the prices of commodities and in the volume of trade, it signifies a ratio, or proportional number, derived from the aggregate of the average wholesale prices of a large number of the principal articles of commerce, compared with a standard, or unit, obtained at some former time in precisely the same manner. It may be derived from Exports or Imports alone, or from both combined,—from

* Parl. paper C-2247.
† Ibid., C-2484 of 1880; C-3079 of 1881; C-4456 of 1885; C-5386 of 1888.

foreign or home products, or both combined, according to the nature of the information desired.

The next step in the process is to compare the price of each article in the years under observation with the price in 1861, and to show the percentage differences, thus indicating the increase or decrease in each year compared with 1861. This is shown in the first part of Mr. Giffen's Table III.

Then these differences, based upon the variations from the standard year of prices 1861, are applied to the relative proportions which each article bore to the total exports of the standard year of quantity, 1875, and the aggregate of the results yields the figure by which the index number of 1875 is to be increased or decreased. This calculation is shown in the second part of Table III.

The whole of the operation may be described by an example. The average price of a horse was according to Table I £80·51 in 1861, and £42·13 in 1865, which by Table III, Part A, is a fall of 47·67 per cent.; but as horses constitute only 0·1 per cent. of the total Exports in the standard year of quantity (1875) the proportionate decrease, calculated on the relative importance of horses to the whole Export, is only 0·05; while the proportion of the aggregate of specified articles in the same year showed an increase of 22·71 per cent., by which figures the index number of 1875 (73·1) has to be increased and thus raised to 95·81, in order to show the difference of total value between the years 1861 and 1865, "irrespective of any decrease in the quantities of trade," which, however, is a most important factor in the calculation.

" In other words, if the index number is a fair one, and if the " articles unenumerated or not entered by quantities have been " subject to similar variations of price, the value of the Exports of " 1865 . . . in comparison with a year like 1861 would fall to be " reduced by 25 per cent. or more. The Exports of British and " Irish produce in . . . 1865 being £165,836,000, a reduction of " 25 per cent., would bring them down to . . . about £125 millions, " in which case they would show a much less increase on 1861 than " they now do." (p. 5). In fact, the Exports of 1861 amounted to almost exactly £125 millions.

Further calculations are required to ascertain from the last result the difference either in volume or price in any given year or series of years. Mr. Giffen does not supply information on either point for a consecutive period, but he gives various illustrations of his method, especially by contrasting the results of its application to years of extreme inflation and depression.

It is unnecessary to carry the description further, but the following remarks may not be misplaced. The method, which is admirable for its ingenuity, is not easily understood, and tho processes are complicated, and require an immense and deterrent amount of computation. The materials also are not available for many months after the expiration of each year. The tables embrace all the Imports, but only Exports of the Produce and Manufactures of the United Kingdom, omitting the Exports of Colonial and Foreign Produce, which amounted in 1886 to £56 millions, or 20·9 per cent. of the whole Exports, upon the assumption that the prices upon exportation are generally governed by those on importation.* The transhipments also, which in the same year amounted to £10·7 millions more, are not included. It may be a question whether, as is assumed, it is a matter of indifference what year is chosen for the basis of quantity, or whether the average can be safely applied to distant years. The years 1861 and 1875 have been taken apparently without reference to their character. The former, which was the standard of prices, was one of depression and low prices of Exports. It is alleged that it does not signify materially which index number of all the years under observation is taken, although it is shown that in the years quoted as an illustration† it does make a difference of 6 to 8 per cent. It is assumed in the composition of the index number that the prices of the unspecified articles, forming one-fifth of the whole Imports and two-fifths of the whole Exports in 1886, will follow in the same direction, and to the same extent, those of the three-fifths or four-fifths on which the index number is calculated. Some information on this point will be furnished in the following pages, which tends to invalidate the assumption.‡ The plan, adopted in order to reduce the labour of computation, of furnishing the calculations only for alternate years, or with longer intervals of omission, some of which are of importance, *e.g.*, the years of inflation 1863-4, disappoints the reader by failing to give a continuous view of the trade, or of the relation of each year to its neighbours. It must further be noted and borne in mind that the standard index number for Exports of 1875 has been changed in the last two reports from 73·1, at which it stood in the preceding reports, to 65·8. The reason for this is that in carrying the inquiry several years further back, it has become necessary, for the purpose of fair comparison, to omit a few articles of which the record does not extend over the whole period. It is not claimed for this method that it furnishes more than an approximation to the truth, and an indication of the direction and amount of the variations in prices, novel in its conception, and of indisputable value, if no more simple and equally reliable method can be employed.

* This point has been investigated at p. 65.
† 1875 and 1861 compared with 1873 at p. 6 of Report of 1879.
‡ See pp. 9 and 51.

§ 2. *Mr. Stephen Bourne's method : Index Numbers.*

Another method, based upon the same data, viz., the declared quantities and value of Imports and Exports, has been proposed by Mr. Bourne in two papers which he read before the British Association at its meetings in 1885 and the present year.   Mr. Bourne has scarcely done justice to his method in his manner of presenting and explaining it, or in his exposition of the value of the results to be derived from the use of it, inasmuch as he has limited the latter to a comparison of the annual aggregates of the value and volume, to which also Mr. Giffen's comparisons are confined, and to a comparative abstract of the results as they affect the principal classes of Exports of British produce and manufactures.   He does not deal with Imports, but his method is equally applicable to them, and it possesses certain distinct and important advantages.

It is simple and easily understood.   He adopts 1883, the first of his series, as a convenient standard year for both price and volume.   He makes 1,000 the unit of total value, and 1·0 the unit of the value, or price, of each of the articles capable of being so enumerated.   These units become common denominators for all the years of the series.   Changes in value are represented by an (percentage) increase or decrease of these figures.

He quotes the average prices from the " Statistical Abstracts," and the index number of each " enumerated " article from the Reports already referred to, p. 2.

The percentage differences in the price of each article and in the total value, in any year of the series compared with the standard year, is found by ordinary simple calculations.

The new index numbers of the value of each article are calculated upon the new total index number of values, and the corresponding index numbers of volume are found by dividing the new index numbers of value by the figures representing the changes in price.

The form of his examples is very convenient.   By the juxtaposition of the changes in the value (price) and in volume (quantity) of each of the enumerated articles, it can be seen at a glance what articles have produced, and to what extent they have contributed to, the change in the aggregates both of value and volume.   It presents also the cardinal advantage of basing the annual calculations upon the actual quantities and value of the year, instead of applying the quantities of a single year to a series of other years, which may differ immensely from the arbitrary standard in this material respect.   Mr. Bourne has pointed out very forcibly the wide opening for error, if not the impossibility of escape from it, in this stage of Mr. Giffen's process.*   Taking

* " Report of the British Association for the Year 1885," p. 868.

the important article of cotton yarn exported, he compares the actual proportions of the quantities and value in three years, taken from the "Statistical Abstracts," with the percentage changes on the standard of 1861, and the corresponding alterations of the index number for this article, as shown in Mr. Giffen's tables, with the following results, which cannot be reconciled with one another:—

	1865.	1875.	1883.
Actual proportions of quantity	104	216	265
„ „ value	10	13	14
Results in Mr. Giffen's tables — Percentage change on standard of 1861	+ 91·23	+ 16·91	− 2·31
Change of Index Number	+ 5·38	+ 1·00	− 0·14

The great value of Mr. Bourne's method may be seen in the following statements derived from the first table in his later paper, in which he compares the Exports of the produce and manufactures of the United Kingdom in the years 1883 and 1887.

He shows that while between these two years the volume of the total Exports had increased from his unit of 1,000* to 1,062, the value had decreased from 1,000 to 922.

Of the 65 articles of which both the quantities and value are annually specified, 26 had increased in volume

15   „   decreased   „
21   „   not changed
3 did not admit of comparison

The increase in these 65 had been greater than in the total Exports, viz., from 673 to 775, or 14·8 per cent., while in unenumerated articles it had been from 249 to 287, or only 11·2 per cent.

The information with regard to value, or price, is still more valuable to the commercial world. Out of the 65 articles, 12, representing 8·3 per cent. of the whole increase of quantity, had increased in price as follows:—

Per cent.
2 representing 0·9 of quantity had increased from 1·0 to 1·27 in price
2   „   0·7   „   „   1·11 and 1·12 in price
8   „   6·7   „   „   1·01 @ 1·08   „
——   ——
12   „   8·3

---

* Mr. Bourne demonstrates the several advantages of adopting this unit, in doing away with the use of the decimal point, and of the signs for *plus* and *minus*, and of establishing a common denominator for the comparison of different years. It would have been adopted in this paper, where practicable, if his suggestion had been noticed sooner.

But 51 out of the 65, representing 67·3 per cent. of the whole increase of quantity, had decreased in price as follows :—

Per cent.

15 representing 12·2 of quantity had decreased from 1·0 to ·90 @ ·99 in price

19	,,	42·8	,,	·	,,	·80	,, ·89	,,
13	,,	10·8	,,		,,	·70	,, ·79	,,
3	,,	1·5	,,		,,	·62	,, ·69	,,
3 not stated								

53   67·3

Of the above 12 which had increased in price only 4 had increased in volume also; of the 26 which had increased in volume all, with those four exceptions, had decreased in value.

The contrast between the above comparison and that shown by Mr. Bourne in his first paper between the years 1883 and 1884, which corresponds with the otherwise ascertained history of the two periods, corroborates the value of his method.

On the other hand his method is open to several of the remarks applied to Mr. Giffen's. It involves a large amount of calculation. The materials are at present only available, like Mr. Giffen's, some months after the close of the year; but this delay, it appears, might be easily curtailed. Mr. Bourne, like Mr. Giffen, deals only with Exports of the produce and manufactures of the United Kingdom. He too assumes that the value of the non-enumerated goods follows the same course as that of the enumerated, and " will give results agreeing with the index number method." But this assumption is not borne out by the figures already quoted from his first table, nor from those to be derived from his second table (of 1888), which show, as seen in the following calculation, that there is no relation as regards extent of rise and fall of prices between the principal classes of British Exports :—

Difference in Price compared with 1883.

	1884.	1885.	1886.	1887.
Textiles	1·4 —	8·4 —	5·4 —	3·3 —
Minerals	8·7 —	16·4 —	18·5 —	9·8 —
Other specified articles	1·0 —	3·0 +	1·0 —	1·0 —
Not enumerated ,,	2·0 —	13·6 —	19·4 —	15·3 —
Total	11·2 —	11·5 —	7·8 —	2·9 —

Notwithstanding these defects, some of which are irremediable, the information to be derived from the results of his method is so valuable, as will be more fully shown in another place,* that an effort should be made to give it to the public in as full a form and

* P. 55.

at as early a date as possible, as a supplement to that proposed in the present paper.

Other methods of estimating the variations in the prices of Imports and Exports by means of index numbers have been proposed by distinguished economists, and the subject is now under investigation by Committees of the British Association and the International Statistical Institute; but they all involve much labour in the collection and computation of data, and they do not take into account the recorded, and therefore available, factor of tonnage actually employed in the trade under examination.

§ 3. *Method of comparing Value with Tonnage.*

It is believed that a sound method of measuring fluctuations in the volume of maritime trade, and in the average value (or price) of the aggregates of Imports and Exports, can be proposed, of the simplest kind, based upon data furnished by the Board of Trade, not only annually but monthly, so that the monthly variations can be shown within seven days after the close of each month, and those of the year within the same period after the last day of it. It involves one simple calculation, and appears to be not inferior in its representation of the fluctuations in prices, while it possesses the advantage of taking into account at the same time the fluctuations in the amount of shipping with cargoes employed in the trade of the Kingdom.

This method consists in a comparison of the total declared value of Imports and Exports with the total registered tonnage of vessels entering and clearing with cargoes,—in simply dividing the total value by the total tonnage. If all the vessels entering into the computation filled up on each voyage, and if they carried nothing but merchandise, the tonnage, which represents roughly their capacity, would supply a factor by which to measure with indisputable accuracy the annual or monthly changes both in volume and value. But vessels do not all fill up, and they carry passengers as well as cargo. During the last thirty years also the character of vessels has greatly changed. Steamers have largely superseded sailing vessels, and the size of steamers and their capacity for stowage have been very greatly increased. The tonnage of large passenger steamers in the trade of the United Kingdom has immensely increased during the last few years.* It might therefore at first be assumed that these circumstances would hinder a fair comparison founded upon the above data. But it must be borne in mind that the fluctuations in the filling up of vessels

---

* Moreover any material change in the method of admeasuring vessels for the purpose of customs entry would disturb a comparison between different years, but there has been no such change since 1st May, 1855. The new method reduced the old measurement on an average by 7·3 per cent.

carrying cargoes (vessels in ballast not being taken into account) do not vary greatly from year to year; that the changes above indicated have been gradual; that the increase of passenger vessels has also been gradual; and above all, that the increased capacity of vessels to carry cargo, and improved methods of package and stowage, have served in some degree to counteract the effect of the increase of passenger traffic.

These suggested objections to the method are open to investigation.

The "Merchant Shipping" Tables presented annually to Parliament afford the means of testing the effect of the passenger traffic, and of the increased size of ships, upon the proposed computation, and they demonstrate beyond all dispute that whatever influence it may exercise is overwhelmed and extinguished by other agencies of greater force.

These tables* show the number and tonnage of ships cleared under the Passengers Acts in which passengers were carried out of the United Kingdom to countries beyond Europe in the years 1853 and 1855, and in each year from 1860 to 1887. The first year in which there was a considerable increase of such tonnage was 1863, when the rise amounted to 255,000 tons. But the average value per ton of Exports in that year, instead of falling, rose from £14·2 to £16·5. The next great rise in passenger tonnage was in 1872, amounting to 221,000 tons. The value per ton rose in that year from £14·9 to £16·3. But, as a contrast, in the preceding year the increase of passenger tonnage was only 80,000; the increase of general traffic was 2,300,000 tons, and the rise of value per ton was only from £14·6 to £14·9. Coming to a later period the increase of passenger tonnage in 1879 was 314,000 tons, and there was a decrease in value from £11·4 to £10·9; but the total increase of tonnage was 1,200,000 tons, to which the increase of passenger tonnage bore a proportion of only a fourth; and in the next year, when there was an increase of general tonnage amounting to 2,800,000 tons, the increase of passenger tonnage was only one-tenth, 275,000 tons, and there was a rise in value from £10·9 to £11·1. Lastly, in 1885, when there was a decrease in the passenger tonnage of 240,000 tons, and the general tonnage remained stationary, the value per ton fell from £10·1 to £9·3. The conclusion from these comparisons is irresistible.

If further confirmation be needed it may be found in the table of passenger traffic, No. XIX, inserted further on at p. 76, from which it appears that:—

1. The proportion of passenger tonnage to the total tonnage clearing with cargoes from the United Kingdom in the twenty-

* Parl. paper No. 198 of 4th June, 1888.

eight years from 1860 to 1887 averaged only 5·5 per cent., and it only once rose as high as 7·3 per cent., in which year (1881) the average value per ton of Exports, with considerable increase of the tonnage cleared, rose, instead of falling, from £11·1 to £11·3 per ton.

2. During the first of the two periods in which the proportion of passenger tonnage rose above the average to 6·2 and 6·3 respectively, viz., 1872-74 and 1879-87, there was a material rise in the average value from £14·9 to £15·9 per ton.

3. In the year 1885, when the passenger tonnage fell from 6·3 to 5·5 per cent., the average value, instead of rising, fell heavily from £10·1 to £9·3 per ton.

4. While the proportion of passenger to total tonnage in the three years 1880, 1884, and 1886 was exactly the same, viz., 6·3 per cent., the average value of Exports was respectively £11·8, £10·1, and £9·2.

5. Between 1860 and 1887 the increase in any one year of passenger tonnage only exceeded 1 per cent. on four occasions. This increase of 1 per cent. just equalled one-half per mille in the total tonnage, and is therefore scarcely appreciable.

As regards the influence of the increased size of vessels, the gradually and generally moderate character of this from year to year is shown in Table XX at p. 77. It has averaged annually on the twenty-six years 1860-87 only 16 tons per vessel. The highest increase, which occurred in 1881, was 36 tons, which was about 7 per cent. on the average size of 1880; but it appears to have been contemporaneous with a decrease in the number of vessels on the registry in that year, amounting to 3 per cent. In five other years it amounted to between 24 and 30 tons, and in four of these it was contemporaneous with a decrease in the number of vessels on the registry.

If it be objected that the passenger tonnage here taken into account does not include the whole of that engaged in the conveyance of emigrants beyond Europe, as shown in the Annual Returns of "Emigration and Immigration" annually laid before Parliament,[*] the reply is that this return does not show the tonnage employed, but that if the same proportion of tonnage be allowed for the additional number of emigrants shown in this return, the addition to be made on the average of twenty-seven years 1861-67 would only be 13·3 per cent. on 5·5 and 7·3 per cent. respectively, which would only increase those proportions to 6·2 and 8·2 respectively. In the last seven years the addition to be made was scarcely 10 per cent.

The passenger traffic with the continent of Europe, carried on

* Parl. paper, No. 2 of 1888, p, 21.

almost entirely in small vessels running daily or weekly, does not affect the above calculations.

Another objection, of a different character, has been suggested against this method, viz., that the quantity and weight of coal exported are so great, compared with those of any, or even all, other articles exported, as to dominate and vitiate the calculations founded upon the relations between tonnage and aggregate value.

On this point it must be remarked :—

1°. The objection does not affect the method applied to Imports, although there may be other articles, such as grain, timber, and iron (ores and metal) which may affect that calculation.

2°. The objection has no weight in the composition of the average price per ton in the first year of the series. It is only in the case, and to the extent of, any extraordinary annual variations in the trade of such articles that the objection would hold good.

3°. It is not the weight or bulkiness of any of these articles which would affect the calculations, but the relations between their quantity and value. If these did not differ widely from the average, fluctuations in quantity would not affect the calculations, because the amount of aggregate value would vary in accordance with those fluctuations. If they should differ widely, as in the case of coal exported, the general average price per ton calculated by this method will range continuously at variance from an average price calculated upon index numbers in which quantities are not taken into account, such as those of the "Economist" and Sauerbeck, or of those others into which the element of bulk does not enter, but only that of quantity *as measured by value* (*price*), such as those of MM. Giffen and Bourne.

4°. Coal exported stands in an exceptional position. While the average value of a ton of cargo exported in 1886 (see table at p. 19) was £9·2, the value of a register ton of coals was much less than £1. As (in 1886) the tonnage employed in the export of coal amounted to more than one-half of the total register tonnage clearing with cargoes (15·5 out of 29·3 millions of tons*), so large a proportion of a low priced article must have had a material influence upon the average value of exports. There is no other article in the Export trade which appears to have any similar influence of much importance. In the Import trade grain and

* A ton avoirdupois of coal averages one "shipping ton," or 40 cubic feet in capacity. A "register ton" is fixed at 100 cubic feet, but of this only 70 to 80 feet are available for stowage. Therefore 100 tons of shipping (sailing and steam) will hold not more than 150 tons of coal, and the 23·3 millions of tons of coal shipped in 1886 required 15·5 million tons of shipping for their conveyance. In this statement of quantity, bunker coal, or coal taken for the consumption of steamers, is not included. A table at p 34 will furnish some useful information with regard to the coal trade.

timber appear to have some influence upon the quantity of tonnage, the former employing in 1886 3·4 millions, and the latter
3·6 millions out of the total register tonnage entered of 26 millions.
But while the average value of a ton of cargo imported in that
year (see table at p. 19) was £14·1, the value of a corresponding
ton of grain was £12·2, and that of timber was £3·12. Consequently neither of these articles affects the calculation of Imports,
as regards either tonnage or value, in the same manner that coal
affects the calculation of Exports.

5°. It is apparent, upon comparing the columns of tonnage in
the tables of Imports and Exports at pp. 18 and 19, with the returns
of grain imported and coal exported in the same years, that there
is a certain extent of parallelism, and that in the years 1872, 1876,
1883, and 1887 the sudden increase in the amount of tonnage
entered was more or less owing to an increased importation of
grain, while in the years 1879, 1880, and 1883 the increase in the
amount of tonnage cleared was more or less owing to an increased
exportation of coal.

The inference to be drawn from the foregoing considerations
appears to be that the method here proposed supplies a ready
means of accurately measuring the whole volume of maritime
trade, inwards and outwards, taking into account the factor of the
tonnage employed, which is in itself the most important single
branch of British commerce; also of calculating the fluctuations
in the value, or price, of the whole mass of Imports and Exports,
with sufficient accuracy as regards Imports, but liable, with regard
to Exports, to be affected by any large variation from year to year,
in the exportation of coal.

It does not therefore supersede, especially as regards Exports,
the method of discovering by means of index numbers, or otherwise, the fluctuations in the prices of the chief articles in the home
and foreign trades, founded upon the prices of a certain number of
selected articles, and unaffected by the preponderating influence of
any one of them. But if the tonnage of ships laden exclusively
with coals exported, and the value of their cargoes, were excluded
from the calculation of Exports, and if in like manner the tonnage
and value of the cargoes of ships laden exclusively with grain and
timber imported were excluded from the calculation of Imports,
which could be done with ease, it is believed that a result equal, if
not superior, to any index number would be obtained.

This subject will be dealt with further on. It need only here
be remarked, that although the exclusion of coal from the Exports
raises the average value of all other Exports very greatly throughout the series, and elevates them above the Imports, it does not
materially affect the review of the general export trade in periods,
nor even from year to year.

'It may not be amiss to place in juxtaposition the results obtained for a series of years by the method now proposed, and by some other of the most important methods based upon index numbers, brought as closely as possible to the common measure of percentage. Mr. R. H. Inglis Palgrave's voluminous and valuable memorandum appended to the third Report of the Royal Commission on the Depression of Trade and Industry (1886) has presented facilities for this. The annexed table exhibits the percentage annual fluctuations for the twenty-nine years from 1858-86, the former year having been selected as the base, or datum line, because it was that from which the return of "The "Economist" started :—*

1. By comparison of total declared value with total tonnage of Imports, Exports, and the mean thereof. Calculated on base of 1858.†

2. By index numbers of Mr. Giffen, based on declared quantities and average prices of all specified articles of Imports, Exports, and the mean thereof. Calculated on base of 1854.‡

3. By index numbers of Mr. Bourne, based on the same data as the last, for Exports only. Calculated on base of 1873.

4. By index numbers of "The Economist," based upon the collective average of prices of twenty-two principal commodities, without reference to their relative importance as regards either value or quantity. Calculated on price in 1858, as estimated on base of average of six years 1845-50.§

5. By index numbers of Mr. Sauerbeck, based upon the collective average of prices of forty-five principal commodities, also without reference to the same conditions. Calculated on base of 1858.||

6. By index numbers of Mr. R. H. Palgrave, based on the same twenty-two commodities and prices as "The Economist," but taking into account the relative importance of each as measured by the quantity *estimated* to remain available for home trade. Calculated on base of average prices of five years 1865-69.¶

* Soetbeer's index numbers have not been overlooked, but they relate to prices in a foreign market, Hamburg.

† See table *infra* at pp. 18 and 19.

‡ "Third Report of Royal Commission on Depression of Trade and Industry," 1886, p. 329, and completed from "Final Report of the Royal 'Gold and Silver' Commission," 1888, p. 17.

§ Ibid., p. 329.

|| Calculated from tables in "Journal of the Royal Statistical Society," September, 1886, p. 617.

¶ Third report as above, p. 343.

Table A.—*Percentage Fluctuations of Prices in the United Kingdom, accord to various Estimates.*

1	2	3	4	5	6	7	8	9	10	11
	By Comparing Value of Total Imports and Exports with Tonnage.			By Comparing Quantities and Prices with Total Value of Imports and of British Exports.				By Index Numbers based on Wholesale Prices of Princip Commodities, British and Forei		
Years.	Rawson.			Giffen.			Bourne.	Without reference to Quantities.		With referen Quanti
	Total Imports.	Total Exports.	Mean.	Total Imports.	British Exports.	Mean.	British Exports	"The Economist."	Sauerbeck.	Palgra
	£ 18·6 =	£ 14·1 =	£ 16·3 =	£ 80·36 = in 1854 100	£ 64·85 = in 1854 100	£ 72·60 = in 1854 100	£ —	118 =	39·28 =	
1858	100	100	100	—	—	—	—	100	100	
'59	106	108	107	99	102	100	—	97	103	
1860	112	108	110	—	—	—	—	103	108	
'61	110	100	105	—	—	—	—	104	107	
'62	113	101	107	—	—	—	—	110	111	
'63	120	117	118	—	—	—	—	134	113	
'64	130	123	126	—	—	—	—	146	115	
'65	120	120	120	118	137	127	—	137	110	Avera of 1865-6 100
'66	119	121	120	—	—	—	—	136	111	
'67	111	108	109	—	—	—	—	116	112	
'68	114	104	109	108	119	113	—	103	111	
'69	110	105	107	—	—	—	—	102	109	
1870	109	103	106	—	—	—	—	103	108	91
'71	108	105	106	—	—	—	1063 =	108	111	90
'72	106	115	110	—	—	—	in 1873	109	122	97
'73	106	115	110	107	132	119	100	113	127	102
'74	104	107	105	—	—	—	94	111	116	100
'75	105	98	101	101	114	107	87	107	110	95
'76	95	84	89	96	105	100	78	104	108	93
'77	95	84	89	99	101	100	78	105	107	94
'78	93	81	87	92	—	—	75	97	100	87
'79	92	77	84	88	92	90	75	85	95	76
1880	92	79	85	93	—	—	87	97	100	87
'81	92	80	86	92	92	92	91	91	97	81
'82	90	79	84	—	—	—	94	94	96	83
'83	89	74	81	89	92	90	94	90	94	79
'84	87	71	79	84	90	87	91	85	87	75
'85	85	66	75	79	87	83	83	80	82	70
'86	77	65	71	74	82	78	83	78	—	69

These estimates have been brought together not because they are comparable, for they are compiled from such different data that they are not comparable, but they throw light upon one another, and in several respects confirm one another. They all exhibit an increasingly rapid fall in prices during the last few years.

The columns which will best bear comparison are those of Imports, Nos. 2 and 5, for they are both derived from the declared value of Imports; but Column 2 is calculated upon the whole value compared with tonnage, and Column 5 is calculated upon the declared value of "enumerated" articles, which form only four-fifths of the total Imports. The near approximation of the results by the two methods points to the approach to adequacy in both. The first has the advantage of simplicity and easy application. Column 3 exhibits the fluctuations of total Exports, including re-exports, which form, as shown at p. 3, rather more than one-fifth of the total Exports, and cannot be compared with Column 6, which shows those only of articles of British (and Irish) produce and manufacture.

The mean of each of the above series founded upon Imports and Exports has been given in Columns 4 and 7, in order to bring them more nearly into comparison with the three series in Columns 9 to 11, which are founded upon market prices of certain principal commodities, half or more of which are of foreign origin; these therefore should be compared with Imports, while the others should be compared with Exports.

The percentages in these three columns, founded as they are upon average prices of a limited number of articles—twenty-two and forty-five respectively—can furnish only an indication of the probable fluctuations in the great mass of other articles, and the discrepancies apparent in some of their figures inculcate the necessity for great caution in using them for any secondary or inferential purpose.

If therefore it be found that a table framed on the method above proposed gives results which are generally consistent with the history of the period, which reflect faithfully the known incidents of inflation and depression, exhibit a remarkable parallel-ism between the Import and Export trades, and can bear the test of comparison, first of one part with another, and then of the whole with corresponding results derived from other data, it is believed that such a table may be accepted as affording an approximate and sufficiently accurate method of measuring the maritime trade of this or any other kingdom which can furnish the same simple data, and of exhibiting the fluctuations both of volume and of price from year to year, and from month to month; that it may in fact serve the purpose of a Commercial Barometer.

CAP. 2. IMPORTS AND EXPORTS.

§ 1. *Quantities, Value, and Average Prices.*

Such a table is now presented, showing for Imports and Exports separately, in each year from 1854 to 1888 :—

1. The total tonnage of vessels entered (or cleared) with cargoes.
2. The total declared value of Imports (or Exports).
3. The average value of one register ton of cargo of Imports (or Exports) in each year.
4. The same in groups of years.

It must be premised that the Exports include the re-exports of

TABLE 1.—*Quantity and Value of Merchandise Imported into, and indicated by the Total Tonnage of Vessels which Entered and and Exported, in each Year from 1854 (the date from which the*

(Compiled from the Annual Statistical

Years.	A.—IMPORTS.					
	Quantity.	Value.	Average Value per Register Ton.			
			Years.	Periods.		
	Milln. tons	Milln. £	£	£	£	
1854	7·9*	152·4	19·3*	19·3		
'55	7·0	143·5	20·4	20·7		
'56	8·2	172·5	20·9			
'57	8·7	187·8	21·5	21·5	20·3	
'58	8·8	164·6	18·6	18·6		
'59	9·1	179·2	19·7	19·7		
1860	10·0	210·5	20·9			
'61	10·6	217·5	20·5	20·8		
'62	10·7	225·7	21·0			
'63	11·1	248·9	22·3	22·3		
'64	11·3	274·9	24·3	24·3	22·8	Increase 12·3%
'65	12·1	271·0	22·3	22·3		
'66	13·3	295·3	22·2			
'67	13·3	275·2	20·6	20·6		
'68	13·8	294·7	21·2	21·2		
'69	14·5	295·5	20·4			
1870	14·9	303·2	20·3	20·2	20·1	Decrease 11·1%
'71	16·4	331·0	20·1			
'72	17·9	354·7	19·8			
'73	18·8	371·3	19·7	19·4		
'74	19·1	370·1	19·4			
'75	19·0	373·9	19·6			
'76	21·0	375·1	17·8	17·8		
'77	22·1	394·4	17·8			
'78	21·3	368·8	17·3		17·4	Decrease 13·4%
'79	21·1	363·0	17·2	17·2		
1880	24·0	411·2	17·1			
'81	23·2	397·0	17·1			
'82	24·8	413·0	16·6			
'83	26·3	426·9	16·2	16·2	16·2	Decrease 5·8%
'84	24·7	390·0	15·8			
'85	25·7	371·0	14·4			
'86	24·7	349·9	14·1	14·1	14·1	Decrease 12·9%
'87	26·0	361·9	13·9			
'88	27·1	386·6	14·3			

* See note at p. 30.

Colonial and Foreign Merchandise, but not transhipments. Mr. Giffen's tables of Exports refer only to Exports of the Produce and Manufactures of the United Kingdom. He could not have readily shown the results for the total Exports, if he had thought it necessary or desirable, because the prices of re-exports are not given in the "Statistical Abstract;" and in the present table the Exports of British Merchandise cannot be shown separately, because in the returns of tonnage no distinction could be made of the origin of the merchandise composing the cargoes. The same remarks apply to Mr. Bourne's tables.

Exported from, the United Kingdom (including re-exports), as Cleared with Cargoes, and the Declared Value of Merchandise Imported Declared Value of Imports has been recorded) to 1888.

Abstracts published by the Board of Trade.)

Years.	Quantity.	Value.	Average Value per Register Ton.			
			Years.	Periods.		
	Milln. tons	Milln. £	£	£	£	
1854.......	7·9*	115·8	14·7* ⎫			
'55.......	8·3	116·7	14·0 ⎪			
'56.......	9·7	139·2	14·4 ⎬	14·2 ⎫		
'57.......	10·3	146·2	14·1 ⎪			
'58.......	9·9	139·8	14·1 ⎭	⎬ 14·4		
'59.......	10·2	155·7	15·2 ⎫	15·2 ⎪		
1860.......	10·8	164·5	15·2 ⎬			
'61.......	11·3	159·6	14·1 ⎬	14·2 ⎭		
'62.......	11·7	166·2	14·2 ⎭			
'63.......	11·9	196·9	16·5 ⎫	16·5 ⎫		
'64.......	12·2	212·6	17·4 ⎪	⎬ 17·0	17·0	Increase
'65.......	12·8	218·8	17·0 ⎬	17·2 ⎭		15·3%
'66.......	14·0	238·9	17·1 ⎭			
'67.......	14·8	225·8	15·2 ⎫			
'68.......	15·5	227·8	14·7 ⎪			
'69.......	15·9	237·0	14·9 ⎬	14·9 ⎫		
1870.......	16·7	244·0	14·6 ⎪			
'71.......	19·0	283·5	14·9 ⎭			
'72.......	19·2	314·6	16·3 ⎫	16·2 ⎬ 15·1		Decrease
'73.......	19·1	311·0	16·2 ⎬			11·1%
'74.......	19·7	297·6	15·1 ⎬	15·1 ⎪		
'75	20·4	281·6	13·8 ⎭	13·8 ⎭		
'76.......	21·5	256·8	11·9 ⎫			
'77.......	21·2	252·3	11·9 ⎪			
'78.......	21·6	245·5	11·4 ⎪			
'79.......	22·8	248·8	10·9 ⎬	11·4	11·4	Decrease
1880.......	25·6	286·4	11·1 ⎪			24·5%
'81.......	26·3	297·1	11·3 ⎪			
'82.......	27·7	306·7	11·1 ⎭			
'83.......	29·4	305·4	10·4 ⎫	10·25	10·25	Decrease
'84.......	29·3	296·0	10·1 ⎭			10·0%
'85.......	29·3	271·4	9·3 ⎫			
'86.......	29·1	268·7	9·2 ⎬	9·3	9·3	Decrease
'87.......	30·2	280·5	9·3 ⎭			9·2%
'88.......	31·7	298·3	9·4			

* See note at p. 30.

A brief examination of the first four or five years of the Table of Imports will best explain the method and the character of the results. Comparing the year 1855 with 1854, the tonnage decreased from 7·900,000 to 7·0 millions, and the value from £152·4 millions to £143·5 millions. But as the decrease in the tonnage was 11·3 per cent., and in the value only 5·1 per cent., or less than one-half, the average value per ton increased from £19·3 (= £19 6s.) to £20·4 (= £20 8s.), which implied a corresponding advance in prices. In 1866 there was a large increase of tonnage amounting to 17·1 per cent., but a still larger proportionate average in the value, viz., 20·2 per cent. The average value therefore increased, but only slightly, to £20·9. By a similar process the average value in the next year increased further to £21·5; but in 1858 the amount of tonnage remained almost stationary, while the total value decreased by £23·2 millions = 12·3 per cent., and the average value fell from £21·5 to £18·6 per ton.

A. *Notes on Table I. Yearly Comparisons.*

Proceeding now to the principal features of the table, and first as regards Imports, it appears that :—

1. The average value per ton in the first year, 1854, was £19·3, that it increased slowly to 1858, when it suddenly fell from £21·5 to £18·6; it recovered slightly in 1859, and continued to rise, with the exception of a single year, 1861, to 1864, when it reached for a single year the highest point in the whole series, viz., £24·3. From that year it continued to fall continuously but slowly, with the single exception of 1868, till 1875, when it suddenly fell from £19·6 to £17·8; and thence continuously, but gradually, to the end, excepting in 1885, when it fell heavily from £15·8 to £14·4; it reached its lowest point of £13·9 in 1887.

2. The difference between the first and last years of the series was 28·0 per cent. ; the rise from 1854 to 1865—eleven years—was 25·9 per cent., and the fall from 1865 to 1887—twenty-two years—was 42·8 per cent.

3. The average of the thirty-four years scarcely differed from the value of the first year, being £19·1, as compared with £19·3.

4. In the first nine years, before the disturbance caused by the American civil war, the extremes of the annual differences were between £18·6 (or excepting 1858, £19·3), and £21·5, or not more than 16·1 per cent. The average of the nine years was £20·3.

5. The four years of the American civil war, 1863-66, formed an exceptional period, of moderate increase of tonnage, and of large increase of value, the latter having risen from £20·3 to £22·8 = 12·3 per cent.

6. During the next nine years 1867 to 1875 the tonnage rose

greatly, from 13·3 millions to 19·0 millions, while the average value fell from £22·2 to £19·6, and returned to about the average of the first nine years, viz., £20·1, a fall of 11·1 per cent.

7. During the Franco-German war, and the two following years, although there was a large increase of tonnage, and an accompanying increase in the volume of Imports, there was no increase, but an actual slight decrease, in prices, viz., from £20·3 to £19·7.

8. The twelve years from 1876 to 1887 divides itself into three periods : in the first, 1876 to 1881, the value per ton remained nearly stationary at an average of £17·4 or 13·4 per cent. below the last period ; in 1882-84 it fell further to £16·2, a decrease of 5·8 per cent. ; and in 1885-87 it averaged £14·1, a decrease of 12·9 per cent.

9. The total fall between 1867-75 and 1885-87 was from £20·1 to £14·1, or 30 per cent.

Examining the Exports in a similar manner, it appears that :—

1. The average value per ton in the first year, 1854, was £14·7 ; it fluctuated slightly below this till 1859-60, in which years it rose to £15·2, but fell again to £14·2 in the next two years, 1861-62. With the American civil war it rose in 1863 to £16·5, and, as in the case of the Imports, it reached the highest point of the series in 1864, viz., £17·4. It did not however recede, as did the Imports, during the two following years, but remained at nearly the same amount. In 1867 it fell heavily from £17·1 to £15·2, and continued to fluctuate till 1872-73, when it rose from £14·9 to £16·3. In 1874 it fell again to £15·1 ; in the following year to £13·8 ; in 1876 to £11·9 ; and from that point it sank gradually to its lowest point, £9·2, in 1886. In 1887 it returned to the rate of 1885, which was £9·3, an insignificant recovery, but indicating a turn of the tide, which is confirmed by an examination of the monthly returns for the past eleven months of 1888.

2. The average of the whole period of thirty-four years was £13·5, being 8·1 per cent. less than the value of the first year, which was £14·7.

3. There is a decided correspondence in the matter of fluctuations of value between Imports and Exports in periods of years, though not in individual years. Thus the first nine years of Exports fluctuated even less than the Imports, viz., between £14 and £15·2, or 8·5 per cent., but there was no exceptional fall in 1858, and there was a fall in 1861-62, which did not occur in the Imports.

4. The increase in the four years 1863-66 was even greater than that of Imports, being from 14·4 in 1854-62, to 17·0, or 15·3 per cent.

5. The decrease in the next nine years to an average of £15·1 corresponds exactly with that in the Imports, both being 11·1 per cent., notwithstanding the exceptional rise in the Exports in 1872-73.

6. The fall in the next period, 1876-82, from 15·1 to 11 4=24·5 per cent., is nearly double, (82 per cent. greater than) the fall in the Imports, which was only 13·4 per cent.

7. In 1883-84 the further fall to £10·25, amounting to 10·0 per cent., was nearly double that of the Imports. But in the last three years the fall in Imports has exceeded that in Exports in the proportion of 12·9 to 9·2 per cent.

8. The difference between the first and last years of the series was 36·7 per cent., being nearly one-fourth greater than the fall in Imports ; the rise from 1854 to 1865 was 18·3 per cent., and the fall to 1887 was 46·5 per cent. The corresponding changes in Imports were 25·9 and 42·8 per cent.

Comparing the Imports and Exports together, the difference in the value per ton on the whole of the period was between £19·1 and £13·5, or 29·3 per cent.; but while in the first year, 1854, the difference was between £19·3 and £14·7 per ton, or 23·8 per cent., in 1887 the difference was between £13·9 and £9·1 per ton, or 33·3 per cent. The whole of this, and of many of the above differences, are however owing to the effect of the large export of coal lowering the aggregate value of Exports.

It must be noticed that the tonnage of Imports and Exports was exactly the same, 7·9 millions,* in the first year, 1854, but in 1887 the tonnage of Imports had increased to 26·0 millions=229 per cent., and the tonnage of Exports had increased to 30·2 millions = 282 per cent., or, approximately, in the proportions of 3 and $3\frac{1}{2}$ fold respectively. Exclusive of coal the tonnage of the Exports had increased from 5·0 to 13·7 millions of tons = 173 per cent.

The differences between the six periods in the table are as follows :—

Periods.	Average Value per Register Ton.		Difference.	
	Imports.	Exports.	Amount.	Per Cent.
	£	£	£	
1854-62.......	20·3	14·4	5·9	29·0
'63-66.......	22 8	17·0	5·8	25·4
'67-75........	20·1	15·1	5·0	24·8
'76-81........	17·4	—	} 6·0	34·5
'76-82........	—	11·4		
'82-84........	16·2	—	} 6·0	37·0
'83-84........	—	10·2		
'85-87........	14·1	9·3	4·8	34·0

* The exact figures were : entered 7,899,742 tons, cleared 7,870,536 tons.

In 1864, when both Imports and Exports reached the highest point, the difference was between £24·3 and £17·4, or 28·3 per cent., being slightly below the above average of the whole period.

It will probably be admitted that this table (at p. 18) bears intrinsic evidence of its adequacy to represent with a sufficient approximation to accuracy the annual fluctuations of maritime trade both in volume and in value. The manner in which sudden and violent changes in the amount of tonnage, or of value, sometimes in agreement with, and at other times in opposition to one another, are reduced into a moderate and reasonable change in the average value of a ton, the parallelism of the results drawn from the tables of Imports and Exports, and the correspondence of those results with the commercial history of the period, seem to combine in establishing the trustworthiness of the table, independently of confirmation from other sources. This however is not wanting, and although a comparison between the results derived from this method and those derived from Mr. Bourne's are not strictly comparable, inasmuch as the former embrace the whole trade, and the latter are confined to the Exports of British produce and manufactures, the remarkable parallelism between the two series for the years 1883-87 affords a strong argument in favour of the acceptance of both methods :—

Changes in Value (Price).

Year.	Bourne. — British Exports only.	Rawson. — Total Exports.
1883	1,000	1,000
'84	971	971
'85	888	894
'86	885	884
'87	922	894

It must however be remarked that in these five years there has been but a slight and gradual change in the quantity of coal exported. The difference in 1887 may be owing to the increased quantity of coal exported in that year.

B. *Notes on Table* II ; *Monthly Comparisons.*

This table shows the average value of a register ton of cargo, calculated in the same manner, for each month of the years 1885-87. It is compiled from the Monthly Accounts of "Trade " and Navigation" published by the Board of Trade, and is computed in the same way as the annual tables.

TABLE II. *Average value per Ton of Cargoes Imported into, and Exported from, the United Kingdom (including re-exports), ascertained by a comparison of the Tonnage of Vessels which Entered and Cleared with Cargoes, with the Declared Value of Imports and Exports, in each month of the years 1885-87.*

Average Value per Register Ton of Cargoes.

Months.	Imports.			Exports.			Average of the Three Years 1885-87.	
	1885.	1886.	1887.	1885.	1886.	1887.	Imports	Exports.
	£	£	£	£	£	£	£	£
January	18·1	16·8	16·4	11·7	10·3	10·1	17·1	10·7
February	17·1	16·8	16·3	11·7	10·9	11·2	16·7	11·3
March	16·6	16·5	15·9	9·7	11·0	10·0	16·3	10·2
April	15·6	14·0	15·0	9·0	9·4	9·1	14·9	9·2
May	14·2	13·4	12·7	8·0	7·7	8·2	13·4	8·0
June	12·1	12·8	12·2	8·7	8·8	8·3	12·4	8·6
July	12·5	12·2	11·7	9·4	8·7	8·8	12·1	9·0
August	11·8	12·2	11·5	8·2	8·8	8·5	11·8	8·5
September	12·9	12·7	12·2	9·2	8·8	8·9	12·6	9·0
October	13·3	13·4	13·5	9·1	8·8	9·3	13·4	9·1
November	14·6	14·9	15·1	8·5	8·7	9·6	14·9	8·9
December	15·9	16·2	16·4	10·1	9·6	9·9	16·2	9·9
Average of year	14·4	14·1	13·9	9·3	9·2	9·3	14·1	9·3

Average of Seasons.		
May to October	12·6	8·7
November to April	16·0	10·0
Excess in winter	27·0	15·0
	p. cent	p. cent

This table reveals the fact that the value of cargoes differs materially, and with great regularity, at the several seasons of the year; that the average value of a ton of Imports in the six months from May to October in the above years was only £12·6, while in the six months of winter it rose to £16·0, a difference of 27 per cent.; and of Exports the corresponding values were £8·7 and £10·0, a difference of 15 per cent. In the preceding years, and in the whole of the six years, the differences stood as follows:—

	Imports.		Percentage Difference.	Exports.		Percentage Difference.
	Summer.	Winter.		Summer.	Winter.	
	£	£	Per cent.	£	£	Per cent.
1882-84	14·9	17·9	20·1	10·0	11·1	11·1
'85-87	12·9	16·0	24·0	8·7	10·0	15·0
1882-87	13·9	17·0	22·3	9·3	10·5	13·0

The records are not available for carrying the comparison much further back; but the combined evidence of the constancy of the difference, of the gradual character of the change, as shown in Table II, and of the total absence of change at a season of commercial quiescence, such as the six months from June to November, 1886, during which the monthly average varied only from £8·8 to £8·7, seems to offer a corroborative proof of the sufficiency of the annual table for its purpose.

It has been suggested as one reason for the winter cargoes being more valuable than those of the summer, that the crops of cotton, corn and wool arrive at the former season; but this would not apply to the value of Export cargoes; and it seems more probable that the trade in coal, wood, and other bulky—and less valuable—articles, carried on in sailing vessels and ships of an inferior quality, is confined to the summer months.

The monthly table presents an equally reliable measure for comparing each month, not with its predecessor, as in the case of the annual table, but with the corresponding month of two, three, or more previous years. Such a comparison, in connection with the upward or downward tendency of the months immediately preceding, seems to offer as correct an indication of the course of prices in maritime trade as that supplied by the annual table.

Taking as an illustration the trade of the last eighteen months, as shown in the preceding and following tables, it will be seen, as regards Imports, that the value per ton during the five months from May to September, 1887, was considerably below the corresponding months of 1886 or 1885, but that in October it began to rise above those of the two preceding years; it continued to rise above either year in November and December; it stood above 1887 in January and February, 1888, but below 1886 or 1885. In March, however, it rose above either of the three preceding years. In April it fell below 1887, but exceeded 1886. In May and June it exceeded 1887, and in the next three months it equalled or exceeded 1887, but fell short of 1886 or 1885. As regards Exports, the turn of the tide began earlier, and indeed in May and July, 1887, the value stood higher than in the corresponding months of 1886. The fall in August, as compared with 1886, was much less than in the Imports; the rise began in September instead of October. In the latter month it advanced more rapidly than in the Imports. It advanced at a lower rate in December and January, showed a slight falling off in February, and rose again in March. In April there was a rise; in May and July a large rise; in August a rise, and in September, for the first time since February, a fall. October exhibits a return to improvement.

On the whole of the year 1888, the Imports show a rise of

2·9 per cent. over 1887, and of 4·2 per cent. over 1886, but have not quite reached the level of 1885. On the other hand the Exports have risen 2·1 per cent. over 1857, 3·2 per cent. over 1886, and have exceeded the level of 1885 by 2·1 per cent.*

TABLE II.—*Continued for the Year* 1888.

	Imports.				Exports.			
	1885.	1886.	1887.	1888.	1885.	1886.	1887.	1888.
	£	£	£	£	£	£	£	£
January	18·1	16·8	16·4	16·7	11·7	10·3	10·1	10·3
February	17·1	16·8	16·3	16·5	11·7	10·9	11·2	10·9
March	16·6	16·5	15·9	16·8	9·7	11·0	10·0	10·3
April	15·6	14·0	15·0	14·5	9·0	9·4	9·1	9·4
May	14·2	13·4	12·7	13·6	8·0	7·7	8·2	9·3
June	12·1	12·8	12·2	12·6	8·7	8·8	8·3	8·4
July	12·5	12·2	11·7	11·7	9·4	8·7	8·8	9·6
August	11·8	12·2	11·5	11·8	8·2	8·8	8·5	8·8
September	12·9	12·7	12·2	12·2	9·2	8·8	8·9	8·4
October	13·3	13·4	13·5	13·6	9·1	8·8	9·3	9·3
November	14·6	14·9	15·1	15·8	8·5	8·7	9·6	9·5
December	15·9	16·2	16·4	16·4	10·1	9·6	9·9	9·4
Average of year	14·4	14·1	13·9	14·3	9·3	9·2	9·3	9·5

If this does not exhibit an exact measure of the actual fluctuations in the course of maritime trade during the last eleven months, it certainly affords a very close indication of them, and one upon which both statesmen and the commercial community may rely. The data on which it is based are furnished periodically by the Government within seven days after the expiration of each month— and the calculations and comparisons are of the simplest kind.

A.—*Notes on Tables of Curves* 3 *and* 4.

Before proceeding to examine the further evidence in support of the sufficiency of these tables for their purpose, which will involve the consideration of other tables leading away from this special point, it will be instructive to inspect the results exhibited

---

* The following statements afford interesting information as to the impulse given to industry and the investment of capital during the first six months of the present year :—

1. The number of vessels under construction in the United Kingdom on 30th June, 1888, was 34 per cent. greater, and the tonnage was 45 per cent. greater than at the corresponding period of last year ; on the 30th September those proportions had advanced to 60 and 77 respectively.

2. The number of new issues quoted on the London Stock Exchange in the first six months of 1888 was £174 millions, identical with the amount quoted in the whole of the preceding year. In ordinary years there is but a slight difference in the amount of new issues between the first and latter halves of the year. It may therefore be anticipated that the issues of 1888 will be double those of 1887.

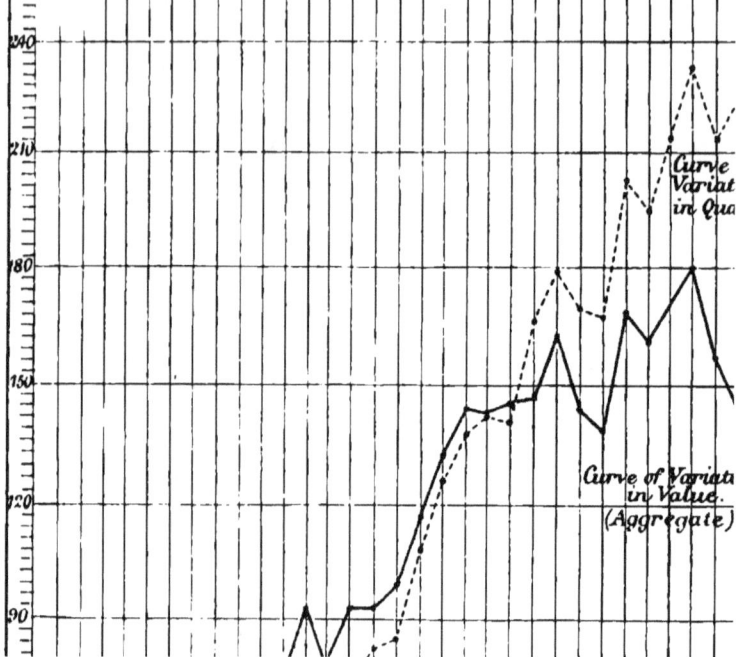

Table 3.

Curves of Imports into the United Kingdom,
1855 to 1887.

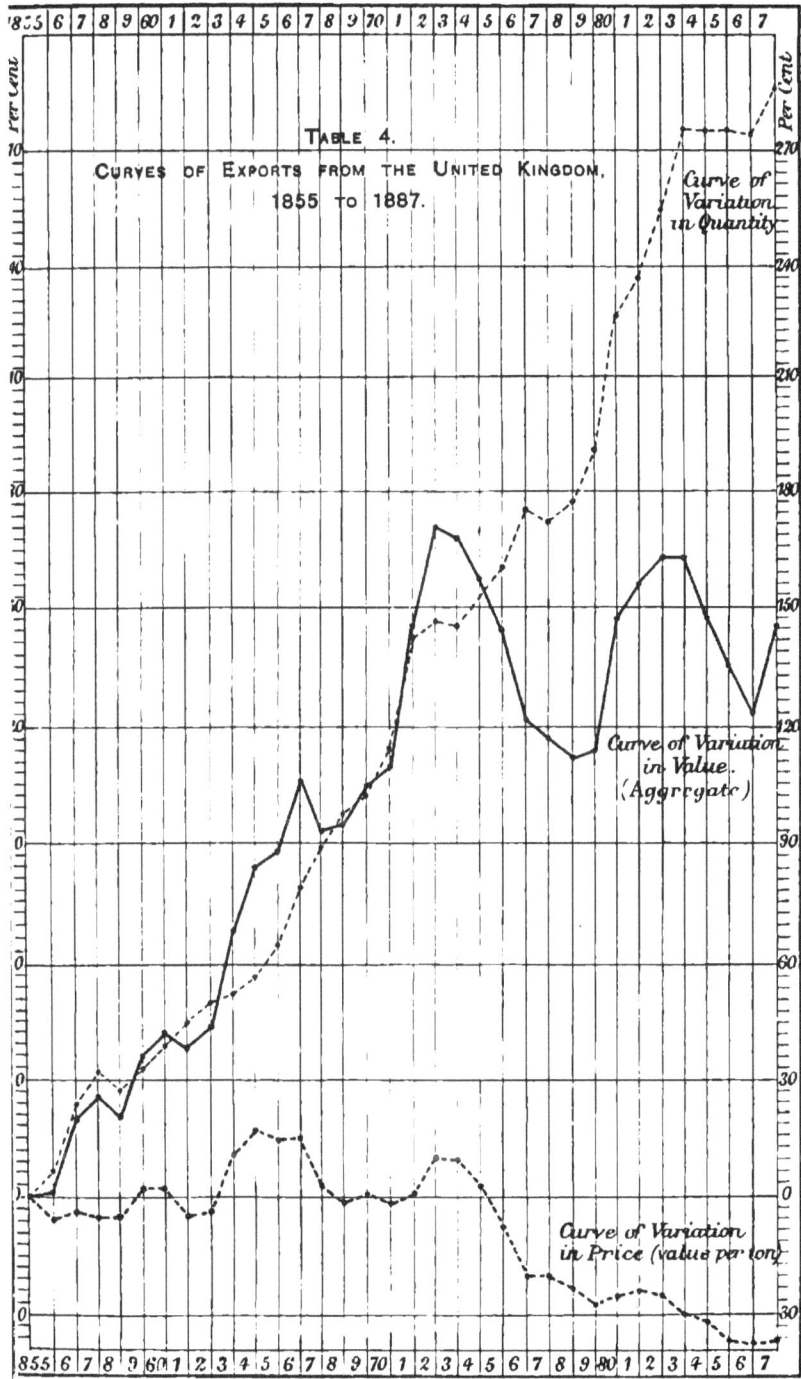

TABLE 4.

CURVES OF EXPORTS FROM THE UNITED KINGDOM,
1855 TO 1887.

Curve of
Variation
in Quantity

Curve of Variation
in Value.
(Aggregate)

Curve of Variation
in Price (value per ton)

in a graphic form in Tables III and IV for Imports and Exports respectively :—

These show the yearly variations :—

1. Of quantity, as represented in Table I by the tonnage of vessels which entered or cleared at the ports of the United Kingdom with cargoes.
2. Of value, as represented by the total declared value of merchandise imported and exported, including foreign and colonial merchandise re-exported.
3. Of price, as represented by the average value per register ton.

The variations of the three factors of quantity, value, and price are calculated as percentage differences from those obtained in 1854, the ordinates representing these differences for each factor, while the abscissæ represent successive years. The scale is the same for Imports and Exports, which therefore are strictly comparable as to magnitude. The influence of price upon value is seen by a simple inspection of the curves of quantity and value, which with a constant price would be parallel, or rather identical.

It will be observed in the table of Imports that—

1. The year 1855, during the Crimean war, was marked by a large decrease of tonnage and of value, but at the same time by a rise in prices.
2. There was a continuous rise in prices till 1858, when there was a sudden and heavy fall below the constant.
3. While prices were rising up to 1865, and until they fell below the constant in 1876, the curve of value ran above that of quantity; but crossed the latter, and in the next year sank rapidly below it, when the curve of price fell permanently below the constant.
4. The curves of quantity and value cross one another, whenever the curve of price crosses the line of constant, to wit in 1858, 1859, and 1876. The two series touch one another without crossing in the year 1874.
5. The effect of a change in prices is conspicuously exhibited in the difference between the curves of quantity and value in the years 1858, 1865, and 1869, when a fall in price produced a fall in value in spite of a rise in quantity; also in 1876, when the difference is even more strongly marked, and again in 1885.
6. There is only one instance of the reverse action, viz., in 1875, when a slight rise in price caused an increase in value, although there was a decrease in quantity.

An examination of the table of Exports and a comparison with that of Imports show the following principal results :—

1. The curves of quantity and value of Exports ran together until 1871, but more irregularly than in the Imports, crossing one another no less than eight times before 1875; when, as in the Imports, they crossed for the last time and took opposite directions, the value falling while the quantity continued to rise.

2. The prices of Exports fell in 1855, during the Crimean war, and remained steady till 1859, unlike those of Imports, which continued to rise until 1858, when they fell heavily. Both began to rise in 1859, but Imports continued to rise until they reached their highest point in 1864, when they fell rapidly and never rose again till the end of the series, except very slightly in two single years, 1868 and 1875. On the other hand Exports remained stationary in 1860, fell in 1861, began to rise rapidly in 1863, and reached their highest point, like the Imports, in 1864.

3. They maintained themselves better than the prices of Imports in 1865-66, but fell more heavily in 1867; made no upward movement in 1868, and fluctuated below those of Imports up to the end of 1871.

4. In 1872-73 they took and maintained an upward course, in which Imports did not share; but in 1874-76 they fell heavily and continuously, while the heavy fall in Imports did not begin till 1876.

5. Prices both of Exports and Imports remained steady in 1877; but since then there has been a continuous fall in both—heaviest in Exports—except in the years 1880-81, when there was a slight rise in Exports, which was scarcely visible in the Imports.

6. The years in which in the table of Exports the effects of a fall in price on the amount of value is most conspicuous are 1861, 1867, 1874 to 1876, and 1878. The year 1872 is noticeable for a sharp rise in prices, which converts a slight rise in quantity into a very large rise in value.

7. There is no instance of the reverse action in the table of Exports.

8. The rise in the value of Exports in 1887 has been higher than that of Imports.

§ 2. *Exports of British Produce and Manufactures*, 1834-88.

a. *Quantities, Value, and Average Prices.*

It has been pointed out that it is only since 1854 that the declared value of Imports has been recorded, and it is only since 1852 that the declared value of re-exports has been recorded. Therefore, although it is possible to carry further back an examination of the annual Exports of British Produce and Manufactures, it is not possible to add to them the value of Colonial and Foreign Merchandise, and to compare this aggregate with the tonnage, as has been done in Table I, and represented in the preceding curves. Yet, as the amount of re-exports has not varied much from year to year, and as the proportion to the total Exports was gradually diminishing in following the years back from 1854, a table may be prepared in which, assuming for the nonce that no re-exports took place, the value of British Exports may be compared with the tonnage, and the value of a ton of merchandise may be estimated minus whatever addition should be made each year for the actual value of the re-exports.

Thus in 1834 2·2 millions of tonnage cleared with cargoes, and the value of British Exports was £41·6 millions, which gives an average of £18·9 per ton,* to which would have to be added from 6 to 12 per cent. for re-exports, in order to obtain an average corresponding to that in Table I. But for the purpose of comparing the price of British Exports in the year 1835 and each following year up to 1886 with its predecessor, and thus constructing a table upon the same principle as Table I, which shall exhibit the annual variation in prices, the omission of the re-exports may be disregarded, and the calculation may be carried on for British Exports only down to the latest year, 1886. Moreover the sufficiency of this calculation may be tested by adding the value of the re-exports from a date when their value was recorded, and comparing the result with that exhibited in Table I, derived from a comparison of the tonnage with the total Exports. The almost completeness of the identity through the whole period from 1854 to 1886 appears to demonstrate the sufficiency of the comparison from year to year, notwithstanding the imperfection of the calculation, as indicative of the average price of each year, to which, in order to show the average value of total Exports, would have to be added a sum varying from £2 to £4 each year for re-exports, according to the experience of the years from 1854 to 1886 during which it was recorded. The average difference during this period was £2·7.

To show these particulars two tables have been prepared: 1. No. V, which exhibits the variations (in the price of British Exports) from 1834 to 1854; 2. No. VI, which continues that table on the same basis up to 1886, and exhibits the result of adding together and showing, in quinquennial periods, the value of British, foreign, and colonial Exports, and a comparison of the figures so corrected with corresponding averages taken from Table I :—

---

* This is the accurate average after allowance for fractions in the factors.

TABLE V.—*Tonnage of Vessels which Cleared with Cargoes, and of the Declare Value of British and Irish Produce and Manufactures Exported, from Port of the United Kingdom, with the Average Value of such Exports per Registe Ton, in each Year from 1834 to 1854.*

(Compiled from "Statistical Abstracts.")

Years.	Tonnage Cleared with Cargoes.	Value of Exports of British and Irish Produce and Manufactures.	Average Value per Register Ton.		Events.
			Years	Periods.	
	Milln. tons	Milln. £	£		
1834	2·2	41·6	18·9*	19·2 ⎫	1834. Slave emancipation.
'35	2·4	47·4	19·6 ⎱21·3	⎪	
'36	2·5	53·3	21·3 ⎰	⎬18·9	'36. U.S. national debt paid off.
'37	2·6	42·0	16·1	16·1	'37. Commercial panic, London.
'38	2·9	50·5	17·4 ⎱17·3	⎭	'38. Famine in India; Affghan war.
'39	3·1	53·2	17·1 ⎰		'39. War with China.
1840	3·4	51·3	15·1 ⎱15·1		1840. Treaty of London; Eastern question.
'41	3·5	51·5	15·0 ⎰		'41-42. Manufacturing depression.
'42	3·7	47·3	12·7 ⎱13·2	⎬14·4	'42. Peace with China.
'43	3·8	52·2	13·7 ⎰		'43. Trade with China opened.
'44	3·7	58·5	15·8 ⎰15·8		'44. Bank Charter Act passed.
'45	4·3	60·1	14·0	14·0	'45. Peel's tariff; railway mania.
'46	4·5	57·8	12·8		'46. Commercial panic; Corn laws repealed Spanish marriages.
				12·7 ⎫	
'47	4·7	58·8	12·5	⎪	'47. Gold discovered in California.
'48	5·0	52·8	10·4	⎪	'48. Chartist demonstration in London; revolutionary movements in Europe
'49	5·4	63·6	11·7	11·4 ⎬12·0	
1850	5·9	71·3	12·1	⎪	
'51	6·5	74·4	11·5		1851. Discovery of gold in Australia.
'52	6·9	78·0	11·3		
'53	7·6	98·8	13·0 ⎱12·7		'53. Australian mint established.
'54	7·9	97·1	12·3 ⎰		'54. Crimean war.

* These are accurate averages allowing for fractions omitted in previous columns.

In this table and the corresponding curve, a correction is necessary to place it in series with the following table, by adding 7·3 per cent. to the tonnage before the 1st January, 1855, and by diminishing the average value per register ton by a corresponding amount. A similar correction is required in Table 1, and the corresponding curves, for the years 1854 and 1855.

TABLE VI.—*Continuation of the preceding Table for each Year from 1855 to 1886; together with Quinquennial Averages, and the Corresponding Average Value of a Ton of Exports of all kinds, including Colonial and Foreign Merchandise, calculated 1 by an addition of the Percentage Value of re-exports, and 2 upon the Average Value of a Register Ton of Total Exports, as shown in Table I.*

(Compiled from "Statistical Abstracts.")

Years.	Tonnage cleared with Cargoes.	Value of Exports of British and Irish Produce and Manufactures.	Years.	Quinquennial Averages.	Calculated by addition of Percentage Proportion of Value of re-exports.	Calculated on Average Value per Ton of Total Exports, according to Table I.
	Milln. tons	Milln. £	£	£	£	£
1855...	8·3	95·7	11·4			
'56....	9·7	115·8	11·9			
'57....	10·3	122·0	11·8	11·9	14·2	14·4
'58....	9·9	116·6	11·7			
'59....	10·2	130·4	12·7			
1860....	10·8	135·9	12·6			
'61....	11·3	125·1	11·0			
'62....	11·7	124·0	10·6	11·9	15·5	15·5
'63....	11·9	146·6	12·3			
'64....	12·2	160·4	13·1			
'65....	12·8	165·8	12·9			
'66....	14·0	188·9	13·4			
'67....	14·8	180·9	12·2	12·4	15·7	15·8
'68....	15·5	179·7	11·6			
'69....	15·9	189·9	11·9			
1870....	16·7	199·6	12·0			
'71....	19·0	223·1	11·7			
'72....	19·2	256·2	13·3	12·5	15·4	15·4
'73....	19·1	265·2	13·3			
'74....	19·7	239·5	12·1			
'75....	20·4	223·5	10·9			
'76....	21·5	200·6	9·3			
'77....	21·2	198·9	9·3	9·4	12·0	12·0
'78....	21·6	192·8	8·9			
'79....	22·8	191·5	8·4			
1880...	25·6	223·0	8·7			
'81....	26·3	234·0	8·8			
'82....	27·7	241·5	8·6	8·3	10·5	10·8
'83....	29·4	239·8	8·1			
'84....	29·3	233·0	7·9			
'85....	29·3	213·0	7·3			
'86....	29·1	212·4	7·3	7·3	9·3	9·2
'87....	30·2	221·4	7·3			
'88....	31·7	233·7	7·4			

The main deduction to be drawn from these tables, which is shown in a striking form in the curves attached to them in Table 7, is, that although prices ranged much higher before the years

1845-46, when Sir R. Peel established his tariff, and the corn laws were repealed, the fluctuations were much more frequent and more violent before those years than subsequently, and that from the year 1848, when the operation of those two great changes may be supposed to have wrought their chief immediate effects, there was an almost continuous uniformity of price down to the year 1874, broken only on rare occasions, generally brought about by external influences, and then only to a slight extent. This will be seen in the following extracts :—

Years.		Average Price. £	Years.		Average Price. £	
1834 '35	} average	19·2	1846 '47	} average	12·7	
'36		21·3	'48-52		11·4	
'37		16·1	'53-54		12·9	
'38 '39	} average	17·3	'55-60		12·0	
'40 '41	} „	15·1	'61-62		10·8	} avge. £12·0
			'63		12·3	
'42 '43	} average	13·2	'64-66		13·1	
			'67-71		11·9	
'44		15·8	'72-73		13·3	
'45		14·0	'74		12·1	

There has been a still greater uniformity since 1876 from year to year, but there has been an almost continuous decline. The great break and sudden decline occurred in the years 1875-76 :—

	£			£
1875	10·9		1878-83	8·6
'76-77	9·3		'84-86	7·3

b. *Curves of the same*, 1834-54.

The Table 7 of the curves of Exports from 1834-54 has been framed to correspond as closely as possible with that of the curves of total Exports from 1854-87, Table 4. The two cannot be made to correspond exactly, because the declared value of re-exports were not recorded in the earlier period; but inasmuch as the amount varied slightly from year to year, and continued to diminish as the series went backward, the curve approximates closely to that which would represent the total Exports; and as it is calculated upon the same basis as that for 1854-87, viz., the tonnage and declared value of 1854, the whole may be viewed as indicative of the actual line of progress from 1834 to 1887.

It will be seen that at the commencement of the earlier period prices ruled very much higher than in 1854, or at any subsequent date, and if the value of re-exports were added, those prices would have been still higher, probably 6 per cent. in the earlier, increasing to 12 per cent. in the later, years. On the other hand the curves of quantity and value at the earlier period are in a corresponding degree below those of 1854 and subsequent years.

TABLE 7.
CURVES OF EXPORTS OF BRITISH PRODUCE
AND MANUFACTURES
1834 TO 1854

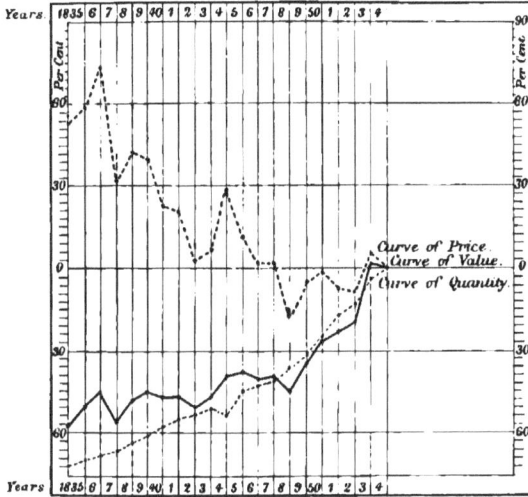

They exhibit in a striking form—

1. The continuous growth of the tonnage, or quantity, increasing slowly during the first half of the period, and with much greater rapidity during the latter half.
2. The rapid fall and extreme variations in the curves of price up to the year 1846.
3. The rapid increase in value subsequent to this date, notwithstanding the heavy fall of prices in 1847, owing to the combined effect of a recovery of prices and an increase of quantity.

§ 3. *Export of Coal; a new Index Number for Exports.*

The annexed table exhibits a view, probably unexpected, of the extent and growth of the exportation of Coal during the years 1854-87, of the amount of tonnage required for its carriage, and of the proportion which such tonnage bore to the total tonnage cleared with cargoes. The balance shows the tonnage employed in the exportation of all other articles in the same years. The table also exhibits the annual fluctuations in the quantities of coal exported, in the amount of tonnage cleared with cargoes, and in the price of coal.

In addition to the remarks at p. 13, it may be noted that while the relation between the quantity of coal exported and the total tonnage cleared in the first five years 1854-58 was 61 to 100, it was 78 to 100 in the five years 1882-86, showing so far the increased influence of the export of coal on the total tonnage. But it must not be overlooked that during this period there has been a very large increase in the carrying capacity of the tonnage employed.

The average annual increase in the export of coal during the whole period has been about half a million tons, and has only thrice amounted to one million or more, viz., in the years 1874-76, and 1880. In the year 1873, when the price of coal reached its highest point, 20s. 5d., the export fell from 13·2 to 12·6 millions of tons.

As regards the value of the coal exported, it amounted upon the average of the whole period to only 2·75 per cent. of the total value of British Exports. In the three years 1872-74, when the average price of the other 30 years rose from 9s. 6d. to 17s. 7d. a ton, the above proportion only rose from 2·75 to 3·8 per cent. The average price of coal in 1854-58 had only fallen in 1884-88 from 9s. 5d. to 8s. 5d. a ton.

TABLE VIIA.—*Export and Price of Coal; Tonnage Cleared with Coal, and all other Articles, in each Year.* 1854-87.

	Quantities of Coal Exported.*		Tonnage of Vessels Cleared with Cargoes.		Percentage Increase or Decrease.		Average Price of Coal per Ton.
	Tons Weight.	Tons Capacity.	Total.	Exclusive of Coal.	Coals.	Total Tonnage.	
	Milln.	Milln.	Milln. tons	Milln. tons			s.
1854....	4·3	2·9	7·9	5·0	....	....	9·5
'55....	5·0	3·2	8·3	5·1	15 +	5·1 +	9·5
'56....	5·0	3·9	9·7	5·7	18 „	15·0 „	9·3
'57....	6·7	4·5	10·3	5·8	14 „	7·0 „	9·3
'58....	6·5	4·3	9·9	5·6	3 −	3·8 −	9·1
'59....	7·0	4·7	10·2	5·6	8 +	3·0 +	9·2
1860....	7·3	4·9	10·8	5·9	4 „	5·3 „	8·9
'61....	7·8	5·2	11·3	6·1	7 „	5·0 „	9·0
'62....	8·3	5·5	11·7	6·2	6 „	3·4 „	8·9
'63....	8·3	5·5	11·9	6·4	0·6„	1·5 „	8·8
'64....	8·8	5·9	12·2	6·8	7 „	2·4 „	9·3
'65....	9·2	6·1	12·8	6·6	4 „	5·4 „	9·5
'66....	9·0	6·6	14·0	7·4	9 „	9·0 „	10·1
'67....	10·4	6·9	14·8	7·9	4 „	5·9 „	10·2
'68....	10·8	7·3	15·5	8·2	4 „	4·2 „	9·7
'69....	10·7	7·2	15·9	8·8	1 −	2·6 „	9·4
1870....	11·7	7·8	16·7	8·9	9 +	6·2 „	9·5
'71....	12·7	8·5	19·0	10·6	8 „	13·9 „	9·6
'72....	13·2	8·8	19·2	10·5	4 „	1·0 „	15·5
'73....	12·6	8·4	19·1	10·7	4 −	0·5 −	20·5
'74....	13·9	9·3	19·7	10·5	10 +	3·2 +	17·0
'75....	14·5	9·7	20·4	10·7	4 „	3·3 „	13·1
'76....	16·3	10·9	21·5	10·6	12 „	5·3 „	10·8
'77....	15·4	10·3	21·2	10·9	5 −	1·5 −	10·0
'78....	15·5	10·3	21·6	11·2	0·6+	1·8 +	9·3
'79....	16·4	11·0	22·8	11·9	6 „	5·9 „	8·6
1880....	18·7	12·5	25·6	13·2	14 „	12·4 „	8·8
'81....	19·6	13·1	26·9	13·8	5 „	2·5 „	8·8
'82....	20·9	14·0	27·7	13·7	6 „	5·2 „	9·0
'83....	22·8	15·2	29·4	13·2	9 „	6·0 „	9·2
'84....	23·3	15·5	29·3	13·5	3 „	0·3 −	9·2
'85....	23·8	15·8	29·3	13·5	2 „	Nil	8·8
'86....	23·3	15·5	29·1	13·6	2 −	1·0 −	8·3
'87....	24·5	16·5	30·2	13·7	5 +	5·7 +	8·1
'88....	27·0	18·0	31·7	13·7	10 „	5·0 „	8·4

* Exclusive of bunker coal, or coal shipped for the consumption of steamers engaged in the foreign trade, which in the last three years, 1886-88, has averaged 6·9 millions of tons.

The next table has been compiled to show in juxta-position the average value per register ton of all Imports and Exports, as calculated in Table I (p. 18), and the value of all Exports other than coal, dividing the trade into periods corresponding closely with those arranged in Table I.

TABLE VIIB.—*Average Value per Register Ton of Total Imports and Exports, also of Exports exclusive of Coal, calculated by the omission of the Estimated Register Tonnage and the Declared Value of that article exported, at Ports of the United Kingdom, in each Year from* 1854 *to* 1887.

Years.	Value per Register Ton.				
	Imports.		Total.	Exports.	
	Total.			Total, Exclusive of Coal.	
	Periods.	Years.		Years.	Periods.
	£	£	£	£	£
1854.......		19·3	14·7	22·7	
'55.......		20·4	14·0	22·3	
'56.......		20·9	14·4	23·7	
'57.......		21·5	14·1	24·4	
'58.......	20·3	18·6	14·1	24·4	25·1
'59.......		19·7	15·2	27·3	
1860.......		20·9	15·2	27·3	
'61.......		20·5	14·1	25·5	
'62.......		21·0	14·2	26·3	
'63.......		22·3	16·5	30·0	
'64.......	22·8	24·3	17·4	30·6	31·1
'65.......		22·3	17·0	32·2	
'66.......		22·2	17·1	31·6	
'67.......		20·6	15·2	28·0	
'68.......		21·2	16·7	27·2	
'69.......	20·5	20·4	14·9	26·4	26·9
1870.......		20·3	14·6	26·7	
'71.......		20·1	14·9	26·3	
'72.......		19·8	16·3	29·1	
'73.......	19·6	19·7	16·2	27·8	28·0
'74.......		19·4	15·1	27·2	
'75.......		19·6	13·8	25·3	
'76.......		17·8	11·9	23·2	23·6
'77.......		17·8	11·9	22·4	
'78.......	17·4	17·3	11·4	21·1	
'79.......		17·2	10·9	20·3	20·8
1880.......		17·1	11·1	21·0	
'81.......		17·1	11·3	20·9	
'82.......		16·6	11·1	21·0	
'83.......	16·2	16·2	10·4	22·3	21·7
'84.......		15·8	10·1	21·1	
'85.......		14·4	9·3	19·3	
'86.......	14·1	14·1	9·2	19·0	19·4
'87.......		13·9	9·3	19·8	
'88.......	14·3	14·3	9·4	20·9	20·9

In examining the preceding table and comparing it with that at pp. 18 and 19, the principal results to be noticed are :—

1°. There is a general parallelism in the periods of changes in price of Exports, whether coal be included or not. There is the same sharp temporary rise in 1859-60, and sudden fall in 1861; the same period of inflation in 1863-66, and sharp fall in 1867; the same rise in 1872-74, and fall in 1875; and lastly the same fall in 1885, and slight recovery in 1887.

The exceptions are that, excluding coal :—

(*a.*) The highest price was reached in 1865 instead of 1864.

(*b.*) There was a slight rise in 1882-84, which was overshadowed in the return of total trade by the increasing export of coal.

2°. The average price per register ton of Imports and Exports inclusive of coal in the latter, was shown to be respectively £19·3 and £13·5, the Exports being 29·3 below the Imports; but if coal be excluded from the Exports, the value was £19·3 and £24·9 per ton, the Imports being 22·5 per cent. below the Exports.

3°. In the last year, 1887, compared with the first, Imports had fallen from £19·3 to £13·9 per ton, or 28·0 per cent.; Exports, exclusive of coal, had fallen from £22·7 to £19·8 per ton, or 12·7 per cent.

4°. The fall in periods of Imports has been unchecked since they reached their highest point in 1863-66; in Exports, exclusive of coal, the fall has not only been less, but has been twice broken by triennial periods of a rise.

5°. The remarkable coincidence of the average prices of Exports in the years 1857-58 and 1859-60, being the same respectively in both scales. A third similar coincidence results from taking the value of British and Irish manufactures only as the dividend, the quotients being 21·3 and 22·4 respectively. Such results from three different series of factors are most remarkable.

6°. A comparison of the tonnage and value of Exports, exclusive of coal, during the last ten years, drawn from the last two tables, affords a striking view of the slow advance of tonnage (quantity) during that period after the sudden start in 1880, and the fluctuations, especially the heavy fall in 1880, of value (price) :—

Annual Exports, Exclusive of Coal.

Years.	Tonnage.	Total Value.	Value per Register Ton.
	Milln. tons	Milln. £	£
1878	11·2	238·2	21·1
'79	11·9	241·6	20·3
1880	13·2	278·0	21·0
'81	13·8	288·3	20·9
'82	13·7	297·1	21·0
'83	13·2	294·8	22·3
'84	13·5	285·2	21·1
'85	13·5	260·8	19·3
'86	13·6	258·9	19·0
'87	13·7	270·8	19·8
'88	13·7	287·0	20·9

7°. A monthly table similar to that at p. 26, but for Exports only, exclusive of coal, brings out more distinctly the fluctuations in the price of general merchandise, and the fact that there has been an improvement in the present year from £19·0 iu 1886 and £19·8 in 1887 to £21·0 per ton.

Monthly Exports, Exclusive of Coal.

Months.	Average Value per Register Ton.			
	1886.	1887.	1888.	Average.
	£	£	£	£
January	20·7	21·6	20·9	20·11
February	20·2	21·2	23·6	21·11
March	22·9	20·7	21·9	21·8
April	17·6	18·2	19·0	18·3
May	16·8	16·7	20·4	17·10
June	19·1	18·5	20·6	19·4
July	17·4	19·6	22·2	19·8
August	19·8	18·3	20·8	19·6
September	18·1	19·6	18·0	18·6
October	18·0	19·7	21·0	19·6
November	18·0	19·3	22·4	19·11
December	21·1	21·1	21·3	21·2
Average of year	19·0	19·8	21·0	19·9

To complete and embody the suggestion of a new index number for Exports, a curve has been prepared, which shows the quantity, value, and price of Exports, exclusive of Coal, in each year from 1834 to 1887, taking, as before, 1854 as the base line, in order to afford the means of comparison with the curves Nos. 4 and 7, which include coal, and show the whole of the Export trade. The figures for the series are given in the next page.

In this table and the corresponding curves the tonnage is stated throughout according to the new admeasurement, and 10 per cent. has been added to the value in order to meet the value of foreign and colonial merchandise re-exported. Some remarks upon these curves are desirable.

1. It will be seen, on comparing them with the preceding curves which include coal, how little the curve of value is changed by its omission between 1834 and 1887. In fact the value of coal exported in the first year of the series amounted to only 4·8 per cent. of the total value of Exports, and in the last year to 3·7 per cent. It is only in years when there was a large increase in the export of coal, such as 1874-76-80, that the curve of total Exports is sensibly modified by the elimination of coal. The contrast between the proportions of value and quantity is very striking. In the first year the proportion of tonnage employed iu

the export of Coal to total Export tonnage was 10·7 per cent.; in 1887 it had increased to 54·7.

2. The curve of Quantity also changed but little before 1854, starting a little below the curve of Value, and rising gradually, not subject to the same violent fluctuations as the curves of Price and Value. From 1854 to 1867 it rose in the same direction as those two curves, but considerably below both. In 1867 the curve of Price, which had reached its highest point in 1865, had begun to fall, but the curve of Quantity continued its upward course in the same direction as that of Value, thus maintaining the latter, notwithstanding the fall in Price, until 1870, when the curve of Value made an extraordinary upward shoot, reaching its highest point in 1872, while the curve of Quantity rose but slowly, with much oscillation, until 1876. It then shot upward until 1879, when it met the curve of Value, which had fallen continuously from 1871 to 1878, and the two ran parallel and close together until 1881, denoting a comparative steadiness of price during that period. The curve of Quantity then fell for a couple of years, 1882-83, when it recovered itself and rose steadily to its highest point in 1887.

3. The difference between the closing point in 1887 of Export Tonnage without Coal, as compared with the same including Coal, was as 136 to 302 millions of tons. The difference in value at the same point was as 271 to 281 million £.

4. As regards the curve of Price, the most conspicuous difference is the lowering of the scale, especially in the years 1848 to 1852, which may be accounted for by an insufficient allowance (10 per cent.) for Re-exports. This arbitrary addition to one of the factors necessarily detracts from the worth of this part of the table, previous to 1854, but does not affect the rest; and the curve when taken in connection with that in Table 7, where no such addition was made, shows distinctly the great fluctuations and heavy falls in prices which occurred before the year 1852, and the commencement in that year of an almost continuous rise up to 1865. From the latter year the curve in its general outline agrees with the curve of total Exports, and confirms the statement made at p. 14, that the elimination of the Export of Coal does not materially affect the review of the general Export trade in periods, or even from year to year, beyond raising the price of the mass of other Exports throughout the whole series.

4. The most striking feature is that although prices have fallen greatly from the height which they reached in 1864, they were but slightly lower in 1885-87 than they were in 1854, and are now higher than they were in 1848-51, after making full allowance for the possible error noticed in the preceding paragraph.

Years 1834 5 6 7 8 9 40 1 2 3 4 5 6 7 8 9 50 1 2 3 4 5 6 7 8 9 60 1 2 3 4 5 6 7 8 9 70 1 2 3 4 5 6 7 8 9 80 1 2 3 4 5 6 7

Per Cent.

210

TABLE 7º

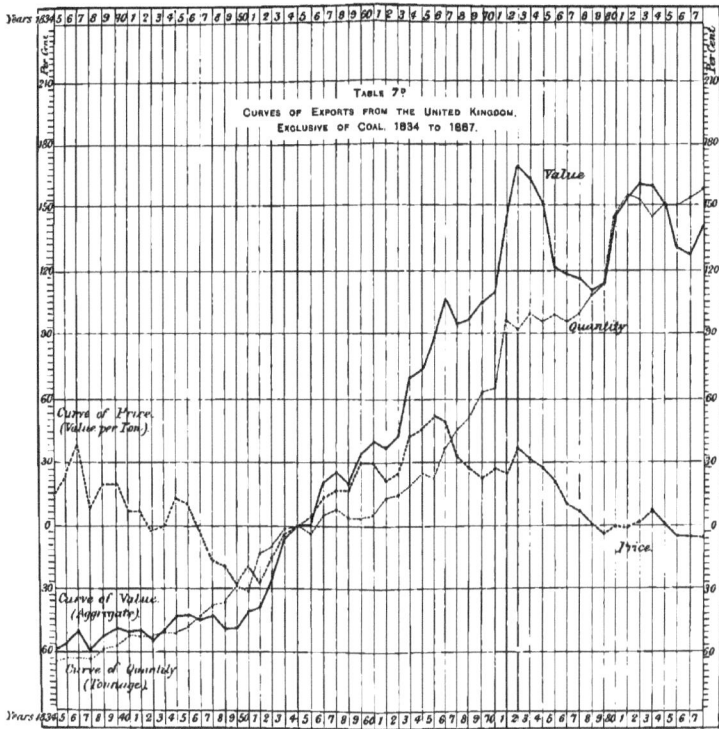

CURVES OF EXPORTS FROM THE UNITED KINGDOM,
EXCLUSIVE OF COAL. 1834 TO 1887.

180

Value

150

120

Quantity

90

60

Curve of Price.
(Value per Ton.)

30

0

Price.

Curve of Value.
(Aggregate.)

30

60

Curve of Quantity
(Tonnage.)

Per Cent.
210
180
150
120
90
60
30
0
30
60

Years 1834 5 6 7 8 9 40 1 2 3 4 5 6 7 8 9 50 1 2 3 4 5 6 7 8 9 60 1 2 3 4 5 6 7 8 9 70 1 2 3 4 5 6 7 8 9 80 1 2 3 4 5 6 7

5. Turning lastly to the table on which these curves are based, it is satisfactory to notice how distinctly it represents periods of inflation and depression. Mr. Giffen notices and defines two of each of these in his report of 1879, viz. :—Of inflation 1863-66 and 1871-73, and of depression 1867-69 and 1875-77; and each of these periods is clearly defined in this table.

In one instance, 1871-73, the change took place a year later than that indicated by Mr. Giffen, and it may be a subject deserving of inquiry whether changes in the declared value of Imports and Exports precede or follow changes in the market prices of commodities. The succession of almost triennial periods of rise and fall in prices during the above period from 1863 to 1878 is worthy of notice.

TABLE VIIc.—*Tonnage cleared with Cargoes and Value of Exports, both exclusive of Coal, and average Value of a Register Ton of Exports exclusive of Coal, in each Year from 1834 to 1887.*

Years.	Exports from the United Kingdom, exclusive of Coal.						
	Tonnage cleared.	Value.	Average Value of Register Ton.	Years.	Tonnage cleared.	Value.	Average Value of Register Ton.
	Milln. tons.	Milln. £	£		Milln. tons.	Milln. £	£
1834	1·9	45·6	24·0	1861	6·1	156·1	25·5
'35	2·0	51·8	25·9	'62	6·2	162·5	26·3
'36	2·0	58·3	28·1	'63	6·4	192·7	30·0
'37	2·0	45·7	22·8	'64	6·8	208·2	30·6
'38	2·2	55·1	25·0	'65	6·6	213·7	32·2
'39	2·3	57·9	25·2	'66	7·4	233·5	31·6
				'67	7·9	221·3	28·0
1840	2·5	55·8	22·3	'68	8·2	222·1	27·2
'41	2·5	55·9	22·4	'69	8·8	231·8	26·4
'42	2·5	50·6	20·2				
'43	2·7	56·7	21·0	1870	8·9	238·4	26·7
'44	2·7	63·6	23·6	'71	10·5	277·3	26·3
'45	2·8	65·0	23·2	'72	10·4	304·2	29·1
'46	3·0	62·5	20·4	'73	10·7	297·8	27·8
'47	3·3	63·7	19·3	'74	10·5	285·6	27·2
'48	3·4	56·9	16·7	'75	10·7	271·9	25·3
'49	3·8	57·8	15·2	'76	10·6	247·9	23·2
				'77	10·7	244·5	22·4
1850	3·9	66·1	16·9	'78	11·2	238·2	21·1
'51	4·5	69·4	15·4	'79	11·9	241·6	20·3
'52	4·8	84·4	17·5				
'53	5·3	107·0	20·2	1880	13·2	278·0	21·0
'54	5·4	113·7	21·0	'81	13·8	288·3	20·9
'55	5·2	114·3	21·9	'82	13·7	297·1	21·6
'56	5·7	136·4	23·7	'83	13·2	294·8	22·3
'57	5·8	143·0	24·4	'84	13·5	285·2	21·1
'58	5·6	136·8	24·4	'85	13·5	260·8	19·3
'59	5·6	152·4	27·3	'86	13·6	258·9	19·0
				'87	13·7	270·8	19·8
1860	5·9	160·9	27·3	'88	13·7	287·8	20·9

§ 3. *Proportions of Chief Constituents.*

The next two tables, the materials for which are gathered from Mr. Giffen's reports, show the proportion in which each of the principal articles of Import and Export enumerated by him enter into the composition of the total amount of the trade of the United Kingdom. The years are not continuous; they are those for which the data are supplied in the reports.

TABLE VIII.—*Percentage Proportion which each of the principal Articles Imported of Years, not consecutive,*

(Compiled from " Board of Trade Reports

	1854.	1855.	1857. 1859.	1861. 1863.	1865.	1866.
A. *Articles of Food.*								
1. Corn, grain, and meal of all kinds	14·25	12·19	10·31	10·07	16·05	10·42	7·64	10·18
2. Sugar, raw, refined, and molasses	7·07	7·65	8·73	6·99	6·09	4·97	4·80	4·14
3. Tea	3·64	3·64	2·49	3·24	3·15	4·28	3·71	3·80
4. Wine	2·37	2·14	2·17	1·55	1·78	1·81	1·44	1·60
5. Butter	1·42	1·43	1·10	1·16	2·25	1·82	2·19	2·02
6. Coffee	1·03	1·18	0·92	1·09	1·21	1·67	1·70	1·38
7. Animals, cattle. and sheep	0·75	1 02	0·81	0·84	0·93	0·98	2·05	1·78
8. Bacon and hams	0·59	0·43	0·56	0·16	0·62	1·10	0·79	0·64
9. Cheese	0·59	0·72	0·52	0·58	0·75	0·76	0·91	0·95
10. Fruit	0 63	0·99	1·08	1·23	0·99	0·92	0·81	0·73
11. Other	5·39	5·19	5·11	3·70	4·66	4·54	4·02	4·13
Total	37·73	36·58	33·80	30·91	38·45	33·27	30·06	31·35
B. *Raw Materials.*								
12. Cotton, raw	13·24	14·52	15·59	19·29	17·77	22·61	24·36	26·26
13. Wood and timber	7·67	5·88	5·15	5·65	5·39	4·98	5·10	4 28
14. Wool, sheep's, and all other	4·26	4·55	5·15	5·48	4·47	4·77	5·51	5·94
15. Silk, raw, thrown and knubs	4 28	3·87	7·78	6·08	3·84	3 95	4·10	2·65
16. Flax and tow, dressed & undressed	2·25	2·32	1·89	2·11	1·58	1·74	2·00	1·52
17. Metals	1·99	2·52	2·46	2·72	2·30	2·80	2·57	2·17
18. Flax and linseed	1·67	1·77	1·63	1·70	1·43	1·35	1·47	1·14
19. Guano	1·66	2·19	1·92	0·43	0·93	1·07	0·99	0·49
20. Tallow and stearine	1·54	1·85	1·76	1·66	1·53	0·99	1·17	1·03
21. Hemp and jute	1·56	1·37	1·03	1·30	0·87	1·37	1·30	1·08
22. Oils, palm	1·14	1·23	0·99	0·86	0·73	0·57	0·54	0·54
23. „ other	2·07	2·54	1·79	1·73	1 48	1·43	1·34	1·08
24. Hides and skins	1·23	1·44	2·38	1·96	1 34	1·28	1·10	1·12
25. Leather	0·32	0·31	0·39	0·35	0·24	0·28	0·31	0·34
26. Indigo	1·10	1·13	1·16	1·08	1·37	0·94	0·74	0·75
27. Other	1·71	1·58	2·54	3·33	2·38	1·94	2·53	3·32
Total	47·69	49·07	53·61	55·43	47·65	52·11	55·13	53·71
C. *Other "enumerated" Articles.* Total	2·66	3·29	2·52	2·54	2·45	3·00	2·92	2·68
Total of "enumerated" articles	88·08	88·94	89·93	88·88	88·58	88·33	88·11	87·74
„ "unenumerated" „	11·92	11·06	10·07	11·12	11·42	11·62	11·89	12·26
Total	100·00	100·00	100·00	100·00	100·00	100 00	100·00	100·00

a. *Imports.*

The Imports extend from 1854 to 1886, and are classed under
four heads:—

- *a.* Articles of food.
- *b.* Raw materials.
- *c.* Other "enumerated" articles.
- *d.* "Unenumerated" articles.

The Exports, which comprise only the Produce and Manufactures of the United Kingdom, do not call for the same distinctions,
and are divided into "enumerated" and "unenumerated." They
extend backwards to the year 1840, and are shown at pp. 42 and 43.

 United Kingdom contributed to the Total Value of such Imports, in a series
ng from 1854 to 1886.
es of Exports and Imports.")

1870.	1871.	1873.	1875.	1877.	1879.	1880.	1881.	1883.	1884.	1885.	1886.
11·26	12·90	13·94	14·20	16·12	16·88	15·29	15·32	15·85	12·31	14·36	12·45
5·79	5·59	5·71	5·87	6·93	6·16	5·59	6·15	5·89	5·08	4·98	4·57
3·33	3·52	3·06	3·68	3·16	3·10	2·82	2·82	2·70	2·69	2·87	3·23
1·59	2·14	2·23	1·82	1·81	1·48	1·57	1·42	1·28	1·37	1·38	1·46
2·24	2·10	1·87	2·27	2·42	2·86	2·95	2·74	2·76	3·22	3·12	3·17
1·63	1·63	1·95	2·01	1·97	1·95	1·67	1·20	1·16	0·96	0·89	0·94
1·28	1·31	1·21	1·63	1·38	1·79	2·30	1·97	2·50	2·37	2·11	1·86
0·58	0·82	1·68	1·87	1·74	2·44	2·68	2·70	2·35	2·24	2·34	2·40
1·08	1·01	1·09	1·26	1·21	1·05	1·24	1·32	1·15	1·28	1·10	1·11
0·71	0·95	0·82	1·02	1·10	1·05	0·80	1·04	0·98	1·09	1·05	0·97
5·13	4·99	5·97	5·52	6·22	6·84	6·35	6·15	6·31	6·50	6·97	6·98
34·02	36·96	39·53	41·15	44·06	45·60	43·26	42·83	42·93	39·11	41·17	39·14
17·63	16 89	14·73	12·37	8·98	9·97	10·40	11·04	10·55	11·41	9·83	10·90
4 34	3·65	5·06	4·12	5·14	2·96	4·07	3·78	4·03	3·86	4·12	3·60
5·21	5·42	5·26	6·27	6·23	6·49	6·41	6·55	5·85	6·80	5·71	6·45
3·07	2·96	1·99	1·06	1·24	1·69	1·00	0·85	0·88	1·18	0·63	0·74
1·99	1·78	1·44	1·20	1·32	1·01	1·02	0 88	0·70	0·80	0·89	0·71
2·20	2·27	2·55	2·81	2·51	2·54	2·47	2·46	2·55	2·72	2·78	2·67
1·82	1·11	1·11	1·37	1·15	1·13	1·04	1·10	1·12	0·98	1·18	1·21
1·15	0·60	0·57	0·35	0·42	0·19	0·20	0·12	0·17	0·11	0·07	0·15
1·09	0·95	0·85	0·55	0 65	0·58	0·56	0·53	0·49	0·54	0·43	0·37
1 44	1·82	1·60	1·28	1·24	1·35	1·41	1·53	1·62	1·46	1·47	1·36
0·52	0 55	0·46	0·40	0·41	0·37	0·37	0·30	0·31	0·36	0·33	0·30
1·05	1·22	1·04	1·03	0 89	0·83	0·69	0·80	0·73	0·65	0·67	0·61
1·54	1·56	1·80	1·54	1·25	1·18	1·39	1·23	1·34	1·53	1·58	1·61
0·42	0·54	0 78	1·00	1·00	0 95	1·10	1·21	1·28	1·39	1·56	1·58
0·90	0·89	0·66	0·43	0·42	0·53	0·42	0·59	0·58	0·64	0 57	0·55
4·16	3·93	3·31	3·76	3 43	2·99	3·55	3·14	4·03	4·55	4·46	4·50
48·03	46·14	43·25	39·54	36·28	34·16	36·10	36·11	36·23	38·98	36·28	37·31
2·67	3·02	2·82	3·04	3·15	2·70	2·50	2·75	2·66	1·93	2·16	2·17
84·72	86·12	85·60	83·73	83·49	82·46	81·86	81·69	81·82	80·02	79·61	78·62
15·28	13·88	14·40	16·27	16·51	17·54	18·14	18·31	18·18	19·98	20·33	21·38
100·00	100·00	100·00	100·00	100·00	100·00	100·00	100·00	100·00	100·00	100·00	100·00

In examining this and the following tables, the remarks made in the note at p. 3 must be borne in mind. The class of "unenumerated" articles contains a large number, of which the value is stated, many of which are of great importance, and which would swell in different proportions the three groups of A. B. C, the latter of which consists chiefly of manufactures. The labour of eliminating and distributing these for the series of years would be too great, but the following epitome for the two extreme years will give an idea of the results of such an operation.

In 1854 this class amounted to 2·5 per cent. of the whole, and consisted of only 4 articles, all manufactures, viz., clocks and watches, and manufactures of hair, silk, and wool. In 1886 it amounted to 11·1 per cent., 'and consisted of 27 articles, of which 3, amounting to 0·6 per cent., belonged to Group A ; 9, amounting to 2·4 per cent., belonged to Group B; and 15, amounting to 8·1 per cent., belonged to Group C.*

The first Table (VIII), relating to Imports, exhibits the following results :—

1. On the average of the twenty-one years the relative proportion of each class was :—

	Per cent.		
Of articles of food	37·99 ⎤		
„ raw materials	44·32 ⎬ 85·00 ⎤		
„ other enumerated articles	2·69 ⎦ ⎬ 100		
„ unenumerated „	15·00 ⎦		

2. The differences between the first and last years of the period, with the necessary correction by apportioning the known items of the unenumerated class, was as follows .—

	1854.	1886.
Of articles of food	37·73	39·74
„ raw materials	47·69	39·71
„ other enumerated articles	5·16	10·27
Total	90·58	89·72
Of unenumerated articles	9·42	10·28
	100·00	100·00

Thus the proportion of articles of

Food has increased	5·3 per cent.
Raw materials has decreased	16·9 „
Other enumerated articles has increased	9·9 „
Unenumerated articles has increased	9·1 „

3. In the year 1886 ten articles in the first class, viz., corn and grain of all kinds, sugar, tea, wine, butter, coffee, cattle and

* The details of these are given at p. 48.

sheep, bacon and hams, cheese and fruit composed 32·2 of the total Imports; corn and grain alone constituted 12·4 per cent. In the years 1880-83 the last named had contributed 15·5 per cent.

4. In comparing the latest year, 1886, with one of the earliest, it is desirable not to take the first or second year, 1854-55, during which commerce was deranged by the Crimean war, nor 1856, which was affected by the reaction consequent upon the peace, and for which, indeed, the data are not given, but rather 1857. Comparing then 1886 with 1857, which was a fairly average year, the total Importation—

Of all food	Had increased from	33·8	to	39·1	per cent.
„ corn and grain	„	10·3	„	12·4	„
„ tea	„	2·5	„	3·2	„
„ butter	„	1·1	„	3·2	„
„ coffee	„	0·9	„	0·9	„
„ cattle and sheep....	„	0·8	„	1·9	„
„ bacon and hams....	„	0·6	„	2·4	„
„ cheese..................	„	0·5	„	1·1	„
„ sugar	Had decreased from	8·7	„	4·6	„
„ wine	„	2·2	„	1·5	„
„ fruit	„	1·1	„	1·0	„
„ other articles........	Had increased from	5·1	„	7·0	„

5. The extremes of fluctuation during the twenty-one years ranged—

For corn and grain	From 7·6 per cent. in 1865 to 16·9 per cent. in 1879
„ sugar	„	4·1	„	'66	„	8·73	„	'57
„ tea....................	„	2·5	„	'57	„	4·3	„	'63
„ wine....................	„	1·3	„	'83	„	2·4	„	'54
„ butter	„	1·1	„	'57	„	3·2	„	'84
„ coffee	„	0·9	„	'85	„	2·0	„	'75
„ cattle and sheep....	„	0·7	„	'54	„	2·5	„	'83
„ bacon and hams	„	0·2	„	'59	„	2·7	„	'81
„ cheese	„	0·5	„	'57	„	1·3	„	'81
„ fruit..........	„	0·6	„	'54	„	1·2	„	'59
„ other articles	„	3·4	„	'68	„	7·0	„	'86

or more than 100 per cent. for most of the articles. The minor articles in this class have fluctuated in like manner between 3·4 per cent. in 1868, and 7 per cent. in 1886.

The population of the United Kingdom increased between the same two years 30·2 per cent.

6. Extending a similar comparison to raw materials, fifteen articles or classes of articles, viz., raw cotton, wood and timber, sheep's wool, silk, flax and tow, metals, flax and linseed, guano, tallow, hemp and jute, oils, hides and skins, leather and indigo, composed 32·8 per cent. of the total Imports in the year 1886, and of this 10·9, or exactly a third, consisted of raw cotton.

7. Comparing the year 1886 with 1857, the following changes, some of which are very notable, have taken place; but it must be borne in mind that the changes are relative, not actual. The proportion of the total importation—

Of all raw materials....	Had decreased from	53·6	to	37·3	per cent.
„ „ cotton	„	15·6	„	10·9	„
„ wood and timber...	„	5·1	„	3·6	„
„ silk	„	7·8	„	0·7	„
„ flax and tow	„	1·9	„	0·7	„
„ „ linseed	„	1·6	„	1·2	„
„ guano	„	1·9	„	0·1	„
„ tallow and stearine	„	1·8	„	0·4	„
„ palm oil	„	1·0	„	0·3	„
„ other oils	„	1·8	„	0·6	„
„ hides and skins	„	2·4* „	1·6	„
„ indigo	„	1·2	„	0·5	„
„ sheep's wool	Had increased from	5·1	„	6·4	„
„ metals	„	2·5	„	2·7	„
„ hemp and jute	„	1·0	„	1·4	„
„ leather..	„	0·4	„	1·6	„
„ other articles	„	2·5	„	4·5	„

8. The extremes of fluctuation during these years had been for each article severally :—

* An exceptionally large importation.

TABLE IX.—*Percentage Proportion which each of the principal Articles of British and Irish of such Exports, in a series of years, not*

(Compiled from the Board of Trade

	1840.	1841.	1845.	1848.	1849.	1852.	1853.	1854.	1855.	1857.	1859.
1. Coals and culm	1·1	1·3	1·5	2·0	1·6	1·7	1·5	2·0	2·4	2·5	2·4
2. Cotton yarn	13·8	14·1	11·6	11·2	10·5	8·5	7·0	6·9	7·5	7·1	7·3
3. „ piece goods	31·8	29·1	30·1	29·7	29·6	27·8	24·2	24·2	27·3	23·6	28·4
4. Linen yarn	1·6	1·9	1·6	0·9	1·2	1·5	1·2	1·0	1·0	1·4	1·3
5. „ manufactures	6·2	6·1	4·6	4·8	4·9	4·8	4·4	3·9	3·9	3·4	3·3
6. Metals, iron and steel	3·1	3·8	3·8	6·9	5·9	6·2	8·1	8·6	7·1	12·3	10·7
7. „ other	2·4	2·6	2·1	2·9	3·7	2·8	2·3	2·5	3·0	3·3	2·7
8. Woollen yarn	0·9	1·1	1·8	1·5	1·7	1·8	1·5	1·6	2·0	2·3	2·2
9. „ manufactures	10·0	10·7	12·3	10·4	11·0	10·8	9·8	9·0	7·5	8·1	8·7
	70·9	70·7	49·6	70·3	70·1	68·9	60·0	60·5	61·7	64·0	67·0
All other "enumerated" articles	8·2	8·6	7·5	6·2	6·0	4·2	7·3	6·9	3·6	3·4	
Total of "enumerated" articles..............	79·1	79·3	77·1	76·5	76·1	73·1	67·3	67·4	70·7	67·6	70·4
„ of articles "unenumerated" and entered *ad valorem*	20·9	20·7	22·9	23·5	23·9	26·9	32·7	32·6	29·3	32·4	29·6
Total	100·0	100·0	100·0	100·0	100·0	100·0	100·0	100·0	100·0	100·0	100·0

NOTE.—The sudden rise in the proportion of iron and steel, and the corresponding fall in that of all other "enumerated" likewise a small proportion of yellow metal and of linen manufactures were similarly arranged under their period.

b. *Exports.*

The second Table (IX), relating to Exports, exhibits the following results :—

Of raw cotton .... From 9·0 per cent. in 1877 to 26·3 per cent. in 1866
„ wood and timber... „ 3·0 „ '79 „ 7·7 „ '54
„ sheep's wool .... „ 4·3 „ '54 „ 6·8 „ '84
„ silk .... „ 0·9 „ '81 „ 7·8 „ '57
„ flax and tow .... „ 0·7 „ '83 „ 2·3 „ '55
„ metals .... „ 2·0 „ '54 „ 2·8 „ '75
„ flax and linseed .... „ 1·0 „ '84 „ 1·8 „ '55
„ guano .... „ 0·1 „ '85 „ 2·2 „ '55
„ tallow .... „ 0·4 „ '86 „ 1·8 „ '55
„ hemp and jute .... „ 0·9 „ '61 „ 1·8 „ '71
„ palm oil .... „ 0·3 „ $\left.\begin{array}{c}\text{'81}\\\text{'86}\end{array}\right\}$ „ 1·2 „ '55
„ other oils.............. „ 0·6 „ '86 „ 2·5 „ '55
„ hides and skins .... „ 1·1 „ '65 „ 2·4 „ '57
„ leather.................. „ 0·2 „ '61 „ 1·6 „ '86
„ indigo .... „ 0·4 „ $\left.\begin{array}{c}\text{'77}\\\text{'80}\end{array}\right\}$ „ 1·4 „ '61
„ other articles .... „ 1·6 „ '55 „ 4·5 „ '84

It will be seen that the fluctuations, which in articles of food did not much exceed 100 per cent., have seldom been less than 300 per cent., and have been in some cases much higher. In both classes variations in price have had a great if not the greatest influence in constituting the proportion of each article in each year.

9. There has been a tolerably steady increase throughout the period of unenumerated articles, interrupted only by a fall in 1861, and a sudden rise, not maintained, in 1870.

Produce and Manufactures Exported from the United Kingdom contributed to the Total Value consecutive, extending from 1840 to 1886.
Reports of Prices of Exports and Imports.)

1861.	1863. 1865.	1866.	1868. 1870.	1871.	1873. 1875.	1877. 1879.	1880.	1881	1883. 1884.	1885.	1886.
2·7	2·4 2·5	2·6	2·9 2·7	2·6	4·8 4·1	3·8 3·5	3·5	3·5	4·2 4·4	4·7	4·3
7·4	5·5 6·2	7·2	8·2 7·4	6·8	6·2 5·9	6·1 6·3	5·3	5·4	5·6 5·9	5·6	5·4
28·9	25·6 27·1	30·7	27·9 26·8	24·0	22·0 24·0	26·4 24·5	25·8	25·3	23·1 22·2	22·6	23·6
1·3	1·7 1·5	1·3	1·3 1·1	1·0	0·8 0·8	0·6 0·6	0·4	0·5	0·4 0·5	0·5	0·4
2·9	4·2 5·3	4·9	4·1 3·8	3·6	3·2 3·5	3·4 3·5	3·4	3·4	3·0 3·0	2·8	2·9
8·9	10·1 9·5	9·1	10·0 12·1	11·6	14·8 11·0	10·2 10·1	12·8	11·8	11·8 10·6	10·3	10·1
2·5	4·0 2·6	2·1	2·6 2·4	2·3	2·1 2·3	2·5 2·4	2·3	2·2	2·1 2·2	2·1	2·0
2·7	3·3 3·1	2·4	3·5 2·5	2·7	2·1 2·3	1·8 1·9	1·5	1·1	1·4 1·7	2·1	2·1
8·5	10·0 11·7	11·0	10·5 10·5	11·7	9·2 9·2	8·2 7·6	7·1	7·2	7·1 8·0	8·2	8·6
65·8	66·8 64·5	71·2	71·0 69·3	66·3	6·2 63·1	63·0 60·4	62·1	60·9	58·7 58·5	58·9	59·4
5·3	2·5 1·7	2·5	2·4 2·7	3·6	2·0 2·7	3·4 3·2	2·0	2·0	2·3 1·9	1·3	2·2
71·1	69·3 71·2	73·7	73·4 72·0	69·9	67·2 65·8	66·4 63·6	64·1	62·9	61·0 60·4	61·2	61·6
28·9	30·7 28·8	28·3	26·6 28·0	30·1	32·8 34·2	33·6 36·4	35·9	37·1	39·0 39·6	38·8	38·4
100·0	100·0 100·0	100·0	100·0 100·0	100·0	100·0 100·0	100·0 100·0	100·0	100·0	100·0 100·0	100·0	100·0

articles in 1857, was caused by the transfer of certain descriptions of the former from the latter category. No proper headings in 1845 and 1852 respectively. The other articles range without change throughout the whole

1. On the average of the same twenty-one years the relative proportion of each class was:—

Of nine principal enumerated articles (quantities stated).... 63·9 per cent.
„ all other enumerated articles   „   .... 3·2   „
„ enumerated articles   (value only stated).... 28·4   „
„ unenumerated   „   .... 4·5   „

                                            100·0

2. The differences between the first and last years of the period, with the changes corresponding to those made in the notes on Imports, were as follows :—

	1854.	1886.
Of nine principal enumerated articles (quantities stated)	60·5	59·4
„ other enumerated articles (quantities stated)	6·9	2·2
„ enumerated articles (value only stated)	27·6	33·4
„ unenumerated articles „	5·0	5·0
	100·0	100·0

3. The proportion in which each of the above nine enumerated articles contributed to the aggregate on the average of twenty-one years was as follows :—

1. Cotton piece goods .... 25·5 per cent.
2. Metals, iron and steel .... 10·7 „
3. Woollen manufactures .... 9·0 „
4. Cotton yarn .... 6·4 „
5. Linen manufactures................ 3·7 „
6. Coals and culm...................... 3·2 „
7. Metals, other....................... 2·5 „
8. Woollen yarn .... 2·1 „
9. Linen   „   .... 0·9 „

Total .... 64·0

4. In comparing the year 1886 with 1857, the proportion of the exportation of—

Coals and culm .... Had increased from   2·5 to 4·3 per cent.
Woollen manufactures ....   „   8·1 „ 8·6   „
Cotton piece goods........... Had remained stationary at 23·6 „ 23·6   „
   „ yarn .... Had decreased from   7·1 „ 5·4   „
Linen „   ....   „   1·4 „ 0·4   „
   „ manufactures ....   „   3·4 „ 2·9   „
Metals, iron and steel ....   „   12·3 „ 10·1   „
   „ other ....   „   3·3 „ 2·0   „
Woollen yarn.................   „   2·3 „ 2·1   „
Other enumerated articles   „   3·6 „ 2·3   „

It must be noted that the comparison for iron and steel is not fair, as 1857 was an exceptional year. The average of 1855-59 and 1861 was only 10·0, instead of 12·3 per cent. as above. This statement affords an illustration of the extent to which new articles of commerce have entered into the aggregate of Exports since 1857.

5. The extremes of fluctuation during the twenty-one years ranged—

For coals	From 2·0 per cent. in 1854	to	4·8 per cent. in 1873
„ cotton yarn	„ 5·3	„	'80	„ 8·2	.,	'68
„ „ piece goods....	„ 22·2	„	'84	„ 30·7	„	'46
„ linen yarn	„ 0·4	„	{'80 '83 '86}	„ 1·7	„	'64
„ „ manufactures..	„ 2·8	„	'85	„ 5·3	„	'65
„ metals, iron and steel	„ 7·1	„	'55	„ 14·8	„	'73
„ „ other	„ 2·0	„	'86	„ 4·0	„	'63
„ woollen yarn	„ 1·4	„	{'81 '83}	„ 3·5	„	'68
„ „ manufactures	„ 7·1	„	{'80 '83}	„ 11·7	„	{'65 '71}

The range, it will be seen, has been less wide than in Imports either of food or raw materials; it has been widest in coal, metals, linen and woollen yarns.

6. The increase in the proportion of articles entered by value only has occurred chiefly within the last seven years, viz., from 1879 to 1886.

It has not been deemed necessary to carry the comparisons further back than the year 1854.

c. *Principal Articles omitted or added.*

A strong indication of changes in the course of trade is furnished by the following statements of the articles which were included among the "principal" commodities of Imports and Exports in 1856, and have since been omitted, and also of those which have been added in the latter years:—

Imports.

A. *Articles included in 1856, and omitted in 1886.*

Value in 1856.

£

1. Dyeing stuffs, geraneine	177,394	Included with madder.
2. Silk manufactures of India	401,645	„ silk goods.
3. Skins, sheep, tanned or dressed	37,567	
4. „ lamb „	2,462	
5. „ goat „	52,826	
6. Spices, Cassia Lignea	46,575	Included with other sorts of spices.
7. „ cloves	32,569	
8. „ nutmegs	54,602	
Total	805,640	

B. *Articles inserted in 1886, and not included in 1856.*

| | Value in 1886. | | |
	Food.	Raw Materials.	Manufactures.
	£	£	£
1. Butterine	2,962,264	—	—
2. Candles of all sorts	—	—	143,652
3. China, porcelain, and earthenware	—	—	521,418
4. Cotton manufactures	—	—	1,858,918
5. Drugs, Peruvian bark	—	801,353	—
6. „ opium	307,666	—	—
7. Dyeing stuffs, unenumerated	—	749,942	—
8. Dye woods	—	415,891	—
9. Feathers, ornamental	—	1,287,595	—
10. Flax, tow, or codilla	—	427,819	—
11. Fruit, raw, exclusive of nuts	2,147,309	—	—
12. Gum of all sorts	—	1,046,345	—
13. Hemp, dressed	included with undressed		
14. Lace and articles thereof	—	—	447,253
15. Leather	—	5,536,225	—
16. Meat, unenumerated, salted or fresh..	1,516,851	—	—
17. „ preserved, other than salted	1,169,777	—	—
18. Metals, iron ore	—	1,894,626	—
19. „ „ and steel, wrought or manufactured	—	2,200,265	—
20. „ zinc, crude, in cakes	—	774,938	—
21. „ „ manufactures	—	—	326,004
22. Musical instruments	—	—	729,805
23. Nuts and kernels, for oil pressing	—	598,529	—
24. Onions, raw	506,710	—	—
25. Painter's colours and pigments	—	778,027	—
26. Paper, for printing or writing	—	—	476,884
27. „ other, except hangings	—	—	1,011,037
28. Petroleum, unrefined and refined	—	—	2,091,276
29. Poultry, game, and rabbits	639,704	—	—
30. Pyrites of iron or copper	—	1,029,839	—
31. Seeds, grass	included with clover		
32. „ cotton	—	1,491,670	—
33. Silk, knubs or husks, and waste	—	815,742	—
34. Skins, furs of all sorts	—	817,565	—
35. Toys	—	—	618,576
36. Woollen and worsted yarn, Berlin, &c.	—	—	263,820
37. „ for weaving	—	2,228,715	—
	9,727,165	22,351,190	8,188,643
		40,266,998	

As regards Imports, it will be seen how few and unimportant are those which have ceased to be classed as "principal"—only 8 out of 112—valued at £805,640 or 0·5 per cent. of the total Imports; while in 1886, 37 articles have been added, valued at £40 millions, or 11·1 per cent. of the total Imports.

Of this addition—

Milln. £
9·7 consisted of food
22·3   „   raw materials
8·2   „   manufactures

In 1856 the value of unenumerated articles amounted to 8·5 per cent. of the total Imports, and in 1886 to 7·7 per cent.

A similar comparison of the following statements of Exports shows the following results:—

The omissions from the list in 1856 are 9 out of 88, valued at £1,161,897, or 1·0 of the total Exports. The additions have been 24 in number, valued at £15· millions, or 7·1 per cent. of the total Exports. It is worthy of notice that 4 out of the 9 omissions since 1856 consist of agricultural implements, bacon and hams, beef and pork, and horses; while among the Exports pictures have assumed a position.

Exports.

A. *Articles included in* 1856, *and omitted in* 1886.

Value in 1856.
£

1. Agricultural implements	154,993	
2. Bacon and hams	214,199	
3. Beef and pork	122,527	
4. Carriages	143,268	
5. Glass, window	35,311	
6. Horses	100,349	
7. Metals, copper, bars, rods, &c.	239,315	Included with other sorts.
8. „ lead ore, red and white lead, and litharge	151,935	
9. Jewellery	—	„ Plate, &c.
Total	1,161,897	

B. *Articles inserted in* 1886, *and not inserted in* 1856.

Value in 1886.
£

1. Biscuit and bread	518,169
2. Bleaching materials	502,919
3. Candles of all sorts	Stearine only in 1856
4. Caoutchouc manufactures	971,108
5. Carriages, railway	913,244
6. Clocks and watches	207,461
7. Coals, products, except dyes	622,398
8. Cotton piece goods, mixed materials	11,536
9. „ stockings and socks	487,378
10. „ thread for sewing	2,586,765
11. Linen yarn, jute	273,315
12. „ manufactures, sails added to sail cloth	—
13. „ thread for sewing	366,774
14. „ jute manufactures	1,807,322
15. Manure	1,614,643
16. Medicines	814,213
17. Metals, steel manufactures, or of iron and steel	403,152
18. Musical instruments	207,842
19. Oil and floor cloth	688,773
20. Pictures	242,491
21. Rags and other materials for paper	383,406
22. Skins and furs, British	490,883
23. „ foreign, British dressed	352,229
24. Umbrellas and parasols	526,348
Total	14,994,674

d. Classification of Articles at Different Periods.

The following statement, compiled from the Return in the Appendix to the Royal Commission, already referred to, furnishes an instructive analysis of the composition of Exports of British and Irish Manufactures and Produce exported at different periods in the years between 1855 and 1884:—

Percentage Proportion of Declared Value of Exports of British Produce.

Quinquennial Periods.	Manufactured Goods.	Articles partly Manufactured.	Raw Materials.	Articles of Food.	Total.
	£	£	£	£	£
1855-59........	74·2	17·2	3·4	5·2	100
1860-64........	75·3	15·9	4·4	4·4	100
1865-69........	76·0	16·7	4·0	3·3	100
1870-74........	74·8	15·8	5·6	3·8	100
1875-79........	76·0	14·0	5·5	4·5	100
1880-84........	76·7	13·0	6·0	4·3	100
Average....	75·5	15·4	4·8	4·3	100

It will be seen how the proportion of Exports of manufactured articles has gradually increased, except in 1870-74, when the increase in raw materials and food diminished it considerably; how that of articles partly manufactured has gradually and largely decreased, except in the years 1865-69, when it increased at the expense of raw materials and food; how raw materials, coal and iron chiefly, have very largely increased, but especially in the years 1870-74; and how articles of food decreased largely between 1855 and 1869, recovered themselves partially between 1870 and 1879, and have fallen off slightly in the last period. This refers only to the relative value. The actual value in the last three periods has been:—

	Raw Materials.	Articles of Food.
	Mil. £	Mil. £
In 1870-74	13	7
„ '75-79	11	9
„ '80-84	14	10

TABLE X.—*Average Prices of the Principal Articles of Food and Raw Materials Imported into the United Kingdom, deduced from the declared Quantities and Values, as stated in the Statistical Abstracts of the United Kingdom, in each Year from 1854 to 1866.*

(Compiled from Board of Trade "Reports on Prices of Exports and Imports.")

A.—FOOD.

Table XI. *Average Price of the Principal Articles of the Produce and Manufactures of the United Kingdom Exported therefrom, deduced from the Declared Quantities and Values, as stated in the Statistical Abstracts of the United Kingdom in each Year from 1854 to 1866.*

(Compiled from Board of Trade Reports on Prices of Exports and Imports.)

§ 5. *Prices of Chief Articles.*

a. *Annual Prices; Tables X and XI.*

This series of tables, compiled from Mr. Giffen's Reports, exhibits the average prices of the principal articles of Imports, distinguishing articles of food from raw materials, and of Exports of the Produce and Manufactures of the United Kingdom, in each year from 1854 to 1886, rising prices being distinguished from falling prices by being placed in a different line, and printed in a different type.

At the bottom of each of these tables the percentage proportion of the value of all articles specified in it to the total value of all articles is stated for those years in which the information has been furnished; and below each is stated the number of articles of which the price rose and fell in each year.

The design of this latter annex is twofold: first to ascertain whether, and to what extent, a rise or fall in prices extends over all the enumerated articles in the same year, and secondly to show in figures the difference already exhibited in the Tables of Curves between the two equal periods of sixteen years into which these tables are divided.

b. *As to Uniformity of Rise and Fall.*

As to the first point, and as regards Imports—

Out of 11 articles of Food—			*Out of 16 articles of Raw Materials—*		
11 rose together in no year			16		
10 " 2 years			15	rose together in no year	
9 " 2 "	7		14		
8 " 3 "			13		6
			12 " 4 years		
			11 " 2 "		
11 fell together in 2 "			16 fell together in 1 "		
10 " 2 "			15 " 1 "		
9 " 4 "	13		14 " 2 "		12
8 " 5 "			13 " 1 "		
		20	12 " 1 "		
			11 " 6 "		18
7 rose together in 2 "			10 fell together in 5 "		
7 fell " 2 "			9 rose " 1 "		
6 rose " 5 "	12		9 fell " 2 "		14
6 fell " 3 "			8 rose and 8 fell 6 "		
Total	32		Total	32	

As regards Exports, out of 12 articles—

$$
\left.
\begin{array}{lll}
12 \text{ rose together in } 2 \text{ years} \\
10 \quad\quad\quad\quad 1 \quad\text{,,} \\
9 \quad\text{,,}\quad\quad\quad 3 \quad\text{,,} \\
8 \quad\text{,,}\quad\quad\quad 1 \quad\text{,,}
\end{array}
\right\} 7
$$

$$
\left.
\begin{array}{lll}
12 \text{ fell together in } 3 \quad\text{,,} \\
11 \quad\text{,,}\quad\quad\quad 3 \quad\text{,,} \\
10 \quad\text{,,}\quad\quad\quad 2 \quad\text{,,} \\
9 \quad\text{,,}\quad\quad\quad 5 \quad\text{,,} \\
8 \quad\text{,,}\quad\quad\quad 4 \quad\text{,,}
\end{array}
\right\} 17
$$

$$\underline{}$$
$$24$$

$$
\left.
\begin{array}{lll}
7 \text{ rose together in } 4 \quad\text{,,} \\
7 \text{ fell} \quad\quad\quad\quad 3 \quad\text{,,} \\
6 \text{ rose and } 6 \text{ fell in } 1 \quad\text{,,}
\end{array}
\right\} 8
$$

$$\underline{}$$
$$32$$

Experts can from the above figures form a judgment as to the extent to which uniformity usually prevails in the rise or fall of prices, and also as to the degree of uncertainty which attends the application of average prices drawn from a limited number of articles to the whole volume of trade.

As to the second point, it is shown that dividing the whole period into two equal terms, viz., from 1854 to 1870, and from 1871 to 1886, the contrast between the two as regards rising and falling prices is very striking:—

	In 1854-70.		In 1871-86.	
	Rising.	Falling.	Rising.	Falling.
Imports—Articles of food	89	87	65	111
Raw materials	123	133	90	166
Total	212	220	155	277
Exports of British Merchandise	90	102	66	126

The excess of falling prices was comparatively small in the first term, but it was very great in the second; and in both terms the excess was greater in Exports than in Imports.

c. *Rise and Fall in Prices.*

An examination of these three tables warrants the assumption that if all the prices were reduced to a single denomination,—that of a shilling would not require many changes,—and if a larger number of articles were included in the calculation, the yearly aggregates would furnish a useful and easily computed index to the yearly variations in the price of the bulk of Imports and Exports. As it is, it has been found that by adding up the very dissimilar items in these tables, composed of the extreme denominations of pounds and pence, and relating to such incongruous things as a ton of iron and a pound of cotton yarn, the aggregates, though meaningless in themselves, when brought into comparison with one another do exhibit a general approximation to the actual rise and fall of prices in each year, and afford a rough means of comparing each year with its predecessor or successor. It is found that a scale of annual prices calculated upon these aggregates, taking for the starting point in 1854 the same figure as that founded upon the relation between tonnage and declared value, exhibits a striking similarity to the scale founded on the latter relation, and that the most striking differences may be accounted for by the insufficiency in the number of articles included in these tables of prices, and the consequent excessive preponderance of some of them upon the average price of the whole mass. Exceptio probat regulam.

As an illustration, when in the years of inflation 1872-73, the extraordinary development of the coal and iron trades caused the average value of a ton of Exports to rise from £14·9 to £16·3 and £16·2, the corresponding rise in this table of prices, in which coal, iron, and steel form comparatively so large a proportion of the articles, was from £14·9 (mark the identity of the starting point) to £19·2 and £21·5. The correspondence in the fall in subsequent years is no less remarkable :—

	Table I.	Calculated on Table XI.
	£	£
1874	15·1	19·0
'75	13·8	17·0
'76	11·9	15·4

The general approximation of the two series is sufficiently close to afford an interesting illustration of the possibility of arriving at an approximation to the truth by the conjunction and comparison of such unequal data. They will therefore be stated side by side in the Appendix.*

d. *Comparison of Prices in* 1857-86.

It would occupy too much time and space to enter into a full examination of these two tables of prices, but it may be well to supplement the preceding comparisons of the proportionate value of the volumes of each article in 1857 and 1886† with a similar comparison of the average price of each in the same years :—

* P. 159.   † P. 43 *et seq.*

	Average Prices.		Percentage Difference in 1886.	
	1857.	1886.	Increase.	Decrease.
IMPORTS— A. FOOD.	Per cent.		Per cent.	Per cent.
Wheat .... per cwt. sh.	12·8	7·5	—	42·0
Wheaten flour .... „ „	18·0	11·0	—	37·8
Sugar, raw .... „ „	35·1	13·1	—	62·8
„ refined .... „ „	46·0	16·7	—	63·6
Tea .... per lb. d.	17·4	11·8	—	32·4
Wine .... per gall. sh.	7·9	7·0	—	11·0
Butter .... per cwt. £	4·7	5·3	12·8	—
Coffee .... „ „	3·3	3·3	—	—
Oxen and bulls .... each „	18·7	18·1	—	3·7
Cheese .... per cwt. „	2·5	2·2	—	10·0
Rice, not in the husk .... „ sh.	11·5	7·5	—	34·8
Average of above 9 articles............	—	—	—	33·1
B.—RAW MATERIALS.				
Cotton, raw .... per cwt £	3·4	2·5	—	26·3
Wood and timber (a) hewn per load „	3·5	2·2	—	38·0
„ (b) split „ „	2·8	2·2	—	21·6
Wool, sheep's and all other per lb. d.	17·9	9·1	—	49·3
Silk, raw .... „ sh.	21·8	13·7	—	36·9
Flax, dressed and undressed per cwt. „	39·0	41·5	6·3	—
Guano .... per ton £	2·9	2·0	—	29·5
Flax or linseed................... per qr. „	12·5	7·8	—	37·6
Tallow and stearine .... per cwt. sh.	54·5	25·7	—	52·9
Hemp, dressed and undressed .... „ „	32·0	28·4	—	11·2
Jute .... „ „	20·9	11·2	—	46·2
Palm oil .... „ „	43·7	20·9	—	52·1
Indigo .... „ £	32·0	22·4	—	30·1
Caoutchouc .... „ „	5·8	11·4	95·3	—
Hides, dry and wet............ „ „	4·1	3·0	—	27·0
Leather................................ per lb. d.	23·9	17·1	—	28·7
Average of above 14 articles	—	—	—	34·8
EXPORTS.				
Coals and culm .... per ton sh.	9·3	8·3	—	10·6
Cotton yarn .... per lb. d.	11·8	10·8	—	8·2
„ piece goods—				
Plain.... per yd. „	3·0	2·2	—	26·1
Printed „ „	4·2	3·2	—	24·0
Linen yarn .... per lb. „	13·7	14·1	3·0	—
„ manufactures—				
white or plain .... per yd. „	7·3	6·0	—	18·6
Metals, iron pig .... per ton sh.	76·2	43·2	—	43·4
„ „ bar .... „ £	8·8	5·1	—	41·6
„ steel (unwrought) „ „	33·5	—	—	—
„ „ (manufactured) „ „	—	30·0	—	—
„ copper (unwrought) per cwt. „	6·0	2·2	- -	63·2
Woollen yarn .... per lb. d.	27·6	23·2	—	16·0
„ cloths .... per yd. „	24·3	39·6	62·5	—
Average of above 9 articles............	—	—	—	28·0

It will be seen that in each table two articles have increased in price or remained stationary, viz., butter, coffee, flax, caoutchouc, linen yarn and woollen cloths, and that the decrease among the other articles has been in each class as follows :—

Imports, articles of food .... 33·1 per cent.
,,   raw materials........ .... 34·8   ,,
Exports .... 28·0   ,,

A still more interesting comparison is that to be derived from Mr. Bourne's tables between the years 1883 and 1887, which is presented in the form in which it might be advantageously given to the public by the Board of Trade monthly—either synchronously with, or soon after, the present monthly accounts of "Trade and "Navigation." The comparison might be either with the corresponding month of the previous year, or with the preceding month of the same year, as might be deemed most useful to the mercantile community. There will be a little trouble, but much convenience, in arranging the articles alphabetically in the three proposed classes. There would be no difficulty in giving at the same time a calculation of the average value of a ton of Imports and Exports after eliminating the trade in grain and timber inwards, and that in coals outwards.

		Proportion of Total Value, showing Volume.		Average Value, showing Price.						Change in Proportion of Volume.		Change in Proportion of Price Above or Below Average of 100.	
		1883.	1887.	1883.			1887.			In-crease	De-crease	In-crease	De-crease
		Per 1,000	Per 1,000	£	s.	d.	£	s.	d.	Per 1,000	Per 1,000	Per 1,000	Per 1,000
A. *Articles Increased in Value.*													
1. Animals, horses	each	2	2		55·62			57·85		—		1·04	—
2. Arms, fire	,,	1	1		27·40			34·75		—	—	1·27	—
3. ,, gunpowder	lb.	2	1			5·83			6·46	—	1	1·11	—
4. Glass, flint...............	cwt.	1	1		44·94			48·64		—	—	1·08	—
5. ,, common	,,	2	2		9·27			9·45		—	—	1·02	—
6. Tin	,,	2	2	4·88			5·48			—	—	1·12	—
7. Silk, broad stuffs	yard	5	8		3·26			4·15		3	—	1·37	—
8. Spirits.......................	gall.	3	4		5·93			6·70		1	—	1·13	—
9. Wool, yarn..................	lb.	14	17			23·41			23·73	—	1	1·01	—
10. ,, cloth	yard	31	41			38·30			40·04	10	—	1·04	—
Total		63	79	—			—			No. of articles 4	1	—	—
B. *Articles Unchanged in Value.*													
1. Zinc............................	cwt.	—	1	13·89			13·91			1	—	—	—
2. Salt	ton	3	2	12·84			12·82			—	1	—	—
Total		3	3	—			—			1	1	—	—

	Proportion of Total Value, showing Volume.		Average Value, showing Price.		Change in Proportion of Volume.		Change in Proportion of Price Above or Below Average of 100.	
	1883.	1887.	1883.	1887.	Increase	Decrease	Increase	Decrease
Articles Decreased in Value.	Per 1,000	Per 1,000	£ s. d.	£ s. d.	Per 1,000	Per 1,000		
Alkali .... cwt.	9	6	6·12	5·66	—	1	—	0·92
Bags .... dozen	5	4	5·16	4·07	—	1	—	0·79
Beer............ brl.	8	7	79·82	76·14	—	1	—	0·96
Books .... cwt.	5	6	9·55	8·81	1	—	—	0·92
Butter............ „	1	1	139·58	112·81	—	—	—	0·81
Candles .... doz. lbs.	1	1	6·72	4·66	—	—	—	0·70
Cement .... cwt.	4	5	2·31	1·94	1	—	—	0·84
Cheese............ „	—	1	84·15	79·26	1	—	—	0·94
Coals .... ton	44	48	9·35	8·32	4	—	—	0·90
Cordage .... cwt.	2	2	51·05	45·67	—	—	—	0·90
Cotton yarn .... lb.	56	53	12·25	10·88	—	3	—	0·89
„ manufactures—								
plain .... yard	142	158	2·61	2·27	16	—	—	0·87
printed .... „	87	90	3·62	3·17	3	—	—	0·88
mixed .... „	2	—	5·81	—	—	—	—	—
stockings ...... dozen	2	2	3·28	—	—	—	—	—
thread .... lb.	10	15	3·27	35·06	5	—	—	0·89
Fish, herrings .... brl.	6	7	29·73	20·62	1	—	—	0·70
Glass, plate .... sq. ft.	1	1	1·42	1·12	—	—	—	0·80
Hats .... dozen	5	6	21·50	19·08	1	—	—	0·90
Leather .... cwt.	7	7	9·34	8·79	—	—	—	0·94
„ boots .... doz. prs.	6	8	60·10	57·94	2	—	—	0·96
Jute yarn .... lb.	1	1	3·05	2·32	—	—	—	0·76
„ manufactures ...... yard	10	10	2·64	2·02	—	—	—	0·78
Linen yarn .... lb.	4	4	14·36	13·77	—	—	—	0·96
„ manufactures—								
white .... yard	13	18	6·95	6·07	—	—	—	0·87
printed .... „	1	1	7·80	6·13	—	—	—	0·78
sail cloth ...... „	1	1	11·73	11·01	—	—	—	0·94
thread............ lb.	1	1	2·61	29·74	—	—	—	0·85
Iron, old............ ton	1	3	3·47	2·86	2	—	—	0·82
„ pig .... „	17	12	52·14	47·26	—	5	—	0·91
„ bar .... „	8	8	7·06	5·50	—	—	—	0·78
„ railroad .... „	25	26	6·19	4·56	1	—	—	0·73
„ wire .... „	4	3	14·80	13·58	—	1	—	0·90
„ sheet............ „	6	3	10·12	9·06	—	3	—	0·90
„ galvanised .... „	7	15	15·18	11·75	8	—	—	0·77
„ hoop .... „	3	3	7·77	16·06	—	—	—	0·78
„ tinned .... „	20	26	17·47	13·56	6	—	—	0·77
„ cast .... „	19	20	12·97	11·16	1	—	—	0·85
Steel, wrought .... „	6	13	19·10	—	7	—	—	
„ manufactures ... „	2	3	42·70	29·93	1	—	—	0·70
Copper, ingots .... cwt.	5	6	3·38	2·26	1	—	—	0·67
„ yellow metal ... „	5	4	2·99	2·09	—	1	—	0·70
„ other kinds...... „	5	7	3·67	2·58	2	—	—	0·66
Brass .... „	2	1	4·47	3·75	—	1	—	0·84
Lead .... ton	2	2	14·07	13·75	—	—	—	0·98
Oil, seed .... gall.	8	8	1·85	1·67	—	—	—	0·90
Paper .... cwt.	5	8	2·15	1·74	3	—	—	0·81
Soap............ „	2	2	22·96	19·93	—	—	—	0·87
Sugar .... „	5	3	21·40	13·19	—	2	—	0·62
Wool .... lb.	4	5	12·71	11·25	1	—	—	0·88
„ flannels	3	5	14·82	12·27	—	3	—	0·89
„ stuffs	32	35	9·94	8·87	4	—	—	0·83
„ carpets............	5	6	28·24	24·26	1	—	—	0·86
Total	640	693	—	—	No. of articles 23	12	—	—
Total of specified articles	706	775	—	—	—	—	—	0·673
All other „	294	287	—	—	—	—	—	0·249
Total	1 000	1,062	—	—	28	14	—	0·922

The table will show at once the number of the 65 specified articles (all for which the information can be furnished) which have increased or decreased in volume and in price, and how many have remained stationary, also the extent to which they have changed in either respect.

Comparing the two years together, inasmuch as in 1887 the total price of the 65 articles had generally fallen from 1·000 to ·922, the volume must have increased from 1·000 to 1·062 in order to produce the sum of £221 millions, as compared with £240 millions in 1883. It must however be borne in mind that the changes in the proportion of the volume of the several articles are relative to the change in the total, and the actual increase or decrease of each must be looked for in the trade returns. The same remarks do not apply to the changes in price which are positive, or actual.

An abstract of this table might be framed in the shape of the table shown at pp. 8-9, indicating in addition the names of the articles in each category.

§ 6. *Prices of Raw Materials compared with those of Manufactured Goods.*

Reverting to the table at p. 52, and comparing the fall in Exports with that in the Imports of raw materials, the results show as follows :—

Change on Imports.			*Change on Exports.*		
		Per Cent.			Per Cent.
Cotton, raw	fall	26·3	Cotton yarn	fall	8·2
			„ piece goods, plain..	„	26·1
			„ „ printed	„	24·0
Flax, dressed and un-dressed	rise	6·3	Linen yarn	rise	3·0
			„ manufactures, white or plain...	fall	18·6
			Woollen yarn	„	16·0
Wool, sheep's, &c.	fall	49·3	„ cloths	rise	62·5

A more detailed comparison of the trade in cottons and woollens will be found in Tables XII and XIII, which show—

1. With regard to cottons : the price of raw cotton on importation, and the prices of cotton yarn and cotton plain piece goods on exportation in each year from 1854 to 1886, with the annual fluctuations in each year above or below the mean of the five years 1855-59, taken as the unit of 100. The year 1854 has been omitted as that of the Crimean war.*

2. With regard to woollens : the price of foreign wool on importation and of British wool on exportation, and the prices of woollen yarn and cloths on exportation ; with a similar account of

---

* 1855 ought to have been omitted for the same reason.

the annual fluctuations, and a comparison between British and foreign wool.

TABLE XII.—*Statement of the Average Price of Raw Cotton on Importation, and of Cotton Yarn and Cotton Plain Piece Goods on Exportation, in the United Kingdom, in each year from 1854 to 1886.*

(Compiled from Table in Appendix to Report of Royal Commission on Depression of Trade and Industry and Statistical Abstracts.)

Years.	Price on Importation.	Price on Exportation.		Annual Fluctuations, the mean of 5 years. 1855-59, being taken as the unit=100.		
	Raw Cotton. Per cwt.	Cotton, Yarn. Per lb.	Cotton, Plain Piece Goods. Per yard.	Raw Cotton Imported. Mean (3·06).	Cotton, Yarn, Exported. Mean (11·23).	Cotton, Plain Piece Goods Exported. Mean (2·93).
	£	d.	d.			
1854....	2·55	10·92	2·85	83	97	97
'55....	2·62	10·44	2·79	85	93	95
'56....	2·89	10·62	2·88	94	94	98
'57....	3·38	11·81	2·99	110	105	102
'58....	3·26	11·49	2·90	106	102	99
'59....	3·16	11·81	3·07	103	105	105
1860....	2·88	12·00	3·09	94	107	105
'61....	3·44	12·54	3·02	112	111	103
'62....	6·65	15·97	3·66	217	142	125
'63....	9·41	26·01	4·97	307	231	169
'64....	9·79	28·80	5·79	320	256	197
'65....	7·56	23·98	5·05	247	213	172
'66....	6·30	23·66	5·09	206	210	173
'67....	4·61	21·11	4·13	150	188	141
'68....	4·65	20·27	3·67	152	180	125
'69....	5·21	20·04	3·79	170	178	129
1870....	4·47	18·92	3·55	146	168	121
'71....	3·52	18·66	3·33	115	166	113
'72....	4·24	18·87	3·51	138	168	120
'73....	4·01	17·76	3·45	131	158	117
'74....	3·62	15·79	3·22	118	140	110
'75....	3·47	14·66	3·13	113	130	107
'76....	3·02	13·19	2·83	99	117	96
'77....	2·93	12·85	2·83	95	114	96
'78....	2·80	12·47	2·76	91	111	94
'79 ...	2·76	12·33	2·65	90	109	90
1880....	2·94	13·25	2·73	96	118	94
'81....	2·92	12·39	2·65	95	110	90
'82....	2·93	12·96	2·71	96	115	92
'83....	2·91	12·25	2·61	95	109	89
'84....	2·85	12·24	2·47	93	109	84
'85....	2·86	11·58	2·33	93	103	79
'86 ...	2·49	10·84	2·21	81	96	75

TABLE XIII.—*Statement of the Average Price of Sheep's Wool, including Wool of Lambs, Alpaca, and the Llama Tribe, Imported: of Sheep and Lambs' Wool of British Produce Exported, and of Woollen and Worsted Yarn, and Woollen Cloths, &c., of British Manufacture Exported, in the United Kingdom in each Year from* 1854-86.

(Compiled from same as last table.)

	Prices of Sheep's Wool.		Prices of Woollen Manufactures on Exportation.		Annual Fluctuations, the Mean of Five Years, 1855-59, being taken as the unit = 100.				Price of British compared with Foreign Wool.
	Foreign and Colonial on Importation.	British on Exportation.	Woollen and Worsted Yarn.	Woollen Cloths, &c.	Foreign and Colonial Wool Imported.	British Wool Exported.	Yarn Exported.	Cloths Exported.	
	Per lb.	Per lb.	Per lb.	Per yard.	Mean (17·25).	Mean (16·14).	Mean (27·01).	Mean (25·99).	
	d.	*d.*	*d.*	*s.*					*d.　d.*
1854....	14·70	14·05	23·76	24·43	85	87	88	94	0·65 –
'55....	15·78	14·62	22·90	26·30	91	90	84	101	1·16 –
'56....	17·89	15·86	24·69	24·34	104	98	91	94	2·03 –
'57....	17·91	17·27	27·60	24·34	104	107	102	94	0·64 –
'58....	16·99	16·09	28·58	25·89	98	99	105	99	0·90 –
'59....	17·69	16·99	31·30	29·09	102	105	116	112	0·70 –
1860....	17·84	18·71	32·46	30·12	103	115	120	116	+0·87
'61...	15·85	17·46	30·13	29·81	92	108	111	115	+1·61
'62...	16·43	17·79	32·47	30·36	95	110	120	117	+1·36
'63....	16·08	20·07	36·92	34·28	93	124	137	132	+3·99
'64....	18·02	22·08	40·30	36·74	104	134	149	141	+4·06
'65....	16·89	23·89	40·31	37·70	98	147	149	145	+7·00
'66....	17·59	22·08	41·06	39·15	102	134	152	150	+4·49
'67....	16·61	21·01	37·28	40·99	96	130	138	157	+4·40
'68....	14·36	18·57	34·78	36·66	83	115	129	141	+2·21
'69....	13·65	17·83	35·74	36·37	79	110	132	139	+4·18
1870....	14·42	15·31	33·73	35·17	83	94	125	135	+0·89
'71....	13·32	16·64	33·49	37·52	77	100	124	144	+3·32
'72....	14·51	19·86	36·91	41·19	84	123	137	158	+5·35
'73....	14·75	21·18	37·26	41·00	85	131	138	158	+6·43
'74....	14·71	21·92	38·14	39·53	85	135	141	152	+7·21
'75....	15·41	21·14	38·58	39·09	89	130	143	150	+5·73
'76...	14·54	18·53	34·36	38·25	84	114	127	147	+3·99
'77....	14·38	17·73	32·12	35·72	83	109	119	137	+3·35
'78....	13·90	19·87	30·07	34·53	80	123	111	133	+5·97
'79...	13·56	14·39	26·71	31·89	79	89	99	122	+0·83
1880....	13·66	16·57	30·33	32·34	79	102	112	124	+2·91
'81....	13·87	15·26	26·04	32·55	80	94	96	125	+1·37
'82...	12·27	15·20	25·62	34·18	71	94	95	131	+2·93
'83....	12·08	12·71	23·41	38·30	70	79	87	147	+0·63
'84...	12·09	10·94	23·78	41·42	70	68	88	159	1·15 –
'85....	10·05	9·55	24·19	40·23	58	59	89	154	0·50 –
'86....	9·08	10·07	23·19	39·56	52	62	85	152	+0·99

The first table brings out the fact that during the last eight years the relation of the price of cotton piece goods exported to that of raw cotton imported has been gradually sinking, to the

disadvantage of the former, while that of cotton yarn has maintained itself better, although it has also been gradually sinking.

The second table shows that between 1854 and 1859 the price
of foreign and colonial wool imported ranged sometimes above,
sometimes below, that of British wool exported; that from 1860 to
1883 the latter ranged the highest, at one time from 40 to 50 per
cent. higher; that in 1884 the foreign again ranked slightly
higher, but in the next year the British recovered its superiority,
and in 1886 made a considerable advance.

It also shows that while the price of foreign wool had fallen
from an average unit of 100·0 in 1855-59 to 60·0 in 1883-86, and
while the price of British wool exported had fallen from 100·0 to
67·0 in the same years, the price of woollen yarn exported had only
fallen from 100 to 87, and the price of woollen cloths exported had
risen from 100·0 to 153·0.

§ 7. *Comparison of Imports with Exports.*

Notes on Table XIV.

This may be a convenient place for inserting a table showing
the proportion which tonnage entering with cargoes bore to
tonnage clearing with cargoes, and the proportion which the value
of Imports bore to that of Exports, in each year 1854-86.

It will be seen that the tonnage cleared has always, with two
exceptions, exceeded the tonnage entered. On the first occasion,
the great change in 1855 was caused by a large decrease in the
Imports of that year, together with an increase in the Exports,
which became permanent, and to which the increasing exportation
of coal contributed. In 1877 the short-lived change was caused
by an increase in the importation of grain in 1876 and several
following years, and in that of iron ores in 1877, which has continued up to the present time. The latter fact, seeing that the
value of such ores has rarely exceeded 15s. a ton, leads to the
conclusion that they should be added to the articles (grain and
timber) which should be deducted from the total Import trade, if
it be desired to arrive at an index number for Imports by the
method now proposed.

TABLE XIV.—*Statement of the Percentage Proportion of the Tonnage which Entered and Cleared with Cargoes, and of the Declared Value of Imports and Exports, including re-Exports; also of the Excess of the Value of Imports over that of Exports, in each Year from 1854-86.*

Years.	Percentage Proportion of Tonnage.		Percentage Proportion of Declared Value.		Percentage Excess of Value of Imports over Exports.
	Entered.	Cleared.	Imports.	Exports.	
1854....	50·1	49·9	56·9	43·1	31·6
'55....	45·7	54·3	55·1	44·9	23·0
'56....	45·8	54·2	55·3	44·7	23·9
'57...	45·8	54·2	56·2	43·8	28·4
'58....	47·0	53·0	54·1	45·9	17·7
'59...	47·1	52·9	53·5	46·5	15·1
1860....	48·1	51·9	56·0	44·0	28·0
'61....	48·4	51·6	57·7	42·3	36·2
'62...	47·7	52·3	57·6	42·4	35·8
'63....	48·2	51·8	55·8	44·2	26·4
'64....	48·1	51·9	56·4	43·6	29·2
'65....	48·6	51·4	55·3	44·7	23·9
'66...	48·3	51·7	55·3	44·7	23·5
'67	47·3	52·7	54·9	45·1	21·8
'68....	47·1	52·9	56·4	43·6	29·3
'69....	47·7	52·3	55·5	44·5	25·1
1870...	47·3	52·7	55·4	44·6	24·2
'71....	46·9	53·1	53·8	46·2	16·7
'72....	48·2	51·8	53·3	46·7	12·7
'73....	49·6	50·4	54·4	45·6	19·4
'74.	49·2	50·8	55·4	44·6	24·7
'75....	48·2	51·8	57·0	43·0	32·6
'76	49·4	50·6	59·3	40·7	46·0
'77....	51·0	49·0	61·0	39·0	56·3
'78....	49·6	50·4	60·0	40·0	50·2
'79....	48·0	52·0	59·3	40·7	45·9
1880....	48·3	51·7	58·9	41·1	43·5
'81...	46·9	53·1	57·2	42·8	33·6
'82....	47·2	52·8	57·3	42·7	34·6
'83...	47·2	52·8	58·3	41·7	39·7
'84..	45·7	54·3	57·0	43·0	31·7
'85	46·7	53·3	57·7	42·3	35·9
'86...	45·9	54·1	56·5	43·5	30·2
'87....	46·2	53·8	56·3	43·7	29·0

The average proportions of the period 1854-86 were—

For tonnage .... Entered .... 47·6. Cleared............ 52·4
Value...................... Imports .... 56·4. Exports .... 43·6

There is but a slight difference, as regards Imports, between the earlier and later years, and not a great difference as regards Exports—

Tonnage, 1855-59 .... Entered .... 45·9. Cleared............ 54·1
   ,,   '82-86 ....   ,, ... 46·5.   ,, ... 53·5
Value,   '55-59 .... Imports .... 55·2. Exports .... 44·8
  ,,   '82-86 ....   ,, ... 57·1.   ,, ... 42·9

In the three years 1876-78, when the difference in the value of Imports and Exports was the greatest in the series, the proportion of tonnage showed no difference—

| Tonnage, 1876-78 .... | Entered .... | 50·0. | Cleared............ | 50·0 |
| Value........................ | Imports .... | 60·1. | Exports .... | 39·9 |

The percentage excess in the value of Imports over that of Exports averaged for the whole period 30·2; but there was a great difference in the earlier and later years. In 1855-59 it averaged 21·6 per cent.; in 1882-86 it averaged 34·6. In 1876-78 it averaged 50·8 per cent. The highest excess in a single year was in 1877, when it rose to 56·3 per cent.; the lowest was in 1872, when it fell to 12·7 per cent. All these differences, as before pointed out, have been caused by the very large and increasing exportation of coal.

§ 8. *Re-export of Colonial and Foreign Merchandise.*

This branch of trade is of sufficient extent to deserve a greater development than can be assigned to it in this review. On the average of 1885-87 it amounted to £58 millions a year, which is equal to 16 per cent. of the total imports, and 21 per cent., or one-fifth, of the total Exports.

The number of articles specified as "principal" in the last annual returns is 71. Of these the relative importance is partially indicated by the following enumeration of the value of those of which the re-export exceeded £500,000 in 1886 :—

	£		£
1. Caoutchouc	1,303,880	13. Rice...............................	1,359,069
2. Coffee.....................	2,629,787	14. Silk manufactures........	564,965
3. Cotton, raw	3,975,567	15. Furs of all sorts	712,849
4. Peruvian bark	547,794	16. Pepper	638,131
5. Indigo.........................	1,170,209	17. Tea	2,226,135
6. Jute	1,095,259	18. Wine	524,605
7. Gum of all sorts	634,076	19. Wool, sheep's, &c........	12,043,266
8. Leather	1,384,505	20. Woollen manufactures	520,242
9. Iron, in bars	613,123		
10. Iron and steel manu-			34,405,891
fuctures	554,432	Other articles enumerated	12,379,312
11. Tin	1,395,612	„ unenumerated	9,449,060
12. Oil, palm	511,785	Total	56,234,263

Another indication is the proportion which the amount of each article exported bore to the amount of the same imported in 1886, which is partially shown in the following enumeration of those articles in which the proportion exceeded 25 per cent.

From 25 to 50 per cent.—Cocoa, cutch and gambier, feathers, hemp, jute, iron and steel manufactured, palm oil, rice, rum, spirits other than rum and brandy, tobacco manufactured, and snuff.

From 50 to 75 per cent.—Caoutchouc, indigo, gums, hides, iron in bars, tin, nuts and kernels, cocoa-nut oil, thrown silk, furs, pepper, spices other than cinnamon, teeth (ivory), wool, sheep's, &c.

Above 75 per cent.—

   Coffee, 78·0 per cent.

   Peruvian bark, 81·0 per cent.

   Cochineal, granilla, and dust, 75·6 per cent.

   Goat skins, undressed, 106·0 per cent. *

   Cinnamon, 80·0 per cent.

Several interesting problems have been raised with regard to this branch of trade.

Is it increasing or decreasing?

The following Table No. XV will show that—

1. In actual amount it has increased from £21 millions in 1854-56 to £58 millions in 1885-87, and that in proportion to Imports it has increased during the same period from 13·5 to 16·0 per cent.

2. Although between the years 1880-84 and 1885-87 there has been a considerable decrease in the actual amount, viz., from £64 to £58 millions, there has been an increase in proportion to the Imports from 15·6 to 16·0 per cent. The average of the whole period was 16·2 per cent.

3. The course of the growth of the trade throughout the period is shown in the following abstract :—

In the Years.	Total Value of re-exportations. Millions £.	In the Years.	Total Value of re-exportations. Millions £.
1854	19	1871	61
'55-59	23	'72-79	56
'60-62	35	'80-84	64
'63-66	51	'85-87	58
'67-70	46		

4. In the proportion to the value of total Exports there has been virtually no fluctuation since 1877, except in the two years 1879-80; in the other years of that period the differences have ranged between 20·7 and 21·3 per cent.

* The excess over importation having been taken out of bond.

TABLE XV.—*Value of Colonial and Foreign Merchandise re-exported, and Proportion which it bore to the Total Imports and Exports in the Trade of the United Kingdom, in each Year from 1854 to 1887.*

(Compiled from "Statistical Abstracts.")

Years.	Value of Colonial and Foreign Merchandise re-exported.	Percentage Proportion to	
		Total Imports.	Total Exports.
	Milln. £	Per cent.	Per cent.
1854	19 ⎫ average 21	12·5 ⎫ average 13·5	16·3 ⎫ average 16·9
'55	21 ⎬	14·7 ⎬	17·9 ⎬
'56	23 ⎭	13·3 ⎭	16·5 ⎭
'57	24	12·7	16·4
'58	23	14·0	16·4
'59	25	14·0	16·1
1860	29	13·8	17·5
'61	35	16·1	20·2
'62	42	18·6	25·3
'63	50	20·0	25·3
'64	52	18·9	24·5
'65	53	19·5	24·2
'66	50	16·9	20·9
'67	45	16·3	20·0
'68	48	16·2	21·1
'69	47	15·9	19·8
1870	44	14·5	18·0
'71	61	18·4	21·4
'72	58	16·3	18·4
'73	56	15·1	18·0
'74	58	15·7	19·4
'75	58	15·5	20·6
'76	56	14·9	21·8
'77	54	13·7	21·3
'78	52	14·1	21·2
'79	57	15·7	22·9
1880	63	15·3	22·0
'81	63	15·8	21·2
'82	65	15·7	21·1
'83	65	15·2	21·3
'84	63	16·	21·2
'85	58 ⎫ average 58	15·6 ⎫ average 16·0	21·3 ⎫ average 21·1
'86	56 ⎬	16·0 ⎬	20·9 ⎬
'87	59 ⎭	16·3 ⎭	21·0 ⎭

Do the re-exports bear any constant proportion to the Imports or Exports? Do they increase or decrease in sympathy with the latter?

The answer appears to be that they do so only occasionally. In 1871-72, when the Imports increased from £303 to £331 and £354 millions, the re-exports increased from £44 to £61 and £58 millions, and the proportion which they bore to the Imports increased from 14·5 to 18·4 and 16·3 per cent. In 1877 they did not increase with the Imports, and the proportion decreased from 14·9 to 13·7. In 1880, when the Imports increased from £363 to £411 millions, the re-exports increased from £57 to £63 millions, but the proportion fell from 15·7 to 15·3 per cent. In 1884, when the Imports fell from £427 to £390 millions, the re-exports fell only from £65 to £63 millions, and consequently the proportion of the re-exports increased from 15·2 to 16·0 per cent.

It has been shown that they bear a very constant proportion to the total Exports.*

Do the prices of re-exports advance beyond, or fall short of, those declared on importation ?

The following comparison of the prices of the twenty chief articles enumerated at p. 62 will supply an answer to that question :—

		Average Price in 1886.	
		On Importation.	On re-exportation.
Caoutchouc	p. cwt.	£11·4	£11·5 increased
Coffee	,,	£3·3	£3·3 no change
Cotton, raw	,,	£2·5	£2·2 decreased
Peruvian bark	,,	£5·6	£4·6 ,,
Indigo	,,	£22·4	£21·6 ,,
Jute	,,	s. 11·2	s. 11·6 increased
Gum of all sorts	,,	£3·3	£3·28 decreased
Leather	p. lb.	d. 17·1	d. 19·4 increased
Iron in bars	p. ton	£9·1	£8·3 decreased
Iron and steel manufactures	p. cwt.	s. 12·4	s. 10·7 ,,
Tin	,,	£4·8	£4·8 no change
Oil, palm	,,	s. 20·9	s. 20·9 ,,
Rice	,,	s. 7·5	s. 9·0 increased
Silk manufactures		entered	by value
Furs of all sorts	each	d. 9·7	d. 13·3 ,,
Pepper	p. lb.	d. 7·4	d. 7·6 ,,
Tea	,,	d. 11·8	d. 11·9 ,,
Wine	p. gall.	s. 7·0	d. 9·1 ,,
Wool, sheep's	p. lb.	d. 9·1	d. 9·5 ,,
Woollen manufactures		entered	by value

Of the eighteen above enumerated articles an equal number, eight, have increased and decreased in price, two have remained stationary. The five articles of which more than 75 per cent. was re-exported show similar differences :—

		On Importation.	On Exportation.
Coffee	p. cwt.	} included in above	
Peruvian bark	,,		
Cochineal	,,	£6·4	£6·8
Goat skins	each	d. 25·4	d. 20·6
Cinnamon	p. lb.	d. 8·1	d. 8·6

* At p. 63.

F

It can scarcely be inferred from the above that the importations have been made with a view to profit on re-exportation, and exports alone can decide how much of the changes are due to a difference of practice in declaring values on entry and clearance, and how much to difference of average quality, depreciation through storage, forced sales, and the other incidents of commerce. It is obvious that the normal value on re-exportation should be increased by the expenses on the double transaction, and by one or more profits.

The following abstract will show the principal countries to which Colonial and Foreign Merchandise has been re-exported, and whether the proportion has increased or decreased within the last thirty years :—

Percentage Proportion of Value of Colonial and Foreign Merchandise re-exported from the United Kingdom.

	1856.	1872.	1886.
Foreign countries—			
Russia	7·5	4·9	3·5
Sweden and Norway	1·9	2·5	2·1
Germany	19·8	19·8	18·9
Holland	10·4	13·9	12·1
Belgium	9·9	11·3	9·1
France	17·2	18·9	11·9
United States	2·9	8·8	19·0
	69·6	80·1	76·6
Other foreign countries	15·9	11·2	11·7
Total	85·5	91·3	88·3
British Possessions, Total	14·5	8·7	11·7
Total	100·0	100·0	100·0

The most conspicuous changes in the above proportions have been the reduction in the comparatively small trade with Russia, and the rapid and great development of the trade with the United States. The apparent decrease in the trade with the Colonies in 1872 was only relative, and caused by the increase in the trade with the Continent and United States in that year.

§ 9. *Transhipments.*

Supplementary to the statistics of Imports and Exports are those of transhipment, which are not included in the preceding statements. The following is the average annual value of each kind during the years 1872-86 :—

Value of Merchandise Transhipped in the United Kingdom.

	£			£
Average of years 1872-74	13,027,467		Average of years 1881-83	12,082,771
„ '75-77	11,711,618			
„ '78-80	11,558,582		„ '84-86	11,172,287

The principal countries from which this merchandise was received in the years 1872 and 1886, and the principal changes in the amount received from each, are shown in the following statement of the percentages at each date. The actual amount in the two years respectively was £13,896,760 and £10,706,065.

Percentage Proportion of Total Value of Imports received for Transhipment.

	1872.	1886.
France	38·7	28·6
Germany	17·1	15·3
Holland	12·1	4·8
Belgium	8·7	5·4
China	4·1	7·9
United States	3·0	8·6
British India	1·4	9·1
	85·1	79·7
Other countries	14·9	20·3
	100·0	100·0

There has been a large decrease in the Imports from France Holland, and Belgium, with a smaller decrease from Germany, and a large proportionate increase in those from British India, the United States, and China. The total decrease of amount between the two years has been 23 per cent.

A similar comparison of the destination of the amount in the same years exhibits the following results:—

Percentage Proportion of Total Value of Imports Transhipped to each Country.

	1872.	1886.
United States	28·8	32·5
Australia	8·7	8·5
Germany	6·0	4·8
Chili	5·5	2·6
Brazil	5·5	1·9
China	5·4	6·2
British India	4·6	8·3
France	4·2	2·2
Argentine Republic	3·9	1·5
New Grenada	3·4	2·4
British North America	3·4	2·0
Belgium	2·6	1·0
Holland	2·6	7·4
	84·6	81·3
Other countries	15·4	18·7
	100·0	100·0

Here again the United States show an increase; also China, British India, and Holland; while Germany, France, Belgium, British North America, and Central and South America, show a decrease.

§ 10. *Diagram representing the Trade of the United Kingdom in each Year, 1854-87, and Supplementary Table showing the Principal Events, Political and Commercial, which influenced, or resulted from, the course of Trade.*

It will be convenient now to resume some of the principal features of the foregoing tables, together with other kindred data derived from the Appendix to the First Report of the Royal Commission appointed to inquire into the depression of trade and industry in 1885, and to present them in a graphic form.

The annexed diagram exhibits the Import and Export trade of the United Kingdom, excluding the coasting trade, in five groups, for each year from 1854-87.

The first, or upper, group shows the total tonnage which entered and cleared with cargoes.

The second shows the total declared value of Imports, also of net Imports, or consumption, and of Exports.

The third shows the value of Exports of British manufactures, and of Imports of raw materials and food. As these are taken from the Report of the Royal Commission, the information does not extend beyond the year 1883. The same remark applies to the second of the curves in the following group.

The fourth shows the value of Colonial and Foreign Merchandise re-exported, and of Colonial and Foreign Manufactures Imported.

The fifth shows the average value per ton both of Imports and Exports, corresponding to the figures contained in Table I. *

The scale of each group is indicated at the sides. Although there are many curves brought together in this table, there is no confusion, as the groups do not interfere with one another, and the number of curves in any single group does not exceed three.

In connection with this diagram an attempt has been made to bring together, and to represent in a supplementary table, the principal events, political and economic, which may have had a disturbing influence upon the trade of this country, as well as several phenomena which may be more properly described as effects, rather than causes, of the most striking fluctuations. Such a catalogue of possible influences and results, brought together as it were in a panorama, may furnish, it is anticipated, the means of forming more correct and broader views of the history of trade, and of economic forces, than when the same events are examined separately, or otherwise than in immediate connection with one another.

* At p. 18.

No. XVI.—*Epitome of the Character of the Trade, and of the Events and Circumstances affecting, or resulting from, the Trade of the United Kingdom, in the Years 1854-87.*

(For actual details and sources of information see Appendix.)

DIAGRAM OF TRADE
OF THE UNITED KINGDOM,
1854 TO 1887.

The following is a list of these events :—

Wars, &c., British.
„   „   Foreign.
Crises in the United Kingdom, commercial, financial, or political.
Famines in India and China.
Special circumstances (for which see table).
Harvest in the United Kingdom.
Price of wheat.
Importation of corn and meal.
Production and price of coal.
„   „   pig iron.
Export of coal.
„   pig iron.
Import and consumption of raw cotton.

Import and re-export of sheep's wool.
Ships built—sailing and steamers.
Emigration.
Gold bu lion and specie, Import - and Exports.
Gold, coined, and excess of Imports.
Price of consols.
Silver bullion and specie, Imports and Exports.
Silver, price.
Bank rate.
Joint stock companies registered.
Railway bills deposited.
Bankruptcies, &c.
New issues of loans and companies.

Where the facts are represented by figures, averages and conspicuous changes only are inserted, in order that the eye, on looking down any year that may be under examination, shall catch only those items which may have contributed more or less to the character of the year, or may have resulted from the events of it. But in order to furnish fuller information, if it should be required, a table has been added in the Appendix which contains the figures for each year. These have mainly been compiled from the Appendix to the Report of the Royal Commission already referred to, and brought up to date from the latest statistical Abstracts.

Most of the leading features of this diagram have already been pointed out in the discussion of the preceding tables, but the following points are worthy of observation :—

In group 1 the tonnage inwards, starting from the same point as the tonnage outwards, drops below it in 1855, and remains below it to the end, except in 1879, when it rises above it for a single year. From 1880 the distance between the two has widened greatly, and while in the last five years the tonnage inwards has fluctuated considerably from year to year, the outward tonnage has not fluctuated at all until 1887, when they both rose together. The increasing number of large passenger steamers employed in frequent periodical voyages to and from the United Kingdom has doubtless contributed somewhat to this difference, but apparently, as has been shown at p. 11, not to the extent that might be anticipated. It is rather to the increasing exportation of coal that the difference is due.

In group 2 the curves of values of Imports and Exports kept pretty closely together up to 1872, though the fluctuations were more strongly marked in the former; but between 1872 and 1877 they were moving in an opposite direction. Since 1877 they have resumed a more simultaneous action, but the fluctuations are more marked in the Imports, and the drop from 1883 to 1886 was sharper. They both rose in 1887.*

In the same group the net Import, or consumption, has, as might be anticipated, followed closely the total Imports.

So, in like manner, in group 3, the curve of value of British Manufactures exported, is almost identical with that of the total Exports, as the value of British raw materials and produce forms but a small proportion of the latter aggregate. During the years 1855-84 they averaged only 9·1 per cent.

The differences however in the Imports of raw materials and food are very striking. It will be seen that in 1854 the former started and remained above the latter until 1862-64, when they came close together, but immediately separated, raw materials rising increasingly higher above food until 1872, when they crossed one another, food rising and raw materials falling more or less continuously until 1879, when the latter took a start upward and continued to rise until 1883. In 1884 food had a sudden and considerable fall. The figures are not given for the subsequent years.

In group 4 the very gradual and equally slow rise of the value of Colonial and Foreign Manufactures imported is conspicuous. The re-exportation of Colonial and Foreign Merchandise has been slightly greater and more irregular.†

In the last group, No. 5, the relation of the annual differences in the prices, as indicated by the average value per ton, is brought into striking relief. They have already been discussed in the notes on the Tables of Curves III and IV, p. 26.

A comparison of the supplementary table with the diagram will amply requite the investigator, but as it must necessarily involve a considerable amount of speculation, and a large amount of details, it has been deemed expedient not to enter upon it in this summary. In this matter the old motto of the Royal Statistical Society offers a suitable guide—"*Aliis Exterendum.*"

---

* For figures see Table I.

Cap. 3. SHIPPING IN THE TRADE OF THE UNITED KINGDOM.

§ 1. *Tonnage Inwards and Outwards.*

The information contained in the foregoing pages relating to the shipping employed in the trade of the United Kingdom is confined to—

1. The total tonnage* of vessels which entered and cleared with cargoes in each year from 1854-87, contained in Table I, and shown in the last described diagrams.

2. The total tonnage of vessels, distinguishing sailing from steam vessels, which were built in the United Kingdom in the same years, contained in the table supplementary to the same diagram.

It is now proposed to show in Table XVII the progress of the shipping trade during the last fifteen years, from 1872-86.† The triad, or triennial period, has been adopted as affording a sufficient average for comparison; single years are manifestly insufficient. The period has been selected as that embraced in the last annual volume of the "Statistical Abstract;" but it must be premised that this shuts out of view the sudden and great increase of tonnage, both inwards and outwards, which occurred in the year 1871, accompanied by a corresponding increase in the aggregate value of Imports and Exports, but without a corresponding change in price, which marks an era in the trade of the country. These changes may be briefly noted :—

		Average of 1868-70.	Average of 1871-73.	Percentage difference.
Imports.	Total tonnage .... milln. tons	14·4	17·7	+ 22·9
,,	,, value .... ,, £	297·8	352·3	+ 18·3
,,	Value of Register ton £	20·6	19·7	− 4·3
Exports.	Total tonnage .... milln. tons	16·0	19·1	+ 19·4
,,	,, value .... ,, £	236·3	303·0	+ 28·7
,,	Value of Register ton £	14·7	15·8	+ 7·4
Exports, exclusive of Coal—				
Tonnage	.... milln. tons	8·6	10·6	+ 23·2
Value	.... ,, £	230·8	293·1	+ 26·5
,,	of register ton........ £	26·8	27·7	+ 3·3

* Tonnage, unless otherwise stated, means net tonnage, see p. 81.

† The figures for 1887-88 have since been added.

TABLE XVII.—*Total Tonnage of Vessels (Sailing and Steamers) distinguishing British from Foreign, which entered into Ports of the United Kingdom with Cargoes and in Ballast; also of such Vessels which entered and cleared with Cargoes only, together with the Percentage Proportion of British to Foreign, and of the increase of British and Foreign respectively, in each Triennial Period from 1872-86, and in each of the last three Years 1884-86.*

(Compiled from " Statistical Abstracts.")

Entered with Cargoes and in Ballast. Annual Average.

Periods.	Tonnage (omitting 1000's).			Percentage Proportion.		Percentage Proportion of Increase or Decrease at each Period.		
	British.	Foreign.	Total.	British.	Foreign.	British.	Foreign.	Total.
1872-74..	14,502,	7,280,	21,782,	66·6	33·4			
'75-77..	16,327,	8,133,	24,460,	66·8	33·2	+ 12·6	+ 11·7	+ 12·3
'78-80..	18,780,	8,019,	26,799,	70·0	30·0	+ 15·0	− 1·4	+ 9·6
'81-83..	21,797,	8,517,	30,314,	72·0	28·0	+ 16·0	+ 6·2	+ 12·1
'84-86..	22,919,	8,809,	31,728,	72·3	27·7	+ 5·1	+ 3·4	+ 4·6
'84......	23,037,	8,651,	31,688,	72·7	27·3	+ 5·7	− 1·5	+ 4·5
'85......	22,980,	8,882,	31,862,	72·1	27·9	+ 0·2	+ 2·7	+ 0·5
'86......	22,741,	8,294,	31,035,	73·3	26·7	− 1·0	− 6·6	− 2·6
'87......	24,303,	8,686,	32,984,	73·7	26·3	+ 6·6	+ 4·7	+ 6·3
'88......	not yet published							

ENTERED WITH CARGOES.

Periods.	British.	Foreign.	Total.	British.	Foreign.	British.	Foreign.	Total.
1872-74..	12,455,	6,139,	18,594,	67·0	33·0			
'75-77..	13,806,	6,926,	20,732,	66·6	33·4	+ 10·8	+ 12·8	+ 11 5
'78-80..	15,523,	6,613,	22,136,	70·1	29·9	+ 12·4	− 4·5	+ 6·7
'81-83..	17,953,	6,829,	24,783,	72·4	27·6	+ 15·6	+ 3·3	+ 11·9
'84-86..	18,396,	6,618,	25,014,	73·6	26·4	+ 2·4	− 3·1	+ 0·9
'84......	18,209,	6,487,	24,696,	73·8	26·2	+ 1·4	− 5·0	− 0·3
'85......	18,759,	6,905,	25,664,	73·1	26·9	+ 3·8	+ 6·4	+ 4·0
'86......	18,220,	6,463,	24,685,	73·9	26·1	− 2·9	− 6·4	− 3·8
'87......	19,311,	6,689,	26,000,	74·3	25·7	+ 6·0	+ 3·5	+ 5·3
'88......	20,116,	6,961,	27,077,	74·3	25·7	+ 4·1	+ 4·0	+ 4 1

CLEARED WITH CARGOES.

Periods.	British.	Foreign.	Total.	British.	Foreign.	British.	Foreign.	Total.
1872-74..	13,746,	5,634,	19,380,	70·4	29·6			
'75-77..	15,004,	6,035,	21,039,	71·3	28·7	+ 9·0	+ 7·1	+ 9·0
'78-80..	17,248,	6,123,	23,371,	73·8	26·2	+ 14·7	+ 1·4	+ 11·1
'81-83..	20,711,	7,091,	27,802,	74·5	25·5	+ 20·1	+ 15·8	+ 18 9
'84-86..	21,965,	7,266,	29,232,	75·2	24·8	+ 6·0	+ 2·5	+ 5·1
'84......	21,946,	7,326,	29,273,	75·0	25·0	+ 5·9	+ 3·3	+ 5·3
'85......	21,885,	7,432,	29,317,	74·7	25·3	− 0·3	+ 1·4	+ 0·1
'86......	22,065,	7,041,	29,107,	75·8	24·2	+ 0·9	− 5·2	− 0·7
'87......	23,116,	7,055,	30,171,	76·6	23·4	+ 4·7	+ 0·2	+ 3·6
'88......	24,127,	7,538,	31,664,	76·2	23·8	+ 4·4	+ 6·8	+ 4·9

a. *Notes on Table* XVII.

This table shows in triads, 1872-86, and in single years, 1884-88—

1. The annual average of the tonnage of vessels, distinguishing British from Foreign, entered in the ports of the United Kingdom with cargoes and in ballast.

2. The same of vessels which entered with cargoes.

3. The same of vessels which cleared with cargoes.

4. The percentage proportion of British and Foreign tonnage.

5. The percentage increase or decrease of British and Foreign tonnage at each period.

The principal results of this table are—

1. The proportion of British to Foreign vessels which entered with cargoes and in ballast rose from 66·6 per cent. in 1872-74 to 72·3 per cent. in 1884-86, and still further to 73·7 per cent. in 1887, the last year for which the figures are published.

The periodical increase in each triad has been favourable to British shipping; foreign tonnage advanced more rapidly than British in 1885, but it lost all the advantage so gained in 1886 and 1887.

2. The returns of vessels entering and clearing with cargoes exhibit similar but less decided results.

3. The increase in the last triad or in any subsequent year, has been greatly inferior to that in any of the preceding triads, as the following comparison of the last two triads will show:—

	1881-83.	1884-86.
Of vessels entering with cargoes and in ballast	16·0	5·1
„ „ only	15·6	2·4
„ clearing „ „	20·1	5·2

4. The percentage proportions do not give an adequate view of the actual relative increase of British and Foreign tonnage, which the following figures supply:—

	1872-74.	1884-86.	Increase.
Of vessels entering with cargoes and in ballast–			Per cent
British, millions of tons	14·8	22·9	54·7
Foreign „	7·3	8·6	17·8
Of vessels entering with cargoes only : —			
British, millions of tons	12·4	18·4	48·4
Foreign „	6·1	6·6	8·2
Of vessels clearing with cargoes only :—			
British, millions of tons	13·7	21·9	59·8
Foreign „	5·6	7·3	30·3

It is only in the last category that the increase of foreign tonnage exhibits a material advance, but this was not maintained in 1886 or 1887, when the advance only amounted to 25·0 per cent. In 1888 it rose again to 33·8 per cent.

The differences in the entrance and clearance of vessels in ballast within the United Kingdom are not without interest. In 1887, of the total tonnage, British and Foreign, which entered, less than a fifth (19·2 per cent.) was in ballast; of the same which cleared, rather more than a twelfth (8·5 per cent.) was in ballast. Of British vessels 18·3 per cent. entered and 4·9 per cent. cleared in ballast. Of foreign vessels the corresponding proportions were 21·6 and 18·7 per cent. Of the total tonnage sailing in ballast, only 0·3 per cent. entered from British Possessions, and 12·4 per cent. cleared for them. Of the total tonnage entered and cleared in ballast more than three-fourths (77 per cent.), was confined to the trade with the four European countries—France, Germany, Holland, and Belgium. But while 44 per cent. of the entrances in ballast came from those four countries, only 11·4 per cent. of the clearances were bound for them, showing that in the trade with those countries a large number of empty vessels come to take away cargoes from ports of the United Kingdom, or which is more probable, that a number of vessels which took cargoes to those countries, very likely colliers, returned empty. There is not a material difference in the proportion of British and Foreign vessels entering in ballast in the trade with those four countries, the percentages being respectively 45·6 and 40·4; but the proportions on clearing are very different, viz., 20·0 and 7·6 per cent., showing that British vessels generally load up for those countries, although many return in ballast.

§ 2. *Nationality of Vessels in Trade beyond Sea.*

Table XVIII shows the nationality of the vessels which entered with cargoes and in ballast at ports of the United Kingdom in the first and last triads of the years 1877-86, from which it results that while the tonnage of British vessels had increased 29·4 per cent., that of foreign vessels had increased only 10·9 per cent. There has been a large percentage increase in Greek, Spanish, Dutch, German, and Danish tonnage, and a lesser increase in French, Swedish, Portuguese, and Norwegian, which has been in some measure counterbalanced by a large decrease in American (United States), Austrian, Italian, and to a less degree in Russian. The increase of the British has been nearly three-tenths, that of the foreign a little over a tenth :—

TABLE XVIII.—*Total Tonnage of Vessels (Sailing and Steamers) belonging to each Nation which entered annually into the Ports of the United Kingdom with Cargoes and in Ballast, on the average of the first and last three Years of the Decennial Period ending in 1886, and showing the percentage Proportion of the Increase or Decrease of the Tonnage of each Nation between these two periods.*

(Compiled from "Statistical Abstracts.")

[000's omitted.]

Nations.	Total Tonnage: Annual Average.			Percentage Proportion of each Nation.		Percentage Increase or Decrease of each Nation between the two Periods.	
	1877-79.	1884-86.	Difference.	1877-79.	1885-86.	+	—
British............	17,707,	22,919,	+5,212	69·0	72·2	29·4	—
Foreign—							
Russian	281,	234,	− 47	1·1	0·8	—	16·7
Swedish........	642,	674,	+ 32	2·5	2·1	5·0	—
Norwegian....	1,858,	1,934,	+ 76	7·2	6·1	4·1	—
Danish	587,	736,	+ 149	2·3	2·3	27·2	—
German	1,378,	1,856,	+ 478	5·4	6·0	34·7	—
Dutch	506,	715,	+ 209	2·0	2·3	41·3	—
Belgian	248,	281,	+ 33	1·0	0·9	13·3	—
French	769,	923,	+ 154	2·9	3·0	22·1	—
Spanish	247,	460,	+ 213	1·0	1·5	86·2	—
Portuguese	20,	21,	+ 1	0·1	0·1	5·0	—
Italian	614,	347,	− 269	2·4	1·1	—	43·4
Austrian	184,	83,	− 101	0·7	0·3	—	54·9
Greek............	35,	79,	+ 44	0·1	0·3	125·0	—
United States	584,	223,	− 361	2·3	0·8	—	61·8
Other............	9,	24,	+ 15	—	—	166·6	—
Total Foreign	7,912,	8,809,	+ 867	31·0	27·8	10·9	
Total	25,649,	31,728,	+6,079	100·0	100·0	23·7	—

§ 3. *Vessels Employed in Passenger Traffic.*

This is an important branch of trade from the United Kingdom, but neither the rate of its increase, nor the increase in the size of the vessels employed in it, has had any important influence upon the total general trade of the country, or in any degree vitiates the soundness of the deductions drawn from a comparison of the tonnage and value of Imports and Exports.

Two Tables, XIX and XX, exhibit—

1. The number and tonnage of vessels, British and Foreign, employed in this traffic, as far as regards emigration from the United Kingdom under the Passengers Acts to countries out of Europe, the number of passengers, and the proportion which the British tonnage bore to the total tonnage clearing with cargoes, in the years 1853-55, and in each year from 1860 to 1887.*

* Parl. Paper No. 198 of 4th June, 1888, p. 34.

2. The average size of passenger vessels compared with that of sailing and steam vessels, and of all vessels, in the same years.*

TABLE XIX.—*Number and Tonnage of Vessels, British and Foreign, which Cleared under the Passengers Acts from the United Kingdom to Ports out of Europe, and the Number of Passengers carried by them in the Years* 1853, 1855, *and in each Year from* 1860 *to* 1887.

(Compiled from Parliamentary Paper No. 198 of 1888, and Statistical Abstracts.)

Years.	Vessels Carrying Passengers Cleared from the United Kingdom.						Passengers Carried.		Total Tonnage Cleared Outwards with Cargoes. Milln. tons.	Percentage Proportion of Passenger to Total Tonnage.
	British.		Foreign.		Total.		In British Vessels.	In Foreign Vessels.		
	Number.	Tons. 000's omitted.	Number.	Tons. 000's omitted.	Number.	Tons. 000's omitted.				
1853....	524	354,	460	480,	984	834,	109,643	192,015	—	—
'55....	263	213,	272	345,	535	558,	58,653	88,403	8·3	6·7
1860....	210	256,	184	249,	394	505,	48,618	50,376	10·8	4·7
'61....	199	257,	108	137,	307	394,	42,339	23,641	11·3	3·5
'62....	277	345,	137	175,	414	52·,	69,050	30,791	11·7	4·4
'63....	402	533,	189	241,	591	774,	124,371	72.362	11·9	6·5
'64....	406	514,	138	186,	544	700,	131,462	58,922	12·2	5·7
'65....	417	566,	92	126,	509	692,	160,805	31,300	12·8	5·4
'66....	414	615,	80	101,	494	716,	149,621	24,015	14·0	5·1
'67....	402	6 0,	52	65,	454	665,	163,838	10,097	14·8	4·6
'68 ...	406	615,	31	40,	437	655,	167.029	9,044	15·5	4·2
'69....	480	751,	26	30,	500	781,	230.385	7,891	15·9	4·9
1870....	539	878,	18	27,	557	905,	229,781	4,805	16·7	5·3
'71....	553	953,	20	31,	573	984,	225,833	4.774	19·0	5·2
'72....	638	1.192,	8	12,	646	1,204,	251,871	1,913	19 2	6·2
'73....	678	1,220,	6	13,	684	1,233,	281,797	970	19·1	6·4
'74....	641	1,157,	21	44,	662	1,221,	266,156	5.294	19·7	6·1
'75....	501	967,	26	52,	527	1,019.	137,378	5,120	20·4	5·0
'76....	424	842,	26	52,	450	894,	98,591	4.397	21·5	4·1
'77....	359	772,	23	46,	382	818,	79,765	4,509	21·2	3·6
'78....	433	952,	25	50,	458	1,002,	105,811	4,842	21·6	4·6
'79....	595	1,282,	32	63,	627	1,345,	174,825	8,142	22·8	5·9
1880....	704	1,551,	35	79,	739	1,621.	285,863	12,498	25·6	6·3
'81...	816	1,851,	34	68,	850	1,919,	347,423	14,564	26·3	7·7
'82 ..	826	1,934,	35	70,	861	2,004,	370,679	14,318	27·7	7·0
'83....	836	2,016,	31	62,	867	2,078,	355,477	9,218	29·4	6·4
'84....	700	1,812,	28	56,	728	1,878,	263,870	8,161	29·3	6 3
'85....	620	1,603,	13	26,	633	1,629.	228,676	4,781	29·3	5·5
'86....	687	1,812.	13	26,	701	1,838,	201,772	4,919	29·1	6 3
'87....	729	1,927,	16	32.	736	1,959,	355,378	7,806	30·2	6·4

Notes on Table XIX.

1. This table shows that in 1853 and 1855 foreign passenger vessels were much larger in size, and carried a much larger number of passengers out of England than British. In 1861

* Parl. Paper, No. 198 of 4th June, 1888, p. 34, and "Annual Statement of Navigation and Shipping for 1887."

however the proportions were equalised, and while the foreign have increased in size, and for many years have averaged 2,000 tons, British passenger vessels have increased to 2,650 tons; and while the British passenger tonnage has increased from 286,000 tons on the average of 1860-62, to 1,781,000 on the average of 1885-87, the Foreign tonnage in the same period has decreased from 187,000 to 28,000 tons.

2. The foreign vessels conveying passengers from the United Kingdom run almost exclusively to the United States.

3. The proportion of passenger tonnage to total tonnage has averaged 5·5 per cent. throughout the whole period. It has ranged from 3·5 (in 1861) to 7·3 per cent., but only on one occasion (in 1881).

TABLE XX.—*Average Size of British Sailing and Steam Vessels, and of British Vessels carrying Passengers, which Cleared from Ports in the United Kingdom in each Year from* 1860 *to* 1887.

(Compiled from Statistical Abstracts and preceding Table.)

Years.	Average Size of British Vessels Cleared from the United Kingdom.							
	Sailing Vessels, with Cargoes.		Steam Vessels, with Cargoes.		Total.		Vessels not Distinguished, with Passengers.	
	Tons.	Annual Increase.	Tons.	Annual Increase.	Tons.	Annual Increase.	Tons.	Annual Increase.
1860....	249	—	332	—	261	—	1,218	—
'61....	240	— 9	335	3	262	1	1,294	72
'62....	249	9	348	13	273	11	1,244	— 46
'63...	258	9	370	22	285	12	1,326	82
'64....	271	13	372	2	300	15	1,266	— 60
'65....	275	4	397	25	312	12	1,597	331
'66....	282	7	414	17	328	16	1,486	—111
'67....	288	7	405	— 9	333	5	1,493	7
'68....	290	1	429	24	343	10	1,514	21
'69....	308	18	438	9	359	16	1,543	29
1870....	290	—18	469	31	366	7	1,628	85
'71....	285	— 5	489	20	370	4	1,722	94
'72 ..	304	19	509	20	400	30	1,8·9	147
'73...	281	—23	525	16	413	13	1,799	— 70
'74..	306	25	532	7	429	16	1.804	5
'75....	320	20	538	6	446	17	1.930	126
'76 ...	325	5	540	2	455	9	1,985	55
'77....	345	20	546	6	470	15	2,150	137
'78...	335	—10	564	18	481	11	2,198	76
'79....	354	19	590	26	511	30	2,155	— 43
1880....	356	2	614	24	528	17	2,203	48
'81....	379	23	640	26	564	36	2,268	—182
'82....	390	—11	648	8	576	12	2,342	321
'83...	406	36	680	32	618	32	2,400	58
'84....	410	4	684	4	629	11	2,589	189
'85....	443	33	704	20	653	24	2.585	— 4
'86....	455	12	728	24	677	24	2,638	53
'87 ...	477	22	732	4	692	15	2,675	37

A glance at the column in this table which shows the annual change in the size of vessels of all kinds clearing with cargoes in each year, will indicate how gradual has been the increase, which has never been interrupted in any single year, although the average of sailing vessels has decreased six times during this series of years. The years 1872, 1879-81, and 1883 show the largest increase on all vessels, 1881-83 and 1885 on sailing vessels, 1863-65-70, 1879-81, and 1883 on steamers. They correspond to some extent with an increased activity in shipbuilding.

2. The average size of sailing vessels has increased from 246 tons in 1860-62, to 458 tons in 1885-87; that of steamers from 333 to 721 tons, an increase of 86 and 116 per cent. respectively. Of the total tonnage the increase has been 116 per cent. Of passenger tonnage the increase has been from 1,250 to 2,633 tons, or 110 per cent. less than that of the total tonnage, affording another proof that the size and increase of passenger traffic does not derange the comparison of tonnage and value.

3. If the whole of the passenger tonnage were deducted from the total tonnage cleared outwards with cargoes in the last five years 1882-86, the average size of the remaining vessels would only be reduced from 652 to 632 tons.

§ 4. *Vessels Employed in Coasting Trade.**

The tonnage of British and Foreign vessels (sailing and steam) which entered and cleared coastwise with cargoes only, at ports of the United Kingdom during the fifteen years from 1872 to 1886, increased between the first and last triad 29·3 per cent.

(000's omitted.)

	Inwards.	Outwards.	Total.
	Tons.	Tons.	Tons.
Average of 1872-74...	20,426,	18,828,	39,254,
„ '84-86........	26,882,	24,333,	51,215,

The increase inwards was somewhat greater than the increase outwards, viz., 31·5 and 29·2 per cent. respectively. At both periods the tonnage inwards exceeded the tonnage outwards by 8·5 and 10·4 respectively. The proportion of foreign tonnage entering into the coasting trade is insignificant. It averaged 0·6 per cent. in 1872-74, and 0·4 per cent. in 1884-86.

The proportion of steamers to sailing vessels in the coasting trade had increased between the two periods from 60·0 to 72·7 per cent., or nearly from three-fifths to three-fourths. In the small

* Compiled from " Statistical Abstracts."

proportion of foreign vessels entering into this trade, steamers have largely displaced sailing vessels between the two periods, having increased from 16 to 50 per cent. of the whole foreign tonnage engaged in it.

§ 5. *Shipping registered as belonging to the United Kingdom.**

In considering the quantity of shipping registered as belonging to the United Kingdom, it is necessary to take into account the number as well as the tonnage of the vessels, for whilst in the period under observation there has been an increase of tonnage, there has been a decrease in the number of vessels, a difference caused by a considerable increase in the average size of the vessels. The following are the principal facts :—

1. The differences in the total number and tonnage of registered vessels were :—

	Number.	Decrease.	Tonnage.	Increase.
		Per cent.	000's omitted.	Per cent.
In 1872-74	25,613	} 7·4 {	5,845,	} 26·6
„ '84-86	23,710		7,400,	

2. This results from a gradual increase in the average size of vessels, both sailing and steamers, which was thrice as great in the latter class.

Average Tonnage.

	Sailing Vessels.	Increase.	Steamers.	Increase.
		Per cent.		Per cent.
In 1872-74	190	} 5·8 {	445	} 26·7
„ '84-86	201		597	

3. There has been a continuous gradual decrease in the number of sailing vessels from 22,103 in 1872, to 16,162 in 1886, amounting to 26·8 per cent., but the tonnage kept slightly increasing up to 1877, from which year it has gradually decreased. The difference in tonnage between the same two years 1872 and 1886 is a decrease from 4,213,295 to 3,396,516, or 19·6 per cent.*

4. On the other hand there has been a continuous gradual increase in both the number and tonnage of steam vessels, except in the last year, 1886, when there was a slight decrease of tonnage, with a still slighter increase of the number of vessels. The number increased from 3,673 in 1872, to 6,653 in 1886, or 81 per cent., and the tonnage from 1,538,032 to 3,965,302, or 157 per cent.†

* Compiled from "Statistical Abstracts."
† In the "Annual Statement of the Navigation and Shipping of the United

§ 6. Vessels Built in the United Kingdom.

a. Tonnage Built, 1872-88.*

The trade of shipbuilding in the United Kingdom has been for a long period of a fluctuating character, as will be seen in the statement of tonnage of sailing and steam vessels built in each year from 1854 to 1886 which is contained in the supplementary table to the Diagram at p. 68. During the last fifteen years it appears to have been peculiarly unstable, as the following figures will show, but to have made an extraordinary stride forward in the present year 1888 :—†

Total Tonnage of Vessels, including War Vessels, Built.

	Sailing Vessels.			Steam Vessels.	
	For Home and the Colonies.	For Foreigners.		For Home and the Colonies.	For Foreigners.
1872 '73 } avge.	71,750	2,442	1872 '73 } avge.	318,009	80,207
'74.............	187,313	1,781	'74		
'75 '76 } avge. '77	230,285	3,368	'75.............	178,905	47,796
			'76.............	123,475	13,457
			'77.............	221,330	15,075
'78............. '79	141,165	7,108	'78 '79 } avge.	292,400	41,029
'80 } avge. '81	69,672	1,466	'80.............	346,361	68,470
			'81.............	408,764	106,346
'82 '83 } avge. '84	151,584	4,785	'82.............	521,575	113,637
			'83.............	621,758	122,368
			'84.............	335,208	79,887
'85.............	208,411	10,683	'85.............	196,975	24,943
'86.............	138,362	6,887	'86.............	154,638	31,641
'87.............	81,279	5,848	'87.............	225,440	64,631
Under construction '88, 30 Sept.	} 45,543	9,5	Under construction '88, 30 Sept.	} 548,663	94,264

" Kingdom for the year 1887," there is an apparently corrected statement of the figures for 1886, viz. :—

	Number.	Tonnage.
Sailing vessels	15,473	3,249,907
Steam ,, ...	6,663	4,085,275
Total.....................	22,136	7,335,182

* Compiled from Tables of Merchant Shipping, Parl. Paper, No. 198 of 1888.
† See also Statement in the note at p. 26.

Of the tonnage built for foreigners there were for—

	Vessels.	Total Tons.	Average size.
			Tons.
Norway	7	9,080	1,297
Germany	13	36,916	2,840
France	4	7,139	1,785
Spain	8	22,056	2,757
Other countries in Europe	11	16,790	1,526
South America	11	6,623	602
Japan (steamer)	3	4,300	1,433
Honolulu (sail)	1	885	885
Total	58	103,789	

In April last Lloyd's Register enumerates 172 British and 155 Foreign war vessels which had been built of late years in private shipyards within the United Kingdom.

Besides the sudden and violent changes in the tonnage of sailing vessels throughout the whole period, and the rapid decrease in the last two years, the most notable facts are the great increase of steamers, both for British owners and foreigners, built in 1881-83; the sudden fall in 1884, accompanied by an increase in the tonnage of sailing vessels, which brought them to an equality on the average of 1885-86, the increase of steamers in 1887, and the great increase in 1888. On the whole period of sixteen years the tonnage of steamers built for foreigners averaged 24 per cent. of that built for British owners.

b. *Size of Vessels.*

The average size of vessels, sailing and steam, both belonging to the country and built in it, is a subject of interest. The figures for each year from 1872 to 1886 are shown in the following table. Net tonnage is stated. The figures for 1887, since published, show a large increase in the size of steamers, returning to the average of 1883, viz., from 502 to 700 tons. The sailing vessels built have further fallen off from 381 to 315 tons, and the number built annually has fallen still further from 363 in 1886 to 258 in 1887. The average size remains the same.

G

Average Size of Vessels.

Years.	Sailing.		Steam.	
	Registered as belonging.	Built.	Registered as belonging.	Built.
	Tons.	Tons.	Tons.	Tons.
1872...........	195 ⎫ avge.	135 ⎫ avge.	418 ⎫ avge.	672 ⎫ avge.
'73...........	188 ⎬ 191	212 ⎬ 241	443 ⎬ 441.	712 ⎬ 692
'74...........	191 ⎭	375 ⎭	463 ⎭	693 ⎭
'75...........	197	427	466	502
'76...........	201	345	462	380
'77...........	201	302	468	569
'78...........	201	241	480	575
'79...........	198	150	499	722
'80...........	190	165	519	730
'81...........	191	257	546	840
'82...........	190	402	573	855
'83...........	191	399	595	771
'84...........	192 ⎫ avge.	376 ⎫ avge.	597 ⎫ avge.	580 ⎫ avge.
'85...........	203 ⎬ 202	454 ⎬ 403	598 ⎬ 597	500 ⎬ 527
'86...........	210 ⎭	381 ⎭	596 ⎭	502 ⎭
Average........	196	313	514	663

From the above it results—

1. That until the year 1885 there was no increase, but rather a falling off, in the average size of sailing vessels belonging to the United Kingdom, which was rather less than 200 tons (196), although the average size of such vessels built in the fifteen years was more than 50 per cent. greater. It must be inferred from this that a proportionately larger number of sailing vessels of large size have disappeared from the register.

2. The average size of sailing vessels built in the last fifteen years has been 60 per cent. higher than that of the average on the register, and in the last three years 100 per cent. higher.

3. The average of those built in the last triad exceeds the higher average of the first by 67 per cent.

4. The average size of steam vessels belonging to the United Kingdom in these fifteen years was 514 tons, and the average size of those built in the same period was 663 tons, or 29 per cent. higher.

5. It is remarkable that while the average size of sailing vessels built has increased within the last three years, that of steam vessels has decreased from 692 to 527 tons, or 23·8 per cent.*

b. *Size of Vessels on Register in* 1887.†

The size of vessels on the register in the United Kingdom,

* See also remarks in § 3 on passenger tonnage, p. 75.

† From "Annual Statement of Navigation and Shipping," Parl. Paper C–5399 of 1888, pp. 239 and 253

including the Isle of Man and Channel Islands, according to
their gross and net tonnage, at the close of 1887, was as follows:—

	Sailing.				Steam.			
	Gross.		Net.		Gross.		Net.	
	Number.	Tons.	Number.	Tons.	Number.	Tons.	Number.	Tons.
Under 50 tons	6,137	199,692	6,297	206,103	645	19,272	1,837	37,253
50 and under 100 tons	4,738	332,746	4,958	352,611	905	66,114	532	38,047
100 „ 200 „	1,774	247,631	1,525	220,977	762	105,678	467	67,550
200 „ 300 „	522	125,659	441	108,785	347	84,840	275	68,440
300 „ 400 „	245	84,083	232	81,018	231	79,912	279	97,860
400 „ 500 „	185	84,209	180	83,213	182	81,067	287	128,638
500 „ 600 „	147	80,751	148	82,244	168	92,453	224	122,797
600 „ 700 „	133	86,426	128	83,790	194	126,050	247	160,209
700 „ 800 „	158	119,139	174	131,141	181	135,327	255	190,704
800 „ 1,000 „	254	227,262	253	227,837	361	324,787	538	483,402
,000 „ 1,200 „	263	290,672	285	316,486	354	390,427	507	558,320
,200 „ 1,500 „	416	556,555	420	561,387	523	705,859	555	747,381
,500 „ 2,000 „	368	630,361	326	558,962	795	1,379,689	354	611,394
,000 „ 2,500 „	112	241,585	93	200,499	467	1,027,831	178	392,950
,500 „ 3,000 „	18	46,079	11	28,769	218	600,119	90	244,411
,000 „ 3,500 „	3	9,274			127	407,689		
,500 „ 4,000 „	—	—			84	315,090		
,000 „ 4,500 „	—	—			60	254,219		
,500 „ 5,000 „	—	—			29	137,490		
,000 „ 5,500 „	—	—			14	72,395		
,500 „ 6,000 „	—	—	2	6,085	4	22,220	38	135,910
,000 „ 6,500 „	—	—			5	31,010		
,500 „ 7,000 „	—	—			1	6,932		
,000 „ 7,500 „	—	—			2	14,661		
,500 „ 8,000 „	—	—			2	15,436		
,000 and above	—	—			2	27,059		
Total, gross	15,473	3,362,724	15,473	3,249,907	6,663	6,523,626	6,663	4,085,275

Total Sailing, Number　15,473　　Tonnage Gross　3,362,724　　Net　3,249,907
„　Steam　　„　6,663　　　　　„　6,523,626　　„　4,085,275

22,136　　　　　　　9,886,350　　　　　7,335,182

It will be seen how widely different are the gross and net ad-
measurements of steamers, and how necessary it is to observe the
distinction.

Briefly summarised according to gross tonnage there were—

	Sailing.		Steam.	
	Number.	Tons (Gross).	Number.	Tons (Gross).
Of vessels under 200 tons	12,649	780,069	2,312	191,064
„ from 200 to 1,000 tons	1,644	807,529	1,664	324,436
„ „ 1,000 „ 3,000 „	1,177	1,765,852	2,357	4,103,925
„ above 3,000 tons	3	9,274	330	1,304,201
Total	15,473	3,362,724	6,663	6,523,626

The net tonnage of steam vessels is 62·7 per cent., little more than three-fifths of the gross tonnage. There is a slight difference between the gross and net tonnage of sailing vessels, 0·4 per cent., which is accounted for by a small allowance made in certain classes of vessels for the accommodation of crews. The allowance in the case of steamers is for the engines and machinery. This is regulated by an Act of Parliament of 1854, very slightly modified by an Act of 1867; there has therefore been no material change to affect calculations founded upon the variations in the tonnage recorded during the period under review.

d. *Increase of Large Steam Vessels.*

Ten years ago, on the 31st December, 1878, the number and tonnage of vessels of 1,000 tons and upwards was—

	Number.	Tons.	Average.
			Tons.
Of sailing vessels	944	1,483,499	1,571
,, steam ,, ...	1,146	1,498,729	1,307

On the 31st December, 1887, there were—

	Number.	Tons.	Average.
			Tons.
Of sailing vessels	1,180	1,775,126	1,504
,, steam ,, ...	2,687	5,408,126	2,012

At the former date there was only one steam vessel of 3,000 tons—which was the only steamer of that size in Europe :* at the present date there are in the United Kingdom 330 of 3,000 to upwards of 8,000 tons gross, with an aggregate tonnage of 1,304,201, averaging 4,000 tons each. According to Lloyd's Register, 4 more were added up to 30th April of the present year, at which date there were owned in foreign countries 188 steam vessels of above 3,000 tons, of which 48 ranged from 4 to 6,000 tons. France owned 68, Germany 33, the United States 20, Spain 17, Italy 15, other countries 25.

e. *Iron and Steel Vessels.*

The first iron vessel appears to have been built in the United Kingdom as early as 1818, although the material did not come into general use until many years later. The first iron regular ocean steamer, the "Sirius," was built in 1837, and the first steel vessel

* According to M. Kiær, in his "Statistique Internationale, Navigation Mari-
"time; Les Marines Marchandes." Christiania, 1881.

in 1862, but it was not till 1877 that mild steel as now used was adopted for the construction of ships. Steel vessels were not distinguished in statistical tables before the year 1879. Their increase will be shown below. Composite vessels, of wood and iron, were not distinguished before 1866. Their number and tonnage has been insignificant since 1870, and in 1886 no vessel of this description was built.

The extent to which iron and steel have supplanted wood in the construction of vessels is shown in the following comparison, compiled from a return obtained from Lloyd's registry office. The figures include vessels built for foreigners:—

Vessels.	Average of Merchant Vessels Built in the United Kingdom.				Proportion of each Class.			
	1860-62.		1884-86.		1860-62.		1884-86.	
	Number.	Tons (Net).	Number.	Tons (Net).	Number.	Tons.	Number.	Tons.
Wood, sailing....	758	123,948	265	16,241	67·0	44·0	28·1	3·7
„ steam	163	65,262	53	1,263	14·4	23·2	5·6	0·3
Iron, sailing	48	26,786	134	123,110	4·2	9·5	14·2	28·0
„ steam........	163	65,262	266	146,437	14·4	23·3	28·1	33·3
Steel, sailing	—	—	39	29,231	—	—	4·1	6·7
„ steam	—	—	187	123,110	—	—	19·9	28·0
Total	1,132	281,258	944	440,056	100·0	100·0	100·0	100·0

The return for 1887 shows that steel is rapidly supplanting iron, and that wood has ceased to be employed except in the construction of small sailing vessels, which averaged only 60 tons, and of (apparently) steam launches averaging 24 tons. The war steamers built for foreigners in 1887, not included in the following statement, consisted of 17 vessels of 3,936 tons, all of steel.

Merchant Vessels Built in 1887.*

	Sailing.		Steam.		
	Number.	Tons.	Number.	Tons (Net).	Tons (Gross).
Iron	44	46,557	76	18,910	34,475
Steel	34	25,235	227	205,907	328,890
Wood	179	9,357	18	610	1,069
Total*	258	81,279	322	225,440	364,453

* Including a few composite vessels.

* Compiled from Annual Statement, &c., for 1887, pp. 280—83.

§ 7. *Vessels struck off the Register.**

From the comparison of the number of vessels belonging to and built in the United Kingdom in each year, the number which disappear annually from the Register as sold, lost, broken up, or otherwise disposed of, can be deduced. The following are the figures for sailing and steam vessels respectively, and of the average annual disappearance for the whole period, which is almost identical in the two classes, and falls short of 5 per cent.:—

	Sailing Vessels.	Steamers.		Sailing Vessels.	Steamers.
	No.	No.		No.	No.
1872	823	206	1881	995	301
'73	733	312	'82	845	360
'74	739	220	'83	793	229
'75	834	155	'84	1,494	350
'76	678	160	'85	1,219	299
'77	696	237			
'78	915	211	Average percentage		
'79	948	254	of number in each	4·3 per cnt.	4·5 p. ct.
'80	972	228	class....................		

* Compiled from " Statistical Abstracts."

CAP. 4. SHIPPING COMPARED WITH THAT OF OTHER MARITIME COUNTRIES.

The Annual Merchant Shipping Tables before referred to (sec note at p. 76) supply the means of making several important and interesting comparisons between the amount and progress of shipping employed and built in the United Kingdom and in the other principal maritime countries of the world. Some of them are exhibited in the following statements :—

a. *Employment of National and Foreign Vessels in each Country.*

The first of these shows the amount and percentage proportion of national and foreign tonnage respectively employed in the trade of each of the principal maritime countries at decennial periods between 1850 and 1880, and in the latest year, 1886 or 1887, for which the information is recorded : —

TABLE XXI.—*Shipping employed in the Foreign Trade of Principal Maritime Countries: Tonnage of National and Foreign Vessels, Sailing and Steamers, with Cargoes and in Ballast, entered and cleared in each Country, in certain Years between 1850 and 1887.*

(Compiled from Tables of "Merchant Shipping," Parl. Paper No. 198 of 1888.) [000's omitted.]

Countries.	Tonnage of Vessels entered and cleared.									
	National.					Foreign.				
	1850.	1860.	1870.	1880.	1886 or 1887.*	1850.	1860.	1870.	1880.	1886 or 1887.*
United Kingdom	9,442,	13,915,	25,072,	41,349,	47,950,*	5,062,	10,774,	11,568,	17,387,	17,212,*
Russia in Europe	—	696,	784,	1,135,	993,*	—	3,518,	6,231,	8,840,	11,508,*
Norway	1,050,	1,513,	2,263,	2,717,	3,023,	347,	517,	968,	1,268,	1,663,
Sweden	—	—	1,374,	2,564,	3,301,†	—	—	2,954,	4,330,	5,715,
Denmark	—	—	‡1,771,	2,352,	3,207,	—	—	‡1,823,	2,110.	2,708,
Germany	—	—	‡4,101,	5,109,	6,979,	—	—	6,640,	7,957,	7,734,
Holland	731,	1,048,	1,034,	2,116,	2,454,	1,017,	1,604,	2,610,	4,728,	5,717,
France	1,891,	3,503,	4,289,	7,522,	9,599,	2,719,	4,954,	9,317,	17,510.	17,151,
Portugal	—	—	297,	371,	347,	—	—	2,213,	5,375,	6,615,
Spain	—	799,	1,312,	3,651,	6,648,‡	—	1,798,	2,230,	10,092,	10,433,‡
Italy	—	—	2,780,	3,425,	2,979,	—	—	4,841,	6,422,	9,260,
United States	5,206,	12,087,	6,993,	6,825,	6,625,	3,504,	4,978,	11,332,	29,249,	24,945,

	PERCENTAGE PROPORTIONS OF NATIONAL AND FOREIGN.									
United Kingdom	65·1	56·3	68·4	70·4	73·6*	34·9	43·7	31·6	29·6	26·4*
Russia in Europe	—	16·5	11·2	11·4	7·9*	—	83·5	88·8	88·6	92·1*
Norway	75·2	74·5	70·0	68·2	64·5	24·8	25·5	30·0	31·8	35·5
Sweden	—	—	31·8	37·2	36·6†	—	—	68·2	62·8	63·4
Denmark	—	—	49·3†	52·7	54·2	—	—	50·7†	47·3	45·8
Germany	—	—	35·9†	39·1	42·8	—	—	64·1†	60·9	57·2
Holland	41·8	39·5	28·4	30·9	30·0	58·2	60·5	71·6	69·1	70·0
France	41·0	41·4	31·5	30·0	35·9	59·0	58·6	68·5	70·0	64·1
Portugal	—	—	11·8	6·5	5·0	—	—	88·2	93·5	95·0
Spain	—	30·7	37·0	26·6	38·9‡	—	69·3	63·0	73·4	61·1‡
Italy	—	—	36·5	34·8	24·3	—	—	63·5	65·2	75·7
United States	59·8	70·8	38·2	18·9	21·0	40·2	29·2	61·8	81·1	79·0

† Year 1885.   ‡ Year 1875.

The chief results to be gathered from it are :—

1. The exceptions to a steady increase of the national shipping throughout the period are observable in Russia, Portugal, Italy, and the United States.

2. The national shipping of the United Kingdom employed in the trade of the kingdom, which in 1870 fell somewhat short of the national shipping employed in the trade of all the other countries, eleven in number, exceeded it in 1880, and in 1886-87, viz. :—

	British.	Other Nations.
In 1870	25,072,000	26,978,000
„ '80	41,349,000	37,797,900
„ '86-87...........	47,950,000	46,155,000

3. The several countries stand in the following order as regards the total tonnage, national and foreign, which entered and cleared in the ports of each in the last year, 1886 or 1887 :—

[000's omitted.]

	Tons.	Percentage.
United Kingdom	65,162,	29·3
„ States...............	30,569,	13·8
France.......................	26,750,	12·0
Germany.................	23,290,	10·5
Spain	17,081,	7·6
Russia.....................	12,501,	5·6
Italy	12,239,	5·5
Sweden	9,016,	4·1
Holland	8,171,	3·7
Portugal.....................	6,962,	3·1
Denmark.....................	5,915,	2·7
Norway	4,686,	2·1
Total	222,351,	100·0

4. Spain has made the greatest proportionate increase in the amount of its national tonnage employed during this period.

5. The percentage proportion of national tonnage employed has increased notably in the United Kingdom, and less considerably during the years for which the record exists in Sweden, Denmark, Germany, and Spain ; and has fallen off more or less heavily in Russia, Norway, Holland, France (with a revival in 1886), Portugal, Italy, and the United States.

6. The order in which each country stood as regards the employment of its national shipping, and its dependence on foreign tonnage, in 1887 was as follows :—

	Employment of	
	National Tonnage.	Foreign Tonnage.
	Per cnt.	Per cnt.
United Kingdom	73·6	26·4
Norway	64·5	35·5
Denmark......................	54·2	45·8
Germany	42·8	57·2
Spain	38·9	61·1
Sweden	36·6	63·4
France.......................	35·9	64·1
Holland	30·0	70·0
Italy	24·3	75·7
United States	21·0	79·0
Russia in Europe	7·9	92·1
Portugal......................	5·0	95·0

b. *Employment of British Vessels in Foreign Countries.*

The next statement shows the extent to which British tonnage has been employed in the trade of the other principal maritime countries during the same years as in the last abstract.

TABLE XXII.—*Percentage Proportion of Tonnage of British Vessels, Sailing and Steamers, with Cargoes and in Ballast, which Entered and Cleared in each Country in certain Years between 1850 and 1887.*

(Compiled from same as Table XXI.)

	Percentage Proportion of British Tonnage Entered and Cleared in Trade of each Country.				
	1850.	1860.	1870.	1880.	1886 or 1887.*
United Kingdom	65·1	56·3	68·4	70·4	73·6 *
Russia in Europe	—	—	37·7 †	42·7 ‡	48·3
Norway	1·0	2·0	11·8	11·8	13·8
Sweden	—	—	11·4 †	13·5	18·2 §
Germany..................................	—	—	31·9 ‖	38·1	34·2
Holland	34·7	37·2	53·8	49·8	51·9
France	29·3	29·8	39·8	40·6	41·7
Portugal..................................	—	—	66·7	63·0	56·0
Italy	—	—	25·8	34·3	48·4
United States...........................	—	24·8	44·1	51·7	50·7

† Year 1875.   ‡ Year 1881.   § Year 1885.
‖ Year 1875, and including coasting trade.

It will be seen that—

1. The proportion of British tonnage employed in the United Kingdom, which appears to have fallen off heavily between 1850 and 1860, recovered itself in 1870, and has increased slowly up to 1887.

2. Between 1870 and 1886-87, for which years the returns are complete, it has increased greatly in Russia, Sweden, Italy, and the United States, and moderately in Norway, Germany, and France; and has decreased in Holland and Portugal.

3. The following is the actual amount of British tonnage employed in the trade of each country in the latest year for which a record is furnished, and the percentage proportion which it bore to the total tonnage in each:—

	Year.	Tons. [000's omitted.]	Proportion to Total Tonnage.
			Per cent.
United States	1886	12,505,	50·7
Russia in Europe	,,	4,837,	48·3
France	,,	11,153,	41·7
Italy	,,	5,925,	48·4
Germany	,,	5,586,	34·2
Holland	,,	4,243,	51·0
Portugal	,,	3,941,	56·6
Sweden	1885	1,643,	18·2
Norway	,,	654,	13·8
Total	—	50,487,	—

4. The total amount, 50,487,000 tons, exceeds by nearly 9 per cent. the total amount of British tonnage employed in the trade of the United Kingdom in the same year, 1886, which amounted to 46,078,299 tons.

5. It represents 50·5 out of 118 millions of tons, or 42·8 per cent., of the total tonnage employed in the trade of the above nine countries in the year 1886.

6. If the above 50·5 millions of tons be added to the 46 millions of British tonnage employed in the trade of the United Kingdom in the same year, the proportion of British tonnage to that of foreign tonnage employed in the trade of these ten countries (including the United Kingdom) will be 96·5 millions of British tonnage to 138·7 millions of foreign tonnage, or 41 per cent. of the shipping trade of the whole.

7. The amount of British shipping employed in the "carrying" "trade" of these eight countries may be ascertained by deducting from the above 46 millions of tons the amount of British tonnage employed in the direct trade between the United Kingdom and those countries, which amounted to 24·5 millions of tons. The difference is 21·5 millions of tons. If to this be added the same proportion (42·8 per cent.) of the other seven principal maritime countries of which the returns for the year 1885 are furnished in the latest Statistical Abstract of foreign countries published by the Board of Trade, viz., Denmark, Belgium, Spain, Austria,

Chili, the Argentine Republic, China, the British tonnage employed in the carrying trade of these fifteen countries will amount to 45·8 millions of tons, or within a fraction of the total amount of tonnage employed in the trade of the United Kingdom in the same year. If on the one hand it be objected that British tonnage in foreign countries includes Colonial, on the other hand it must be noted that a probably much larger addition must be made to the above 45·8 millions of tons on account of the British shipping employed in the carrying trade of all the rest of the world, including all British Possessions.

8. The foreign tonnage employed in the trade of the United Kingdom in 1886 was 16·7 millions of tons, out of a total trade of 62·8 millions, or 26·7 per cent. In 1887 it was slightly reduced to 17·2 millions, out of 65 millions, or 26·4 per cent.

c. *Tonnage of Vessels belonging to each Country.*

The next statement exhibits the total tonnage belonging to each country in the same years.

Tonnage of the Merchant Navies of the principal Maritime Countries in certain Years between 1850 *and* 1887.
(Compiled from same as Table XXI.)
[000's omitted.]

Countries.	Total Tonnage belonging to each Country.				
	1850.	1860.	1870.	1880.	1886 or 1887.*
United Kingdom	3,505,	4,587,	5,618,	6,520,	7,296,
British Possessions	727,	1,124,	1,531,	1,927,	1,839,
Total, British Empire	4,232,	5,611,	7,149,	8,447,	9,237,
Russia	—	—	—	468,	492,
Norway	298,	559,	1,022,	1,519,	1,524,
Sweden	—	—	347,	543,	517,†
Denmark	—	—	179,	249,	272,
Hamburg	71,	142,	184,	244,	341,
Bremen	68,	122,	172,	270,	334,
German Empire, total	—	—	982,	1,182,	1,285,
Holland	293,	434,	390,	328,	286,
Belgium	35,	33,	30,	76,	87,
France	688,	996,	1,072,	919,	993,
Italy	—	—	1,012,	999,	946,
Austria-Hungary	—	—	329,	291,	262,
Greece	—	263,	404,	—	259.*
United States, foreign trade	1,586,	2,546,	1,517,	1,353,	1,016,
„ home and internal ditto	1,900,	2,753,	2,678,	2,715,	3,090,*

† Year 1885.

It shows with regard to those countries for which the returns run through the whole period thus :—

The tonnage between 1850 and 1886-87 has doubled in the United Kingdom; more than doubled in the British Possessions and Belgium; has increased five-fold in Norway, Hamburg, and Bremen; increased in Holland in 1860-70, and decreased in 1886 below the amount at which it stood in 1850; has remained stationary in France since 1860; had increased in the United States as regards shipping employed in foreign trade in 1860, but has since decreased to one-third below the amount at which it stood in 1850; as regards the river, lake, and home trade it has increased slowly since 1860.

As regards the other countries: the tonnage since 1870 has increased considerably in Sweden, Denmark, and the German Empire; has fallen off in Italy and Austria-Hungary; has increased slightly in Russia since 1880.

d. *Steam Vessels belonging to each Country.*

The next statement shows a similar return of the tonnage of steamers only, in which the progress among foreign nations has been somewhat more rapid, and in the latest year of the series has in several instances outstripped the United Kingdom; but a glance at the relative proportion between the steamer tonnage of all the countries put together and that of the United Kingdom, and an examination of the remaining tables of this series, will remove all apprehension of any serious disturbance of the present proportions.

Tonnage of Steam Vessels belonging to the Merchant Navies of the principal Maritime Countries in certain years between 1850 and 1887.
(Compiled from same as Table XXI.)   [000's omitted.]

	Tonnage of Steam Vessels belonging to each Country.				
	1850.	1860.	1870.	1880.	1886 or 1887.*
United Kingdom	168,	452,	1,111,	2,721,	4,081,
British Possessions	20,	48,	91,	228,	329,
Total, British Empire	188,	500,	1,202,	2,941,	4,410,
Russia	—	—	—	89,	130,
Norway	—	—	14,	58,	113,
Sweden	—	—	—	81,	110,†
Denmark	—	—	10,	52,	88,
Hamburg	3,	10,	32,	99,	206,
Bremen	—	8,	41,	59,	116,
German Empire, total	—	—	82,	216,	454,
Holland	3,	10,	19,	64,	109,
Belgium	2,	4,	9,	65,	81,
France	14,	68,	154,	278,	500,
Italy	—	—	32,	77,	144,
Austria-Hungary	—	—	50,	63,	90,
Greece	—	—	5,	—	31,*
United States, foreign trade	45,	17,	192,	147,	173,*
„ home and internal trade	481,	770,	883,	1,065,	1,369,*

† Year 1885.

The principal results of this abstract are:—

1. The steam tonnage of all countries (exclusive of that employed in the United States in the river, lake, and home trade) was, as compared with British:—

	British Empire.	Other Countries.
In 1870	1,201,000	640,000 = 34 per cent. of the total
„ '80	2,949,000	1,346,000 = 31 „
„ '86-87............	4,410,000	2,335,000 = 33 „

2. The steam tonnage of the United States employed exclusively in the river, lake, and home trade has nearly doubled since 1860, and now amounts to 1,369,000 tons. If this be added to the above total of other nations, British steam tonnage will still show an excess of nearly a million tons.

In connection with the preceding comparisons, it should be noted that according to "Lloyd's Universal Register" the number of British vessels belonging to the United Kingdom on 30th April 1888, was—

Sailing vessels	3,403
Steam „	4,966
	8,369

and that at the same date the number of vessels belonging to the British colonies and foreign countries which had been built in the United Kingdom was—

Sailing vessels................	1,328 = 37·0 per cent.	} of the number belonging
Steam „	2,373 — 47·7 „	} to the United Kingdom
	3,701	

Deducting the number belonging to British colonies, (741) 2,960 had been supplied by British shipbuilders to foreign countries, which is just 35 per cent. of the number on the register of the United Kingdom.

e. *Increase of Tonnage in each Country.*

This is shown in the two following statements, the first exhibiting the total tonnage added in each of the principal maritime countries of Europe at decennial intervals from 1850 to 1880, and in each year from 1881 to 1886-87; and the second comparing the addition made in the United Kingdom, and in all the other European countries, in each year from 1878 to 1886-87.

Tonnage of Shipping added to the Merchant Navies of the Principal Maritime Countries of Europe in certain Years between 1850 and 1886.

(Compiled from same as Table XXI.)

Yrs.	Total Tonnage to Merchant Navy of each Country.								
	United Kingdom.	Norway.	Sweden.	Denmark.	Germany.	Holland.	France.	Italy.	Total of preceding Foreign Countries.
1850	133,695	11,115	—	—	—	18,572	44,032	—	—
'60	301,535	20,884	—	—	—	11,866	43,823	—	—
'70	391,831	69,415	25,434	—	—	19,406	63,372	106,162	—
'80	411,736	71,427	13,152	12,273	80,827	14,690	46,830	31,863	271,062
'81	561,750	78,748	18,274	18,455	88,537	18,883	55,644	41,090	319,631
'82	714,521	74,776	15,171	17,146	118,728	12,777	135,206	43,548	428,352
'83	751,950	88,311	18,201	20,259	128,145	27,560	84,610	41,055	408,141
'84	549,896	84,896	26,237	17,654	85,919	17,032	77,634	39,619	348,991
'85	423,711	69,421	17,158	9,197	44,179	13,433	25,611	30,165	209,464
'86	323,897	37,495	—	5,908	52,405	8,443	41,467	49,473	212,649
'87	384,537	—	—	—	—	—	—	—	—

Tonnage of Shipping added to the Merchant Navies of the United Kingdom, and of the other Principal Maritime Countries of Europe, viz., Norway, Sweden, Denmark, Germany, Holland, France, and Italy, in each Year from 1878 to 1887.

(Compiled from same as Table XXI.)

Years.	United Kingdom.		Other European Countries.	
1878	464,511	average 429,300	268,711	average 269,000
'79	410,804		266,578	
'80	411,736		271,062	
'81	561,750	644,000	319,631	376,000
'82	714,521		428,352	
'83	751,950		408,141	
'84	549,896		348,991	
'85	423,711	374,000	209,464	211,000
'86	323,897		212,649	
'87	384,537		—	

From the latter it will be seen that simultaneously with the great increase in shipbuilding in the United Kingdom during the four years 1881-84, which averaged 50 per cent. above the mean of 1878-80, there was an increase on the continent which averaged 40 per cent. This increase was greatest in Norway, Germany, and France.

2. The sudden decrease commencing in 1884 was spread alike over the United Kingdom and continental Europe. In the two

years 1885-86 it amounted to 42 per cent. in the former, and 40 per cent. in the latter.

3. The rate of increase of the continental mercantile marine has been diminishing at each period, as compared with that of the British, viz.:—

	Total Annual Increase.	Percentage Proportion of Increase.	
		British.	Foreign.
	Tons.		
Average of 1878-80	698,000	62	38
„ '81-84	1,020,000	63	37
„ '85-86	585,000	64	36

4. The addition to the tonnage of Europe in the nine years 1878-86 was 7,374,000 tons, of which the United Kingdom furnished 4,613,000 tons, or 62·6 per cent. In the last year, 1886, the United Kingdom furnished 60 per cent.

5. Of the 37·4 per cent. added by continental Europe—

10·3 per cent.	was furnished by		Germany.
8·5	„	„	Norway.
7·5	„	„	France.
4·9	„	„	Italy.
2·2	„	„	Holland.
2·0	„	„	Sweden.
2·0	„	„	Denmark.

37·4

6. Although France is among the European countries in which the addition to its shipping has been the greatest, a large proportion since 1872, when the distinction was first made in the returns, has been by purchase from foreigners, viz.:—

From 1872 to 1886........Built at home	493,000 tons =	56 per cent.
Bought from foreigners........	396,000 „ =	44 „
	889,000	100

The sales to foreigners during the same period have amounted to 238,000 tons, equal to 27 per cent. of the total built and bought.

Part IV.—TRADE OF THE BRITISH EMPIRE, 1872-86.

§ 1. *Aggregate of British Possessions.*

The fourth and last part of this review will comprise the Imports and Exports of the whole Empire, and of its several parts, for a period of fifteen years, from 1872 to 1886, being the usual term comprised in the annual, "Statistical Abstract," and the comparisons being brought down to the latest date of publication. It might have been better, as the years 1872-74 were a period of exceptional commercial inflation in the United Kingdom, to have commenced the comparison from an earlier date, but the trouble and delay of computation created an obstacle to this, and it will be sufficient to keep the point in mind, and, where practicable, to carry the starting point further back, in order to make the comparisons as fair as possible. At the same time it is in these tables that the difficulty caused by variations in prices, and in the case of the United Kingdom by the continuous and heavy fall in the prices both of Imports and Exports during the last fifteen years, comes into full force, and calls for the exercise of the greatest caution in drawing conclusions from the simple figures as to the volume of trade at different dates. Nothing is known—or at least recorded—as to the variation of prices in the several Possessions, but it may reasonably be assumed that if they have fallen, their fall has not been generally comparable with that which has occurred in the United Kingdom.

Notes on Tables XXIII *and* XXIV.

These two tables contain a return of the average annual value of Imports into and Exports from each part of the British Empire, calculated in triads. from 1872-74 to 1884-86, with the percentage difference of increase or decrease at each triennial period.

TABLE XXIII.—*Total Value of Imports (including Bullion and Specie) into each part of the British Empire in each Triennial Period between* 1872 *and* 1886 ; *also the Percentage Proportion of the Difference at each period.*

(Compiled from " Statistical Abstracts.")

[000's omitted.]

	Total Value of Imports (Annual Average).					Percentage. Difference at each Period.			
	1872-74.	1875-77.	1878-80.	1881-83.	1884-86.	1875-77.	1878-80.	1881-83.	1884-86.
	£	£	£	£	£				
India	39,903.	45,811,	52,166,	62,696,	69,627,	14·8	13·9	20·2	11·0
Straits Settlements.............	11,92?,	12,193,	14,135,	16,967,	19,155.	2·3	15·9	20·0	12·9
Ceylon	5,360,	5,603,	5.008,	4 43?,	4,277,	4·5	−10·6	−11·3	− 3·6
Mauritius	2,575,	2,279,	2,275,	2,705,	2,571,	−11·5	− 0·2	19·0	− 4·9
Labuan	100,	133,	157,	129,	83,	33·0	18·0	−17·9	−35·7
Australasia—									
New South Wales	9,962,	13,923,	14,306,	19,883.	22,4?2,	39·7	2·7	39·0	12·8
Victoria..........................	15,726,	16,251,	15 251,	17,737,	18,592,	3·3	− 6·1	16·3	4·8
South Australia	3,542,	4,46s,	5,43s,	6,0s0,	5,297,	26·2	21·7	11·8	−12·9
Western Australia	296,	366,	380,	477.	643,	23·7	3.8	25·5	34·8
Tasmania	1,057,	1,209,	1,320.	1,645,	1,723,	14·4	9·2	24·6	4·7
New Zealand	6,576,	7,303,	7,764,	8,013,	7,301,	11·1,	6.3	3·2	− 8·9
Queensland	2,5s3,	3,50s,	3.201,	5,53s,	6,302,	35·8	− 8·7	73·0	13·8
Fiji	...	137,	200,	375,	325,	...	46·0	87·5	−13·3
Cape of Good Hope............	5.789,	5,683.	7,449.	8,709,	4,741,	− 1·s,	31·1	16·9	−45·5
Natal	986,	1,153,	2,077,	1,959,	1,50s	16·9	80·1	− 5·7	−23·0
St. Helena......................	79,	10?,	96,	77,	61,	3s·1	−12·0	−19·8	−21·0
Lagos	325,	517.	473,	426,	479,	5·1	− 8·5	− 9·9	12·4
Gold Coast......................	26 ,	379,	351,	391,	456,	45·9	− 7·4	11·4	16 6
Sierra Leone....................	411,	340,	476,	402,	351,	−17·3	40·0	−15·5	−12·7
Gambia	122,	10s,	182,	179,	126,	−11·5	68·5	− 1·7	−29·6
Canada	25,532,	21,917,	18,162,	24,792,	22,900,	−14·1	−17·1	36·5	− 7·6
Newfoundland	1,447.	1,523,	1,465,	1,691,	1,444	5·2	− 3·s	15·4	−14·6
Bermuda	25s,	256,	246,	261,	266,	− 0·8	− 3·9	6·1	4·3
Honduras	194,	168,	196,	234,	243,	−13·3	16·7	19·4	3·s
British West Indies—									
Bahamas	204,	160,	179,	206,	202,	21·5	−11·9	15·1	− 1·9
Turk's Islands	24,	23,	23,	26,	28,	− 4·2	...	13·0	7·7
Jamaica	1,6s5,	1,671,	1,43s,	1,435,	1,442,	− 0·8	−13·9	− 0·2	0·5
St. Lucia	133,	123	115,	14s	121,	− 7·5	− 6·5	28·7	−18·2
St. Vincent	15s,	154,	154,	143,	105,	− 2·5	...	− 7·1	−26·6
Barbados	1,117,	1,120,	1,099,	1,136,	970,	0·3	− 1·9	4·3	−15·3
Grenada	127,	120,	142,	134,	140,	− 5·5	5·9	− 5·7	4·5
Tobago	49,	60,	41,	51,	28,	22·5	−31·6	24·4	−45·1
Virgin Islands.................	4,	5,	6.	6,	5,	25·0	20·0	...	−16·6
St. Kitts.........	159,	135,	173,	179,	} 186,	(−15·1	2s·1	3·5	} −15·1
Nevis	46,	32,	34,	40,		(−30·5	6·3	17·7	
Antigua	172,	1f5,	1s9,	172,	14s,	− 4·1	2·4	1·8	−14·0
Montserrat	24,	25,	26,	29,	22,	4·2	4·0	7·7	−21·4
Dominica	63,	61,	64,	69,	53,	− 3·2	5·0	7·8	−23·2
Trinidad.........................	1,300,	1,627,	2.169,	2 429,	2,610,	25·1	33.3	12·0	7·4
British Guiana.................	1,8s4,	2,016,	2,073,	2,036,	1,634,	7·0	2·7	− 1·8	−19·7
Falkland Islands...............	29,	34,	36.	43,	63,	17·0	0·6	19·4	46 5
ABSTRACT.									
India	39,903,	45,811,	52,166,	62,696,	69,627,	14·8	13·9	20 2	11·0
Asia and Mauritius...........	19,957,	20,208,	21,575,	24,240,	26,086,	1·3	6·7	12·3	7·6
Australasia	39,742,	47,165,	47,860,	59.7 8,	62·405,	18·1	1·5	24·s	4·s
African............................	7,972,	8.2s9,	11,104,	12,143,	7,722,	4·0	33·9	9·3	−36·4
America—North	27,431,	23,864,	20,069,	26,978,	24,853,	−13·0	−15·9	34·4	− 7·9
West Indies	5,265,	5,4s1,	5,872,	6,212	6,060,	4·1	6·4	6·5	− 2·4
South	1, 13,	2,050,	2,109,	2.079,	1,697,	7·1	2·9	− 1·4	−18·3
Total of British Possessions	142,1s3,	152,868,	160,715,	194,096,	198,650,	7·5	5·1	20·8	2·3
,, United Kingdom...	396,550,	416,995,	405,275,	431,547,	391,634,	5·2	− 2·8	6·5	− 9·2
,, British Empire......	538,733,	569,863,	565,990,	625,613	590,234,	5·8	− 0·7	10·5	− 5·6

H

TABLE XXIV.—*Total Value of Exports (including Bullion and Specie) from each part of the British Empire in each Triennial Period between 1872 and 1886; also the Percentage Proportion of the Difference at each Period.*

(Compiled from "Statistical Abstracts.")

[000's omitted.]

	Total Value of Exports (Annual Average).					Percentage Difference at each Period.			
	1872-74.	1875-77.	1878-80.	1881-83.	1884-86.	1875-77.	1878-80.	1881-83.	1884-86.
	£	£	£	£	£				
India	59,381,	61,106,	67,200,	81,205,	86,467,	2·9	9·9	20·8	6·5
Straits Settlements	11,178,	11,576,	13,396,	15,002,	17,214,	3·6	15·7	12·0	14·7
Ceylon	4,321,	5,205,	4,714,	3,378,	3,093,	20·4	-9·4	-28·3	-8·4
Mauritius	3,213,	3,332,	3,563,	3,807,	3,575,	3·7	6·9	6·9	-6·1
Labuan	106	126,	163,	136,	83,	18·9	29·4	-16·6	-39·0
Australasia—									
New South Wales	*5,759,	13,267,	13,859,	17,551,	16,783,	51·5	4·4	26·6	-4·4
Victoria	14,872,	14,707,	14,444,	16,281,	14,466,	-1·1	-1·7	12·7	-11·1
South Australia	4,243,	4,749,	5,231,	4,884,	5,510,	11·9	10·1	-6·6	12·8
Western Australia	301,	387,	468,	511,	494,	28·6	18·4	11·6	-3·3
Tasmania	910,	1,211,	1,376,	1,625,	1,373,	33·1	13·6	18·1	-15·5
New Zealand	5,351,	5,943,	6,037,	6,605,	6,861,	11·1	1·6	9·4	3·9
Queensland	*3,180,	3,930,	3,357,	4,117,	4,950,	23·6	-14·6	22·7	20·2
Fiji	...	113,	197,	239,	318,	...	74·3	21·3	33·1
Natal	681,	728,	723,	777,	932,	6·9	-0·7	7·4	19·9
Cape of Good Hope	4,436,	3,897,	4,030,	4,609,	3,920,	-12·1	3·4	14·3	14·9
St. Helena	32,	51,	44,	29,	20.	59·4	-13·7	-34·1	-31·0
Lagos	446,	624.	603,	545,	608,	39·9	-3·4	-9·6	11·6
Gold Coast	†385,	393,	435,	359,	457,	2·1	10·7	-17·4	27·3
Sierra Leone,	461,	345,	386,	409,	343,	-25·1	11·9	5·9	-16·1
Gambia	139,	120,	183,	201,	133,	-13·7	52·5	9·8	-33·8
Canada	18,179,	16,300,	16,578,	20,730,	18,465,	-10·3	1·7	25·0	-10·9
Newfoundland	1,359,	1,377,	1,193,	1,519,	1,122,	1·3	-13·4	27·3	-26·1
Bermuda	71,	70,	73,	96,	83,	-1·4	4·3	31·5	-13·5
Honduras	220,	178,	190,	267,	281,	-19·1	6·7	40·5	5·2
British West Indies—									
Bahamas	141,	109,	134,	141,	151,	-22·7	22·9	5·2	7·1
Turk's Islands	27,	27,	24,	28,	32,	...	-11·1	16·7	14·3
Jamaica	1,362,	1,462,	1,360,	1,399,	1,391,	7·3	-7·0	2·8	-0·6
St. Lucia	161,	161,	185,	202,	124,	...	14·9	9·2	-38·6
St. Vincent	217,	189,	160,	154,	106,	-12·9	-15·3	-3·7	-31·2
Barbados	1,062,	1,179,	1,168,	1,158,	1,021,	11·0	-0·9	-0·8	-11·8
Grenada	150,	165,	157,	191,	191,	10·0	-4·9	21·7	...
Tobago	58,	80,	72,	59,	33,	37·9	-10·0	-18·1	-44·1
Virgin Islands	5,	5,	5,	5,	4,	...	...	...	-20·0
St. Kitts	157.	148,	188,	‡237,	} §204,	-5·7	27·0	26·1	} -31·6
Nevis	60,	54,	48,	†61.		-10·0	-11·1	27·1	
Antigua	143,	201,	244,	224,	165,	40·5	21·3	-8·2	-26·3
Montserrat	33,	31,	32.	35,	23,	-6·1	3·2	9·4	-34·3
Dominica	70,	75,	74,	61,	50,	7·1	-1·3	-17·6	-18·0
Trinidad	1,529,	1,785,	2,096,	2,413,	2,508,	16·7	17·4	15·1	3·9
British Guiana	2,481,	2,806,	2,613,	2,993,	1,988,	13·1	-6·8	14·5	-33·6
Falkland Islands	38,	45,	70,	83,	102,	18·4	55·5	18·6	22·9
ABSTRACT.									
India	59,381,	61,106,	67,200,	81,205,	86,467,	2·9	9·9	20·8	6·5
Asia and Mauritius	18,821,	20,239,	21,836,	22,323,	23,965,	7·5	7·9	2·2	7·3
Australasia	37,616,	44,307,	44,959,	51,813,	50,755,	12·5	1·5	15·2	-2·0
Africa	6,580,	6,158,	6,404,	6,929,	6,413,	-6·4	4·0	8·2	-7·4
America—North	19,829,	17,925,	18,034,	22,612	19,951,	-9·6	0·6	25·3	-11·8
West Indies	5,175,	5,671,	5,947,	6,368,	6,003,	9·6	4·9	7·1	-5·7
South	2,519,	2,851,	2,653,	3,076,	2,090.	13·2	-5·8	14·6	-32·0
Total of British Possessions	149,921,	158,257,	167,063,	194,326,	195,644,	5·6	5·5	16·3	0·7
„ United Kingdom ...	335,111,	295,879,	284,947,	323,029	300,276,	-11·7	-3·7	13·3	-7·0
„ British Empire	485,032,	454,136,	452,010,	517,355.	495,920,	-6·3	-0·5	14·4	-4·1

* Exclusive of overland traffic.   † Figures of 1872.   ‡ Average of 1881-82.   § Figures of 1883-86.

a. British Possessions examined separately.

The several Possessions have been grouped in the same manner as previously in Part II, and the figures for the United Kingdom have been added, although for the reason above stated there is strong ground for believing that a fair comparison cannot be instituted between the aggregates of the Possessions and those of the United Kingdom, while the increase in the former disappears, and the aggregate of the Empire is dragged down by the fall in prices in the last triad of the period.

The trade of all the British Possessions taken together may be examined first. There has been a continuous increase both of Imports and Exports in each triad, but the increase in the years 1881-83 has been in both three or four times as great as in any of the other triads. Thus:—

Trade of the British Possessions.

	Total Value [000's omitted].		Percentage Increase at each Period.	
	Imports.	Exports.	Imports.	Exports.
	£	£	Per cent.	Per cent.
1872–74	142,183,	149,921,	—	—
'75–77.........	152,868,	158,257,	7·5	5·6
'78–80.........	160,715,	167,063,	5·1	5·5
'81–83.........	194,096,	194,326,	20·8	16·3
'84–86.........	198,650,	195,644,	2·3	0·7

On the above it may be noted—

1. That the increase has been greater in Imports than in Exports in three out of the four periods.

2. That the actual amount of Exports exceeded that of Imports in each of the first four periods, but the excess was gradually diminishing, and had nearly disappeared in the fourth; and that in the fifth and last the Imports had begun to exceed the Exports, indicating in this respect a growing approximation to the proportions which have long existed in the United Kingdom and the majority of old countries.

3. The total increase between the first and last triad has been for Imports 39·8 per cent., and for Exports 30·5 per cent., the increase in both having been small in the last period, after the very large increase in the one immediately preceding it.

b. British Possessions compared with the United Kingdom.

The corresponding figures for the United Kingdom tell a different tale, as far as the recorded value of the trade is concerned; but if the variations in prices in the British Possessions could be ascertained, and if it should turn out that there has been no such fall as in the United Kingdom, the difference would not be so striking, and a comparison between the two might be fairly instituted; but this is now, and will probably remain for some time, an impossibility. As they stand, the figures run thus:—

Trade of the United Kingdom.

	Total Value (000's omitted).		Percentage Difference at each Period.	
	Imports.	Exports.	Imports.	Exports.
	£	£	Per cent.	Per cent.
1872-74	396,550,	335,111,	....	....
'75-77	416,995,	295,879,	+ 5·2	− 11·7
'78-80	405,275,	284,947,	− 2·8	− 3·7
'81-83	431,547,	323,029,	+ 6·5	+ 13·3
'84-86	391,634,	300,276,	− 9·2	− 7·0

1. Here, instead of a continuous increase, there has been generally a decrease, except in the years 1881-83, in which, as in the British Possessions, there was a notable increase both in Imports and Exports.

2. The Imports have always largely exceeded the Exports. On the average of the fifteen years the excess was just a third, or 32·8 per cent.

3. Instead of an increase between the two extreme triads, there has been a falling off in Imports of 1·2 per cent., and in Exports of 10·1. But it must not be overlooked that 1872-74 was a period of great inflation. If the comparison be made with the years 1869-71,* there has been an increase of 16·8 per cent. in Imports, and of 8 per cent. in Exports.

c. *Estimated increase of Quantity at Prices of* 1872-74.

The method employed in this review, of measuring the average prices in each year, supplies the means of calculating what the value of Imports and Exports into and from the United Kingdom in each triad would have been, if the prices had remained stationary, the same as they were in the first triad. The comparative results are shown in the following statements:—

* Declared value of Imports in 1869-71.............. 339,276,000
   „   Exports   „   277,907,090

Imports into the United Kingdom.

	As recorded.		Calculated on Prices of First Triad.		Percentage Increase on calculated rices at each Period.
	Amount. [000's omitted.]	Average Price per Ton.	Amount [000's omitted.]	Average Price per Ton.	
	£	£	£	£	Per cent.
1872-74........	396,550,	19·6	396,550,	19·6	—
'75-77........	416,995,	18·1	450,155,	,,	13·5
'78-80	405,275,	17·2	461,825,	,,	2·6
'81-83........	431,547,	16·7	506,486,	,,	9·6
'84-86........	391,634,	14·8	518,650,	,,	2·4

which shows an increase of 30·8 per cent. between the first and last triads, comparable with the increase of 39·8 per cent. in the corresponding Imports into the British Possessions.

Exports from the United Kingdom.

	As recorded.		Calculated at Price of First Triad.		Percentage Increase at calculated Prices at each Period.
	Amount, [000's omitted.]	Average Price per Ton.	Amount. [000's omitted.]	Average Price per Ton.	
	£	£	£	£	Per cent.
1872-74........	335,111,	15·9	335,111,	15·9	—
'75-77........	295,879,	12·9	364,688,	,,	8·7
'78-80........	284.947,	11·1	406,365,	,,	11·4
'81-84........	323,029,	10·9	471,207,	,,	13·2
'84-86........	300,276,	9·5	502,567,	.,	6·6

which shows an increase of 50 per cent. between the first and last triads, largely exceeding the increase of 30·5 per cent. in the corresponding value of Exports from the British Possessions.

For the reason above given it does not appear expedient to exhibit here the aggregate of the United Kingdom and the Possessions, as the results would give a misleading view of the total trade, but the figures are available for examination in the table; and for the same reason, in comparing the proportion which the trade of the United Kingdom and the Possessions bore to one another at the two ends of the period, it appears desirable to show the calculation both for the actual declared value, and for the estimated value on the supposition that the prices had remained stationary.

	Calculated on Declared Value.		Calculated on Stationary Value.	
	Percentage Proportion of		Percentage Proportion of	
	United Kingdom.	British Possessions.	United Kingdom.	British Possessions.
Imports.				
1872-74.......	74·0	26·0	74·0	26·0
'84-86........	66·3	33·7	72·3	27·7
Exports.				
1872-74.......	69·0	31·0	69·0	31·0
'84-86........	60·6	39·4	72·0	28·0

The proportions are not so much changed as might be anticipated, and it may be assumed that the real proportions lie about
midway, and that the proportion at the present time of Import
trade of the Empire carried on by the Possessions is about 30 per
cent., and of the Export trade about 35 per cent.

§ 2. *British Possessions in Groups.*

As regards the progress of trade in different parts of the
Empire, Table XXIII shows, with respect to Imports, that—

1. There has been a continuous increase at each triad in India,
Asia, and Australasia, the amount of which has been very steady
in India, and very variable in the other two sections.   In all three
the greatest increase was in 1881-83.

2. In Africa there was an increase in the earlier triads, with a
heavy falling off of 36·4 per cent. in the last.   The increase in
1878-80 was very large, one-third (33·9 per cent.).

3. In North America there was a heavy falling off in the earlier
periods, a large increase, 34·4 per cent., in 1881-83, and a moderate
falling off in the following triad.

4. The West Indies exhibit a moderate continuous increase
in all but the last triad, in which there was a small falling off of
2·4 per cent.

5. In South America the first two comparisons exhibit a
moderate or small increase, and the latter two one small and
one large decrease.

6. There was a large increase in 1881-83 in India, Asia,
Australasia, and North America, and only a small increase or a
falling off in Africa, the West Indies, and South America.

Similar comparisons with regard to Exports derived from
Table XXIV exhibit the following results.   There has been—

1. A continuous but an unsteady increase in India and Asia.

2. An increase in Australasia and the West Indies—very

unsteady in the former—and a small falling off in the last triad in both.

3. A decrease in the second and last triads in both Africa and North America, and great unsteadiness, culminating in a heavy falling off, in the last triad in South America.

4. There was a large increase in 1881-83 only in India and North America, a moderate increase in the same triad in Australasia and South America, with a small increase in Asia, Africa, and the West Indies.

An examination of the trade of each Possession will be presently made in connection with the shipping, and the distribution of the trade of each.

Before quitting this branch of the subject it will be interesting to ascertain whether, and to what extent, the trade of the British Possessions taken collectively has increased in proportion to that of the United Kingdom, and the following statement shows that it has increased considerably and continuously, and also to the same extent both in Imports and Exports, during the last fifteen years :—

Years.	Imports.		Exports.	
	United Kingdom.	British Possessions.	United Kingdom.	British Possessions.
1872-74.......	73·6	26·4	69·1	30·9
'75-77.......	73·2	26·8	65·2	34·8
'78-80	71·6	28·4	63·1	36·9
'81-83	69·0	31·0	62.5	37·5
'84-86.......	66·4	33·6	60·6	39·4

On the whole period the proportion of Imports into the British Possessions as compared with those into the United Kingdom, has increased 27·2 per cent., and that of Exports therefrom has increased 27·5 per cent., with a corresponding decrease of the proportions contributed by the United Kingdom. The Exports from British Possessions took a great start in the years 1875-77.

Cap. 2.—Shipping in the British Possessions.

§ 1. *Character of Shipping in Trade of each Possession.*

The character and growth of the shipping employed in the trade of the Possessions are shown in Tables XXV and XXVI. The former gives for the latest year, 1886, a very complete description of its character by showing, in addition to the total tonnage entered and cleared—

1. The average value per ton of the cargoes conveyed.
2. The proportion of British to Foreign tonnage.
3. The same of sailing to steam vessels.

The results of the co-ordination of each of the Possessions in these several categories are very instructive and interesting.

The second table furnishes a comparison of the total tonnage, British and Foreign, and of the proportion of each on the average of the triennial periods 1877-79 and 1884-87, and of the increase of British and Foreign tonnage respectively in the latter period.

It must be premised that the tables are compiled from the Statistical Abstract for the Colonies, which gives only the total tonnage entered and declared, without distinction of vessels in ballast, and the total value of Imports and Exports without distinguishing them. From these data the average value of a ton of merchandise has been calculated for each Possession, and the remarkable differences indicate in a striking manner the character of the trade of each.

a. *Average Value per Ton, Imports and Exports combined.*

The first comparison exhibits the order in which each British Possession stands with regard to the relative value of Imports and Exports to each ton of shipping employed in the trade, inwards and outwards, in the year 1886. The classes into which they have been here divided are somewhat numerous, as there appeared to be a significance in some of them, but they can be easily thrown together in a smaller number:—

TABLE XXV.—*Statement showing the character of the Shipping employed in the Trade of each part of the British Empire, viz., the Total Tonnage Entered and Cleared, with Cargoes and in Ballast (exclusive of the Coasting Trade), the Total Value of Imports and Exports, the proportion of such Value to each Ton of Shipping, the proportions of British and Foreign Tonnage, and of the Tonnage of Sailing and Steam Vessels, in the Year 1886.*

(Compiled from "Statistical Abstracts.")   [000's omitted].

	Total Tonnage Entered and Cleared with Cargoes and in Ballast.	Total Value of Imports and Exports.	Value of Imports and Exports to each Ton of Shipping	Percentage Proportion of Tonnage (Average of 1884-86). British.	Foreign.	Percentage Proportion of Tonnage. Sailing.	Steam.
India	7,294,	156,123,	21·4	82·5	17·5	34·7	65·3
Straits Settlements	6,978	37,611,	5·4	64·6	35·4	6·2	93·8
Ceylon	3,923,	6,551,	1·7	82·7	17·3	—	—
Mauritius	681,	5,785,	8·5	54·6	45·4	50·3	49·7
Labuan	52,	163,	3·1	91·8	8·2	1·3	98·7
Hong Kong	9,080,	—	—	76·2	23·8	—	—
Australasia—							
New South Wales	4,258,	36,529,	8·6	88·6	11·4	29·9	70·1
Victoria	3,735,	30,325,	8·1	87·4	12·6	21·9	78·1
South Australia	1,558,	9,341,	5·9	83·4	16·6	—	—
Western Australia	501,	1,388,	2·8	96·5	3·5	19·8	80·2
Tasmania	692,	3,088,	4·5	98·8	1·2	14·0	86·0
New Zealand	990,	13,431,	13·5	91·3	8·7	—	—
Queensland	3,275,	11,037,	3·4	99·3	0·7	—	—
Fiji	105,	514,	4·9	89·8	9·7	34·9	65·1
Natal	392,	2,291,	5·8	91·5	8·5	—	—
Cape of Good Hope	1,554,	7,772,	5·0	85·6	14·4	22·2	77·8
St. Helena......	127,	8.,	0·7	90·4	9·6	29·9	70·1
Lagos	448,	896,	2·0	82·1	17·9	4·7	95·3
Gold Coast	605,	783,	1·3	84·1	15·9	2·5	97·5
Sierra Leone..................	436,	590,	1·3	88·4	11·6	6·2	93·8
Gambia	136,	148,	1·1	71·3	28·7	9·5	90·5
Canada	8,044.	39,515,	4·9	60·4	39·6	40.8	59·2
Newfoundland	612,	2,267,	3·7	97·3	2·7	45·2	54·8
Bermuda	281,	355,	1·2	84·6	15·4	22·0	78·0
Honduras	237,	616,	2·6	43·5	56·5	25·1	74·9
British West Indies—							
Bahamas	209,	339,	1·6	27·5	72·5	31·7	68·3
Turk's Islands	232,	62,	0·3	25·7	74·3	38·0	62·0
Jamaica........................	928,	2,601,	2·8	76·3	23·7	21·2	78·8
St. Lucia	435,	227,	0·5	87·4	12·6	5·5	94·5
St. Vincent	346,	161,	0·4	93·6†	6·4†	8·8	91·2
Barbados	916,	1,603,	1·7	89·7	10·3	—	—
Grenada.......................	298,	310.	1·0	98·0	1·9	8·3	91·7
Tobago	87,	38,	0·1	98·9	1·1	9·4	90·6
Virgin Islands	10,	7,	0·7	97·0	3·0	100·0	—
St. Kitts and Nevis........	380,	330,	0·8	94·6	5·4	13·3	86·7
Antigua........................	380,	291,	0·7	94·9	5·1	12·2	87·8
Montserrat	325,	42,	0·1	99·0	1·0	4·0	96·0
Dominica	304,	101.	0·3	98·9	1·1	3·9	96·1
Trinidad........................	1 196,	5,012,	4·2	66·5	33·5	23·5	76·5
British Guiana	627,	3,278,	5·2	64·7	35·3	55·5	44·5
Falkland Islands	59,	182,	3·1	35·9	65·0	43·5	56·5
ABSTRACT.							
India	7,294,	156,123,	21·4	82·5	17·5	34·7	65·3
Asia and Mauritius..........	21,227,	50 110,	2·3	72·5	27·5	9·5	90·5
Australasia	15,114,	105,653	7·0	91·0	9·0	25·1	74·9
Africa	3,698,	12,567,	3·4	85·7	14·4	14·0	86·0
America: North	9,174,	42,753,	4·6	63·2	36·8	40·1	59·9
West Indies	6,046,	11,124,	1·8	79·7	20·3	16·6	83·4
South	686,	3,460,	5·0	63·0	37·0	54·5	45·5
Total of British Possessions*	63,239,	381,790,	6·0	78·3	21·7	18·4	81·6
„ United Kingdom ...	62,811,	660,402,	10 5	72·7	27·3	21·4	78·6
„ British Empire ...	126,080,	1,042,192,	8·3	75·4	24·6	19·9	80·1

* Exclusive of Malta and Gibraltar, from which the returns are not comparable with the others, and Heligoland, from which there is no return.   † Average of 1884 and 1885.

TABLE XXVI.—*Total Tonnage of Vessels, British and Foreign, which Entered and Cleared wit Cargoes and in Ballast (exclusive of the Coasting Trade), in each part of the British Empir in the two Triennial Periods 1877-79 and 1884-86; also the Percentage Proportion of th Foreign Tonnage at each period, and the Increase and Decrease of British and Forei respectively between the two periods.*

[000's omitted.]

	Total Tonnage Entered and Cleared.						Percentage Proportion of Foreign.		Percentage Dif ference betwee the two Periods	
	1877-79. Annual Average.			1884-86. Annual Average.						
	British.	Foreign.	Total.	British.	Foreign.	Total.	1877-79.	1884-86.	British.	Foreig
India	4,600.	985,	5,585,	5,829,	1,235,	7,064,	17·6	17·5	26·8	25·
Straits Settlements	2,843,	1,336,	4,179,	4,370,	2,391,	6,761,	31·9	35·4	53·7	78·
Labuan	18,	2,	20,	45,	4,	49,	10·0	8·2	150·0	100·
Hong Kong	3,780,	1,228,	5,008,	6,034,	1,899,	7,933,	26·5	23·8	59·6	54·
Ceylon	2,176,	381,	2,557,	3,033,	632,	3,665,	15·0	17·3	39·4	66·
Mauritius	343,	209,	552,	373,	310,	683,	37·8	45·4	9·0	48·
Australasia—										
New South Wales	2,173,	239,	2,412,	3,854,	497,	4,351,	9·9	11·4	77·3	108·
Queensland	1.049,	44,	1,093,	3,320,	24,	3,344,	4·0	0·7	216·5	-45·
Victoria	1,764.	145,	1,909,	2,958,	424,	3,382,	7·5	12·6	67·7	192·
South Australia	760,	77,	837,	1,446,	287,	1,733,	9·1	16·6	90·2	272·
Western ,,	152,	9,	161,	454,	16,	470,	5·5	3·5	19·7	77·
Tasmania	338,	1,	339,	653,	8.	661,	0·2	1·2	93·2	700·
New Zealand	742,	132,	874,	939,	89,	1,028,	15·1	8·7	26·5	-32·
Fiji	33,	15,	48,	103,	11,	114,	31·2	9·7	212·1	-26·
Cape of Good Hope	1,011,	203,	1,214,	1,351,	226,	1,577.	16·7	14·4	33·6	11·
Natal	259,	29,	288,	368,	33,	401,	10·4	8·5	42·1	14·
St. Helena	109,	20,	129,	111,	11,	122,	15·5	9·6	1·9	-45·
Lagos	280,	67,	347,	346,	75,	421,	19·5	17·9	23·6	11·
Gold Coast	109,	32,	141,	492,	93,	585,	22·6	15·9	351·4	190·
Sierra Leone	277,	55,	332,	369,	49,	418,	16·5	11·6	33·2	-10·
Gambia	97,	49,	146,	107,	43,	150,	33·5	28·7	10·3	12·
Can·da	4,076.	2,396,	6,472,	4,073,	3,185,	8,058,	35·4	39·6	19·5	32·
Newfoundland	537,	56,	593,	625,	17,	642,	8·0	2·7	16·2	-69·
Bermuda	138,	45,	183,	208,	38,	246,	24·6	15·4	50·8	-18·
Honduras	53	34,	87,	102,	132,	234,	38·9	56·5	92·4	258·
British West Indies—										
Bahamas	50,	119,	169,	60,	159,	219,	70·4	72·5	20·0	33·
Turk's Islands	27,	69,	96,	64,	185,	249,	71·9	74·3	133·3	169·
Jamaica	552.	185,	737,	723,	225,	948,	25·1	23·7	30·9	21·
St. Lucia	105,	46,	151,	376,	54,	430,	30·5	12·6	258·1	17·
St. Vincent	37,	5,	42,	161,	11,	172.†	12·0	6·4	335·1	100·
Barbados	319,	93,	412,	786,	93.	879,	22·8	10·6	146·4	...
Grenada	129,	19,	148,	263,	5,	268,	12·9	1·9	103·9	-73·
Tobago	12,	...	12,	98,	1,	99,	...	1·1	716·6	...
Virgin Islands	9,	...	9,	10,	...	10,	0·0	0·0	11·1	...
St. Kitts and Nevis	61,	33.	94,	367.	21,	388,	35·1	5·4	501·6	-36·
Antigua	82,	17,	99,	363,	19,	382,	17·1	5·1	34·3	11·
Montserrat	15.	2,	17,	204,	2,	206,	11·8	1·0	1,260·0	...
Dominica	19,	7,	26,	277,	3,	280,	26·9	1·0	1,357·8	-57·
Trinidad	445,	251,	696,	736,	369,	1,105,	36·1	33·5	65·4	47·
British Guiana	not dist	nguished	537,	422,	230,	652,	...	35·3	...	...
Falkland Islands	20,	3,	23,	14,	26,	40,	13·0	65·0	5·0	834·
ABSTRACT.										
India	4,60·.	985,	5,585,	5,829,	1,235,	7,064,	17·6	17·5	26·8	25·
Asia and Mauritius	9,160,	3,156	12,316,	13,855,	5,236,	19,091,	25·6	27·5	51·2	68·
Australasia	7,011,	662,	7,673,	13,727,	1,356,	15,083,	8·6	9·0	95·8	104·
Africa	2,142,	455,	2,597,	3,144,	530,	3,674.	17·5	14·4	46·8	16·
America, North	4,804,	2,531,	7,335,	5,808,	3,372,	9,180,	34·5	36·8	20·9	33·
West Indies	1,862,	846,	2,708,	4,488,	1,147,	5,635,	31·2	20·3	141·0	35·
South	not dist	nguished	560,	436,	256,	692,	...	37·0	...	...
Total of British Possessions*	29,579,	8,535,	38,774,	47,287,	13,132,	60,419,	22·0	21·7	60·0	53·
,, United Kingdom ...	35,830,	16.117,	51,947.	46,380,	17,418,	63,798,	31·0	27·3	29·4	8·
,, British Empire	65,409,	24,652,	90,721,	93,667,	30,550,	124,217,	27·1	24·6	43·2	23·

* Exclusive of Malta and Gibraltar, from which the returns are not comparable with the others, and Heligola from which there is no return.   † Average for 1884-85.

Class.
1. £21·4   per ton.   British India.
2. £13·5   ,,   New Zealand.
3. £10·5   ,,   United Kingdom.
4. £8 to £9 .,   New South Wales, Mauritius, Victoria.
5. £5 to £6 ,,   South Australia, Natal, Straits Settlements, British Guiana, Cape of Good Hope.
6. £4 to £5 ..   Canada, Fiji, Tasmania, Trinidad.
7. £3 to £4 ,,   Newfoundland, Queensland, Labuan, Falkland Islands.
8. £2 to £3 .,   Western Australia, Jamaica, Honduras, Lagos.
9. £1 to £2 ,,   Ceylon, Barbados, Bahamas, Gold Coast, Sierra Leone, Bermuda, Gambia, Grenada.
10. £0·5 to £1 ,,   St. Kitts and Nevis, St. Helena, Virgin Islands, Antigua.
11. Under £0·5 ,,   St. Lucia, St. Vincent, Tobago, Turk's Islands, Dominica, Montserrat.

Similar order of groups :—

	£		£
1. India	21·4	5. North America	4·6
2. United Kingdom	10·5	6. Africa	3·4
3. Australasia	7·0	7. Asia	2·3
4. South America	5·0	8. West Indies	1·8

Upon these statements it may be observed—

1. It is difficult to account for the immense difference between India and the United Kingdom ; one cause may be a difference in the proportion of vessels in ballast : another may be the difference in the proportion of steam vessels ; a third will be the proportionately large importation of bullion and specie into India ; and possibly one cause may be a greater proportion both of Imports and Exports of low value in England.

2. The high proportion of New Zealand compared with the Australian and other Possessions, may partly be accounted for by the small proportion of its inter-Colonial trade, which was only 20 per cent. compared with 49·2 per cent. in the Australian Colonies. It may be assumed that the proportion of vessels in ballast is much larger in an inter-colonial trade with neighbours than in a trade with distant countries.

3. The position of the several Australian Colonies in this table corresponds somewhat with the proportionate amount of the trade with British (chiefly Australian) Colonies, and with the United Kingdom and foreign countries, shown in Table VIII A of Part I of this work. Western Australia and Tasmania may have been depressed in the scale by steamers entering somewhat more largely into their trade.

Average Value per ton.		Percentage Proportion of Total Trade with	
		British Colonies.	United Kingdom and Foreign Countries.
£			
8 to 9	New South Wales	40·8	59·2
„	Victoria	38·3	61·7
5 „ 6	South Australia	38·0	62·0
4 „ 5	Tasmania	71·8	28·2
3 „ 4	Queensland	61·0	39·0
2 „ 3	Western Australia	45·2	54·8

4. Three causes have a material effect in producing the average value per ton in the several Possessions. One is shown conspicuously in the next statement, namely, the proportion of steamer tonnage, as exemplified in the trades of West Africa and the West Indies, where the periodical visits of passenger steamers swell the aggregates of tonnage, but contribute comparatively little to the aggregates of Imports and Exports.

Another cause is the proportion of small native craft which move about constantly, but carry little cargo that is recorded at the customs.

A third cause is the proximity of a Possession to some other territory with which a constant intercourse is kept up, but which contributes little to the record of Imports and Exports.

Ceylon offers a conspicuous example of the operation of all these causes, reducing the average value of a ton to £1·7. In the returns from this island the tonnage of steamers is not distinguished from that of sailing vessels, but the large proportion of it may be inferred from the fact that of the total tonnage which entered and cleared in 1885, nearly 4 million of tons, 1½ millions (38 per cent.) sailed in ballast. Of the 5,828 vessels which entered and cleared in the same year, 1,635, or 28 per cent., were British, of an average size of 1,734 tons, evidently chiefly passenger steamers, and 4,193, or 72 per cent., were Colonial vessels, chiefly native craft, of an average size of 82 tons. Of the total trade of the island in the same year 71 per cent. of the Imports and 19 per cent. of the Exports were shipped to or from India, to which must be added the large passenger traffic in coolies. Furthermore it appears that while the value of Imports and Exports has decreased of late years, the tonnage (especially of foreign vessels) has increased considerably, which, to whatever cause it may be attributed, helps to account for the very low average value of cargoes.

b. *Proportion of Steamer Tonnage.*

The next statement shows the order in which each British Possession stands with regard to the proportion of tonnage of steamers compared with that of sailing vessels, employed in its trade, inwards and outwards collectively.

Proportion of Steamer Tonnage.

	Per cent.			Per cent.
1. Labuan	98·7		22. Honduras	74·9
2. Gold Coast	97·5		23. New South Wales	70·1
3. Dominica	96·1		24. St. Helena	70·1
4. Montserrat	96·0		25. Bahamas	68·3
5. Lagos	95·3		26. India	65·3
6. St. Lucia	94·5		27. Fiji	65·1
7. Sierra Leone	93·8		28. Turk's Islands	62·0
8. Straits Settlements	93·8		29. Canada	59·2
9. Grenada	91·7		30. Falkland Islands	56·5
10. St. Vincent	91·2		31. Newfoundland	54·8
11. Tobago	90·6		32. Mauritius	49·7
12. Gambia	90·5		33. British Guiana	44·5
13. Antigua	87·8		34. Virgin Islands	Nil
14. St. Kitts and Nevis	86·7			
15. Tasmania	86·0		35. Ceylon	⎫
16. Western Australia	80·2		36. Hong Kong	⎪
17. Jamaica	78·8		37. South Australia	⎪ No returns
18. Victoria	78·1		38. New Zealand	⎬
19. Bermuda	78·0		39. Queensland	⎪
20. Cape of Good Hope	77·8		40. Natal	⎪
21. Trinidad	76·5		41. Barbados	⎭

It will be seen that in Labuan, the West African Possessions, and all the smaller West Indian Islands, a large proportion of the tonnage consists of the passenger steamers which visit them periodically. Returns are wanting from several important Colonies.

c. *Proportion of Foreign Tonnage.*

The next statement, deduced from Table XXV, shows the order in which each British Possession stands with regard to the proportion of foreign tonnage employed in its trade, inwards and outwards collectively, upon the average of the years 1884-86.

Proportion of Foreign Tonnage.

	Per cent.		Per cent.
1. Turk's Islands	74·3	22. Sierra Leone	11·6
2. Bahamas	72·5	23. New South Wales	11·4
3. Falkland Islands	64·1	24. Barbados	10·3
4. Honduras	56·5	25. Fiji	10·2
5. Mauritius	45·4		
6. Canada	39 6	26. St. Helena	9·6
7. Straits Settlements	35·4	27. New Zealand	8·7
8. British Guiana	35·3	28. Natal	8·5
9. Trinidad	33·5	29. Labuan	8 2
		30. St. Vincent	6·4
10. Gambia	28·7	31. St. Kitts and Nevis	5·4
11. Hong Kong	23·8	32. Antigua	5·1
12. Jamaica	23·7	33. Western Australia	3·5
13. Lagos	17·9	34. Virgin Islands	3·0
14. India	17·5	35. Newfoundland	2·7
15. Ceylon	17·3	36. Grenada	2·0
16. South Australia	16·6	37. Tasmania	1·2
17. Gold Coast	15·9	38. Tobago	1·1
18. Bermuda	15·4	39. Dominica	1·1
19. Cape of Good Hope	14·4	40. Montserrat	1·0
20. Victoria	12·6	41. Queensland	0·7
21. St. Lucia	12·6		

The above are divided into three classes: 1, those in which the proportion of foreign tonnage exceeds a third; 2, those in which it ranges from 10 to 30 per cent.; and 3, those in which it is less than 10 per cent.

The four Possessions in which the proportion exceeds 50 per cent. are not important for the amount of their trade, but five important Possessions employ from 33 to 45 per cent. of foreign tonnage. Among these is Canada. The Australian Colonies employ but a small proportion; Queensland less than 1 per cent.

d. *Comparison with the United Kingdom*

Taking a summary view of this table, the average value of a ton in the whole Empire was £8·3, in the United Kingdom £10·5, and in the Possessions £6·0. In these latter the average ranged from £21·4 in India to £1 8 in the West Indies.

The proportions of British and foreign tonnage employed in the trade of the Empire were as close as possible 75 and 25 per cent. respectively. In the United Kingdom the proportion of foreign was somewhat greater, viz., 27·3; in the Possessions that of British was to the same extent greater, viz., 78·3.

The several groups of Colonies exhibit very different proportions :—

Percentage Proportion
of Foreign Tonnage.

South America	37·0
North ,,	36·8
Asia and Mauritius	27·5
West Indies	20·2
India	17·5
Africa	14·4
Australasia	9·0
Average	21·7

The proportion of steam to sailing tonnage in the trade of the Empire is 80 to 20 per cent. In the trade of the United Kingdom it is slightly lower, 78·6, and in that of the Possessions slightly higher, 81·6 per cent. The order in which the several groups stand is :—

Percentage Proportion
of Steam Tonnage.

Asia and Mauritius	90·5
Africa	86·0
West Indies	83·4
Australasia	74·9
India	65·3
North America	59·9
South ,,	45·5
Average	81·6

§ 2. *Comparisons of British and Foreign Tonnage in each Possession.*

Table XXVI compares the total tonnage entered and cleared, distinguishing British and foreign, in the first and last triad of the ten years 1877-86. It shows that—

1. The total tonnage employed in the trade of the Empire, inwards and outwards, had increased from 90·7 millions of tons to 124·2 millions, or 37·1 per cent. British tonnage had increased from 65·4 to 93·7 millions, or 43·2 per cent.; foreign tonnage had increased from 24·6 to 30·7 millions, or 24 per cent.

2. In the trade of the United Kingdom separately the corresponding changes were :—

British from 35·8 to 46·4 million tons	= 29·4 per cent.
Foreign ,, 16·1 ,, 17·4 ,,	= 8·1 ,,
Total.... 51·9 63·8 ,,	= 22·7 ,,

4. And in the trade of the British Possessions :—

British from 29·6 to 47·3 million tons	= 60·0 per cent.
Foreign ,, 8·5 ,, 13·1 ,,	= 54·0 ,,
Total.... 38·2 60·4 ,,	= 57·3 ,,

§ 3. *Tonnage in Trade of all Possessions, 1885.*

Tables XXVII and XXVIII contain an epitome of a series of tables prepared for the Defence Committee of the Imperial Federation League, which may be consulted in the office of the League. They contain a return of the tonnage, distinguishing British from Foreign, which was employed in the trade of each British Possession, carried on inwards and outwards, with each country, in the year 1885. These are brought together in different groups according to their locality, and the groups into a single aggregate, showing the shipping trade of the British Possessions in the latest year for which the returns were available. These tables are too voluminous and too detailed for this review, but some of the most interesting features are shown in the abstracts published herewith, and others will be brought out in the following remarks.

TABLE XXVII.—*Percentage Proportions of the Total Tonnage, British and Foreign, employed in the Trade, Inwards and Outwards, of all the British Possessions, exclusive of the United Kingdom, with different Countries, in the Year 1885.*

(Computed from returns compiled from Blue Books of the several Possessions.)

In Trade with	Percentage Proportions of Total Tonnage of British Possessions.		
	Inwards.	Outwards.	Total.
United Kingdom .	24·6	20·2	22·40
British Possessions—			
Australasia	15·1	15·6	15·35
India	9·0	9·7	9·35
West Indies	3·6	3·6	3·60
Hong Kong	2·4	2·7	2·55
North America	1·2	1·3	1·25
Africa	1·2	1·5	1 35
Mauritius	0·5	0·5	0·50
British Guiana	0·3	0·3	0·30
Other	1·0	0·6	0·80
Total of British Possessions....	34·3	35·8	35·85
Foreign Countries—			
China and Japan	14·0	14·6	14 30
United States	9·0	9·2	9·10
Asia	8·1	9·0	8·55
Europe and Egypt	4·0	5·8	4·90
Africa	1·8	1·9	1·85
Foreign West Indies	1·4	1·6	1·50
Central America	0·9	1·1	1·00
South America	0·8	0·6	0·70
All other, and Fisheries	0·4	0·2	0 30
Total of Foreign Countries	41·1	44·0	42 55
Total	100·0	100·0	100·00

Proportions in Trade with Different Countries.

Notes on Table XXVII.

It must be borne in mind that these tables relate exclusively to the shipping trade of the British Possessions. The first shows the percentage proportion of tonnage, not distinguishing British from Foreign, employed in the trade of all the British Possessions with different countries. The notable results are—

1. The proportion employed in the total trade with the United Kingdom, inwards and outwards, is between a fourth and a fifth, viz., 22·4 per cent. The intercolonial trade amounts to 35·05 per cent., and the trade with Foreign Countries to 42·55.

2. There are some differences sufficiently great to be worthy of notice in the inward and outward trades. The proportion of tonnage arriving from the United Kingdom exceeds that despatched thither by 4·4 per cent. On the other hand that of tonnage despatched to other Colonies is 1·5 per cent. in excess, and that despatched to Foreign Countries is 2·9 in excess. This seems to indicate, if tonnage affords any measure of trade, that the Possessions import more from the United Kingdom than they export thither, and that they export more to other Colonies and to Foreign Countries than they import from them.

The annual statements of Navigation and Shipping afford the means of comparing the proportions of the tonnage employed in the United Kingdom in the Foreign and Colonial trades respectively with those so employed in the British Possessions. Thus in the year 1885—

	Tonnage, 00's omitted.		
	Inwards.	Outwards.	Total.
Trade of British Possessions—			
In trade with United Kingdom	7,890,	6,349,	14,239,
„ other Countries	24,173,	25,094,	49,267,
Total............	32,063,	31,443,	63,506,
Trade of United Kingdom—			
In trade with British Possessions....	4,155,	6,105,	10,260,
„ Foreign Countries	27,707,	26,314,	54,021,
Total..............	31,862,	32,419,	64,281,

The chief points to be noted in the above figures are—

1. The total tonnage in the trade of the United Kingdom in the year 1885 exceeded slightly that in the trade of all the British Possessions.

2. In the British Possessions the total tonnage inwards

1

exceeded the tonnage outwards; in the United Kingdom the excess lay in the opposite direction in about the same proportions.

3. These proportions however are found to differ both in the United Kingdom and the British Possessions when the trades between them and between Foreign Countries are examined separately. In the United Kingdom the imports from Foreign Countries exceed in the proportion of 51 to 49, but the Exports to the Possessions exceed in the proportion of 60 to 40. In the Possessions the Imports from the United Kingdom exceed in the proportion of 55 to 45, while the Exports to Foreign Countries exceed in the proportion of 51 to 49. The identity of this latter proportion in the two cases is remarkable, as is also the near approximation in the other proportion, which will be best seen in the following statement:—

	Proportions of Tonnage.	
	Inwards.	Outwards.
Trade of British Possessions—	Per cent.	Per cent.
In trade with United Kingdom	55	45
,, other Countries.................	49	51
Trade of United Kingdom—		
In trade with British Possessions............	40	60
,, Foreign Countries	51	49

3. There is one feature in the above figures which requires investigation and explanation : how the 6·1 millions of tons which cleared from the United Kingdom figured as 7·9 millions on arrival in the Possessions : and how the 6·3 millions of tons which cleared from the Possessions figured as only 4·1 on their arrival in the United Kingdom. Of course they were not the same ships— but the difference is too great to be accounted for by the fluctuations in the annual trade.

4. After deducting the double entry of trade between the United Kingdom and the British Possessions, the aggregate of tonnage employed in the trade of the British Empire in 1885 stood thus :—

		Tons, 000's omitted.
Trade of the United Kingdom with British Possessions............		12,250,*
,, ,, Foreign Countries		54,021,
,, British Possessions with other British Possessions		22,283,
,, ,, Foreign Countries		26,984,
	Total................	115,538,

4. The trade with China, Japan, and the rest of Asia is slightly greater than that with the United Kingdom, being 22·8 and 22·4 respectively; and is greater than that with all other countries

* Taking the mean of the figures in the statement at p. 111.

put together, being 22·8 and 19·7 respectively; the trade with China and Japan is only inferior to that with Australasia; the trade with India and the United States is nearly equal, being 9·3 and 9·1 respectively; but the most striking feature is that the direct trade with all foreign European countries and Egypt is less than 5 per cent.

§ 4. *Tonnage in Trade of Groups of Possessions.*

Notes on Table XXVIII.

This table has been prepared for the purpose of showing the proportions in which British and Foreign tonnage is employed in the trade of the British Possessions, and in the several groups into which they have been divided. The same obstacle exists as in the case of the last table, to combining the returns for the United Kingdom in the same form, and so exhibiting the aggregate of the British Empire.

TABLE XXVIII.—*Percentage Proportion of British and Foreign Tonnage employed in the Trade, Inwards and Outwards, of the British Possessions in different parts of the World, exclusive of the United Kingdom, distinguishing the Trade with the United Kingdom, other British Possessions, and Foreign Countries, in the Year* 1885.

(Compiled from same returns as Table XXVIII.)

	INWARDS.							
	United Kingdom.		British Colonies.		Foreign Countries.		Total.	
	British.	Foreign	British.	Foreign.	British.	Foreign.	British.	Foreign.
British Asia	92·7	7·3	83·0	17·0	51·2	48·8	68·0	32·0
Australasia	99·2	0·8	96·3	3·7	29·1	70·9	90·7	9·3
British Africa	88·4	11·6	94·1	5·9	78·1	21·9	85·4	14·6
„ N. America	85·2	14·8	95·8	4·2	43·5	56·5	62·9	37·1
„ West Indies	95·8	4·2	93·0	7·0	57·7	42·3	80·0	20·0
„ S. America	64·0	36·0	83·4	16·6	29·6	70·4	62·4	37·6
Total	91·9	8 1	90·9	9·1	50·5	49·5	74·7	25·3

	OUTWARDS.							
British Asia	91·1	8·9	84·4	15·6	53·9	46·1	67·7	32·3
Australasia	95·9	4·1	94·9	5·1	57·2	42·8	90·7	9·3
British Africa	97·8	2·2	92·8	7·2	70·9	29·1	84·1	15·9
„ N. America	78·3	21·7	81·2	18·8	45·3	54·7	53·1	46·9
„ West Indies	91·1	8·9	95·8	4·2	61·7	38·3	79·5	20·5
„ S. America	86·9	13·1	71·0	29·0	34·9	65·1	61·1	38·9
Total	88·7	11·3	82·3	17·7	54·2	45·8	74·4	25·6

The table divides the British Possessions into six groups, viz.:—

> British Asia.
> Australasia.
> British Africa.
> ,,   North America.
> ,,   West Indies.
> ,,   South America.

And it shows the percentage proportion of British and Foreign tonnage respectively which entered and cleared in each group during the year 1885, in trade with the United Kingdom, other British Colonies, and Foreign Countries respectively. The principal results are :—

1. In the home (United Kingdom) and inter-colonial trades inwards, the proportion of foreign tonnage employed does not amount to 10 per cent In the outward trade with the United Kingdom it is considerably higher than in the inwards trade, being 8·1 and 11·3 respectively. In the inter-colonial trade the proportion of foreign in the outwards trade is nearly double that in the inwards. These facts may be easily explained. In exporting merchandise from the United Kingdom to the Possessions, British bottoms obtain the preference, and can always be engaged; while in the Possessions British bottoms may not always be available, and foreign bottoms will be eager to obtain cargoes.

2. There is a considerable difference in the proportion of foreign tonnage employed in the different groups in the above trades. In the Australasian groups it is less than 1 per cent. in the inwards trade from the United Kingdom. In the large home trade of British North America it rises to 14·8 and 21·7 inwards and outwards respectively, and in the smaller trade of British South America (chiefly British Guiana) it mounts to 36·0 of inward tonnage.

3. The very low proportion in the Australasian trade tends to lower materially the average of the aggregate.

4. As regards the trade with Foreign Countries British shipping appropriates a full moiety and considerably more in the outward trade. In the direct trade with Foreign European Countries and Egypt, the proportion inwards is 27·5, and outwards 49·1 per cent., indicating the preference given by each country to its own flag, when available.

5. The contrast between the employment of foreign shipping in the trade with the United Kingdom and British Possessions, and of British shipping in the trade with Foreign Countries, is very striking :—

Shipping: British Possessions.	British.	Foreign.
	Per cent.	Per cent.
Trade—inwards and outwards, with United Kingdom	91·3	9·7
„ inwards and outwards, with British Possessions	90·9	9·1
„ inwards, with all Foreign Countries	50·5	49·5
„ outwards „	54·2	45·8
„ inwards, with foreign Europe, and Egypt	27 4	72·6
„ outwards, with foreign Europe, and Egypt	49·1	50·9

6. The returns do not show the nationality of the foreign vessels, only the countries in the trade with which they are employed. But it may be assumed that to a great extent the trade of each country is carried on under its own flag, if not in British vessels. In such a case as that of Australasia, where the whole of the inward trade with France, and most of the trade with French Possessions, is carried on in foreign bottoms, it may safely be assumed that the vessels were French. The same remark applies to the trade of Australasia with Germany.

7. The proportion of foreign vessels in the total trade, inwards and outwards, was about the same, and slightly exceeded one-fourth, viz. :—

Inwards .... 26·1 per cent.
Outwards .... 25·6 „

This approximates in a remarkable manner to the proportion in the trade of the United Kingdom in the same year, where the proportions were—

Inwards .... 27·9 per cent.
Outwards .... 27·7 „

The proportions for the whole of the Empire were —

Inwards .... 26·7 per cent.
Outwards .... The same.

§ 5. *Shipping belonging to the British Empire.*

The annual statements of the Navigation and Shipping of the United Kingdom contain several returns relating to British Possessions, among these are returns of the shipping belonging to each Possession, and of the shipping built in each. From the last statement for the year 1887, published during the present year, have been abstracted three tables, showing :—

1. Table XXIX.—The number and tonnage of vessels, sailing and steam, classed according to their tonnage, which belonged to all the British Possessions, the United Kingdom, and the British Empire respectively.

2. Table XXX.—The number and tonnage of vessels, sailing and steam, belonging to each Possession, with the average size of such vessels, at the close of the year 1887.

3. Table XXXI.—The number and tonnage of vessels, sailing and steam, and distinguishing those made of iron, which were built in each Possession in the year 1887.

The most noteworthy facts to be derived from an examination of these tables are :—

1. Of the total number of vessels belonging to the Empire, viz., 36,752, 60 per cent. belonged to the United Kingdom and 40 per cent. to the British Possessions.

2. Of the total tonnage of vessels belonging to the Empire, viz., 9,135,512, 80 per cent. belonged to the United Kingdom, and 20 (19·7) per cent. to the Possessions, the difference in the proportions compared with those of the number of vessels arising from the difference in their size.

3. Of the sailing vessels belonging to the Empire, 27,599, with a tonnage of 4,725,509, the proportions belonging to the United Kingdom and Possessions respectively were of ships 56 and 44, and of tonnage 69 and 31 per cent.

4. Of the steam vessels belonging to the Empire, numbering 9,153, with a tonnage of 4,410,000, the proportions belonging to the United Kingdom and Possessions respectively were of vessels 73 and 27, and of tonnage 92·7 and 7·3 per cent.

5. The average size of sailing vessels was 210 tons in the United Kingdom, and 121 tons in the Possessions, and the average size of steam vessels was 613 tons in the former, and 130 in the latter. There were 60 sailing vessels and 9 steamers in the Possessions exceeding 1,500 tons, and in the United Kingdom the corresponding numbers were 432 and 660.

6. The character of the shipping belonging to each Possession, which to a great extent may be taken as indicative of the character of its trade, is shown in the following arrangement of the Possessions in the order of the average size of the sailing vessels belonging to them in 1887 :—

Average size (Tonnage) of Vessels belonging to each Possession.

	Sailing Vessels.	Steamers.
1. India	363	239
2. Hong Kong	326	525
3. Victoria	183	254
4. Gibraltar	181	208
5. Canada	170	99
6. Bermuda	159	—
7. New Zealand	140	235
8. New South Wales	118	108
9. South Australia	117	123
10. Falkland Islands	115	—
11. Cape of Good Hope and Natal	99	35
12. Mauritius	90	31
13. Malta	89	105
14. Queensland	85	60
15. Straits Settlements	82	214
16. Fiji	71	19
17. Tasmania	68	172
18. Western Australia	60	92
19. Ceylon	68	255*
20. West Indies, not distinguished	56	41
21. Jamaica	52	758*
22. Bahamas	43	247
23. Newfoundland	42	195
24. British Guiana	41	94
25. Trinidad	32	65
26. Honduras	23	82
27. West Africa	19	41
28. Heligoland	10	—

* One only.

The principal features of this statement are :—

1°. With few exceptions the ships belonging to the several Possessions are of a size suitable for coasting and short voyages, rather than for a trans-oceanic trade to distant countries. Many of the Possessions therefore are wholly or mainly dependent upon English or foreign vessels for this branch of their commerce.

2°. The average size of ships belonging to India is twice as great, and that of Hong Kong is nearly twice as great as that of ships belonging to any other British Possession, while the size of steamers belonging to Hong Kong is double that of steamers belonging to India.

3°. The other Colonies divide themselves into classes :—

a. Victoria, New Zealand, Canada, Gibraltar, and Bermuda average from 183 to 140 tons. The high position of the latter two is noteworthy.

b. New South Wales, South Australia, Falkland Islands, and Cape of Good Hope, with Natal, from 118 to 99.

c. Among the rest, including several important colonies, e.g., Queensland and Tasmania, Ceylon and Mauritius, British Guiana and Trinidad, the average size dwindles from 90 to 10 tons.

TABLE XXIX.—*Number and Tonnage of Vessels, Sailing and Steam, classed according to their Tonnage, which were Registered under the Merchant Shipping Acts in the British Possessions, United Kingdom, and British Empire respectively, on the 31st December, 1887.*

(Compiled from Annual Statement of Navigation and Shipping.)

[000's omitted in tonnage columns.]

Tonnage.	British Possessions.				United Kingdom.				British Empire.					
	Sailing.		Steam.		Sailing.		Steam.		Sailing.		Steam.		Total.	
	Number.	Tons.	Number.	Tons.	Number.	Tons.	Number.	Tons.	Number.	Tons.	Number.	Tons.	Number.	Tons.
Under 50 tons	6,705	168,	1,329	27,	6,297	206,	1,837	37,	13,002	374,	3,166	61,	16,168	438,
Of 50 and under 100 tons	2,607	182,	445	32,	4,958	353,	532	38,	7,565	535,	977	70,	8,512	605,
,, 100 ,, 200 ,,	1,287	178,	290	39,	4,525	221,	467	68,	2,412	399,	747	107,	3,559	506,
,, 200 ,, 300 ,,	422	101,	144	35,	441	109,	275	68,	863	213,	449	104,	1,312	317,
,, 300 ,, 400 ,,	304	105,	77	27,	232	81,	279	98,	536	186,	356	125,	892	311,
,, 400 ,, 500 ,,	123	55,	56	25,	180	83,	287	129,	303	138,	343	153,	646	291,
,, 500 ,, 600 ,,	84	46,	44	24,	148	82,	224	123,	232	129,	268	147,	500	276,
,, 600 ,, 700 ,,	72	47,	24	17,	128	84,	247	160,	200	131,	273	177,	473	308,
,, 700 ,, 800 ,,	67	51,	13	10,	174	131,	235	191,	211	182,	268	200,	509	382,
,, 800 ,, 1,000 ,,	129	118,	32	29,	253	228,	538	488,	382	346,	570	512,	952	858,
,, 1,000 ,, 1,200 ,,	153	170,	19	21,	285	316,	507	558,	438	486,	526	579,	964	1,065,
,, 1,200 ,, 1,500 ,,	113	152,	16	21,	420	561,	555	747,	533	713,	571	769,	1,101	1,482,
,, 1,500 ,, 2,000 ,,	57	73,	6	11,	326	559,	354	611,	383	652,	360	621,	743	1,273,
,, 2,000 ,, 2,500 ,,	3	6,	—	—	93	200,	178	393,	96	207,	178	383,	274	600,
,, 2,500 ,, 3,000 ,,	—	—	3	8,	11	29,	90	214,	11	29,	93	252,	104	281,
,, 3,000 tons and above	—	—	—	—	2	6,	38	136,	2	6,	38	136,	40	142,
Total	12,126	1,475,	2,490	325,	15,473	3,250,	6,663	4,085,	27,590,	4,725,	9,153	4,410,	36,752	9,135,
	14,616.		1,800.		22,136.		7,335.		36,752.		9,135.			

TABLE XXX.—*Number and Tonnage of Vessels, Sailing and Steam, with their Average size, which were Registered in each of the British Possessions on the* 31st *December,* 1887.

(Compiled from same as Table XXIX.)

Possessions.	Sailing.		Steam.		Average Size.	
	Number	Tons.	Number	Tons.	Sailing	Steam.
India	101	36,692	71	17,012	363	239
Straits Settlements	305	25.219	80	17,124	82	214
Hong Kong	25	8.152	37	19,466	326	525
Ceylon	208	14,238	1	255	68	255
Mauritius	77	6,936	3	92	90	31
Australasia—						
New South Wales	643	75,974	485	52,660	118	108
Queensland	108	9,225	82	4,920	85	60
Victoria	260	47 610	115	29,223	183	254
South Australia	230	27,084	96	11,810	117	123
Western Australia	106	6,436	8	737	60	92
Tasmania	170	11 537	33	5,378	68	172
New Zealand	388	54,451	168	39,516	140	235
Fiji	14	1.004	1	19	71	19
Cape of Good Hope and Natal	29	2,873	17	605	99	35
West Africa (Bathurst, Freetown, and Lagos)	} 133	2,543	6	244	19	41
Canada*	5,755	982,196	1,194	108,814	170	99
Newfoundland	2,026	86 017	26	5,079	42	195
Bermuda	23	3,673	—	—	159	—
Honduras	106	3,937	3	246	23	82
British West Indies—						
Bahamas	557	23,886	17	4,210	43	247
Jamaica	66	3,439	1	758	52	758
Trinidad	85	2,696	1	65	32	65
Other Islands	337	19,091	6	247	56	41
British Guiana	133	5,566	9	849	41	94
Falkland Islands	7	805	—	—	115	—
Gibraltar	27	4,893	11	2.296	181	208
Malta	100	8,938	19	2,005	89	105
Heligoland	47	461	—	—	10	—
Total	—	—	—	—	121	130
Average of United Kingdom					210	613

* Including vessels registered for inland navigation only.

Lloyd's Universal Register of British and Foreign Shipping furnishes the means of comparing the shipping belonging to the British Empire with that belonging to the rest of the world in the month of April of the present year. The figures do not agree with the above, because all vessels under 100 tons are excluded. The chief results are as follows:—

1. Of the total number of ships, sailing and steam, 33,200, and of the total net tonnage of the same 20·7 millions of tons, 37 and 51 per cent. respectively are British.

2. The corresponding proportions of British sailing vessels are 28 and 37·5 per cent., and of steam vessels 58 and 61 per cent.

3. The countries which approach nearest to the British Empire are, for sailing vessels, the United States, which show a percentage of vessels of 14 per cent., and of tonnage 14·6 per cent.; for steam vessels, Germany, which shows a percentage of number of steamers amounting to 6 per cent., and of France, a percentage of tonnage of steamers amounting to 6·8 per cent.

4. The average size of British steamers is 838 tons net, of British colonial 334, and of foreign 648 tons. The average size of sailing vessels is of British 646, of British colonial 433, and of foreign 364 tons.

5. There is a somewhat greater difference in the relation of net to gross tonnage in foreign than in British steamers, viz., 67 per cent. in the former, and 63 per cent. in the latter.

Vessels Built in each Possession.

7. The total number of vessels built and registered in the Possessions in 1887 was 421, of 31,227 tons. The number built in the United Kingdom in the same year was 580 of 306,719 tons. The proportion built in the Possessions was 42 per cent. of the total number, but only 9·2 per cent. of the total tonnage.

8. Of the total tonnage built in the Possessions in 1887, 76 per cent. was built in Canada, 15 per cent. in Australia, and 5 per cent. in India, leaving only 4 per cent. distributed over the remaining Possessions.

TABLE XXXI.—*Number and Tonnage of Vessels, Sailing and Steam, Wood and Iron, Built and Registered in each British Possession, in the Year* 1887.

(Compiled from same as Table XXIX.)

	Sailing.		Steam.		Total.	
	Number.	Tons.	Number.	Tons.	Number.	Tons.
India............................	20	1,592	1	3	23	1,637
„ .... iron	—	—	2	42		
Hong Kong	—	—	1	20	1	20
Mauritius.....................	2	36	—	—	2	36
Australia and New Zealand	30	1,358	23	741	65*	4,748*
Ditto .... iron	7	1,974	4	656		
South Africa	2	58	—	—	2	58
British North America	199	21,148	83	2,391	285	23,831
„ iron	—	—	2	283		
British West Indies	35	664	—	—	35	664
„ Honduras ...	4	37	—	—	4	37
„ Guiana	1	18	—	—	1	18
Malta	2	48	—	—	2	48
Total...............	303	26,963	118*	4,164*	421*	31,127*

* Including composite vessels.

CAP. 3. SUMMARY OF TRADE OF EACH BRITISH POSSESSION.

It remains to furnish an epitome of the trade—Imports, Exports, and Shipping—of each British Possession. This must necessarily be brief, and in order to make it as concise and as complete as possible, the same information, arranged in the same order, will be given in a form which will render it more suitable for reference than for perusal, but which will give the essence of several of the tables in this and the first part of the work in a shape the most illustrative of the commercial position of each Colony, and the most useful to the general inquirer.

The several tables from which the following descriptions are compiled are Nos. VIII and VIIIA, XI, XII, and XIII of Parts I and II, and Nos. XXIII, XXIV, XXV, XXVI, XXX, and XXXI of Parts III and IV, with the Statistical Abstracts of the United Kingdom.

As the several Possessions are arranged in the following pages in their geographical order, it may be well to help the reader to form an idea of their relative importance and contribution to the trade of the Empire by presenting them in a table showing the order of that importance. Hong Kong, Malta, Gibraltar, and Heligoland are necessarily omitted for reasons explained in the first Part.

This and the following table will supply a new, and probably unexpected, view of the proportions in which the several portions of the Empire contribute to the trade of the whole Empire, and to that of the United Kingdom.

1. As regards the Empire, the United Kingdom and India contribute more than three-fourths, 77·4 per cent., New South Wales, Canada, the Straits Settlements, and Victoria each from 3·8 to 3·2 per cent.; New Zealand, Queensland, Cape of Good Hope, and South Australia each from 1·3 to 1·0 per cent.: the next eleven colonies each from 0·7 to 0·1 per cent., and the remaining twenty colonies taken together a trifle over 0·5 per cent.

2. As regards the trade of the United Kingdom nearly three-fourths, 73·6, are carried on with foreign countries—9·8 per cent. with India, and the remaining 16·6 per cent. with all the other colonies, to which last figure Australasia contributes 8·0 per cent., and Canada 2·9 per cent.

These figures suggest many weighty considerations. The large export of coal constitutes only 1 per cent. of the proportion contributed by the United Kingdom to the value of Imports and Exports of the Empire.

TABLE XXXII.—*Showing the Order in which the several Parts of the British Empire contributed to the Total Declared Value of Imports and Exports, and the Percentage Proportion of the Trade of each, in the Year 1885.*

(Compiled from Table VIIIA in Part II.)

[000's omitted.]

Divisions of British Empire.	Total Value of Imports and Exports.	Per-centage Pro-portion.	Divisions of British Empire.	Total Value of Imports and Exports.	Per-centage Pro-portion.
Total of British Empire	£ 1,046,342,				
1. United Kingdom	642,372,	61·4*			
2. India	167,160,	16·0	22. Gold Coast	963,	⎫
3. New South Wales	40,007,	3·8	23. Sierra Leone	651,	⎪
4. Canada..................	39,991,	3·8	24. Fiji.....................	634,	⎪
5. Straits Settlements....	35,559,	3·4	25. Honduras	499,	⎪
6. Victoria	33,596,	3·2	26. Bahamas	415,	⎬ 0·4
7. New Zealand	14,300,	1·3	27. St. Kitts and Nevis	352,	⎪
8. Queensland	11,666,	1·1	28. Bermuda	322,	⎪
9. Cape of Good Hope	11,216,	1·1	29. Grenada..............	317,	⎪
10. South Australia	10,706,	1·0	30. Antigua	303,	⎭
11. Ceylon	7,586,	0·7	31. St. Vincent	231,	⎫
12. Mauritius..............	5,748,	0·5	32. Gambia	217,	⎪
13. Trinidad	4,488,	0·4	33. St. Lucia	215,	⎬ 0·1
14. British Guiana	3,268,	0·3	34. Labuan	166,	⎪
15. Tasmania..............	3,071.	0·3	35. Falkland Islands ..	146,	⎪
16. Jamaica	2,896,	0·3	36. Dominica	103,	⎭
17. Natal	2,396,	0·2	37. St. Helena..............	74,	⎫
18. Newfoundland	2,380,	0·2	38. Tobago	69,	⎪
19. Barbados	1,894,	0·2	39. Turks Islands	59,	⎬ 0·02
20. Lagos	1,157,	0·1	40. Montserrat	37,	⎪
21. Western Australia	1,097,	0·1	41. Virgin Islands	35,	⎭
				38·08†	0·52
				100·0	

* Of which with British Possessions 16·2 ⎱ 61·4. If transhipments were added, this
  Foreign Countries 45·2 ⎰ proportion would be increased to 62·6 per cent.

† Of which with United Kingdom and British Possessions 18·7 ⎱ 38·1
  Foreign Countries 19·4 ⎰

A similar table showing the proportion borne by each Posses-sion in the trade of the United Kingdom cannot be given, as the Statistical Abstracts do not furnish the information in the same detail, but the following table will supply it for the several groups as arranged in those abstracts, for the same year.

TABLE XXXIII.—*Showing the Order in which the several Groups of the Possessions of the British Empire contributed to the Total Declared Value of the Imports and Exports of the United Kingdom, and the Percentage Proportion of the Trade of each, in the Year 1885.*

(Compiled from " Statistical Abstract.")

[000's omitted.]

Countries.	Total Value of Imports and Exports.	Percentage Proportion.
	£	
Total of United Kingdom	642,371	100·
„ with Foreign Countries	472,545	73·6
With British Possessions—		
1. India	62,761,	9·8
2. Australasia	51,429,	8·0
3. British North America	18,722,	2·9
4. Cape of Good Hope and Natal ...	8,638,	1·3
5. Straits Settlements	6,967,	1·1
6. West Indies and British Guiana ..	6,608,	1·0
7. Hong Kong	5,012,	0·8
8. Ceylon	2,955,	0·5
9. Channel Islands	1,518,	0·2
10. Malta	1,257,	0·2
11. Gold Coast	1,242,	0·2
12. Gibraltar	731,	0·1
13. Mauritius	601,	0·1
14. Honduras	338,	0·05
15. West African Settlements	390,	0·05
16. Other	643,	0·1
Total	169,826	26·4

India.—The trade of British India is so important as to call for a detailed notice. For purposes of reference it may best be shown in a semi-tabular form, which might be applied to each Possession if time and space permitted :—

British India.

Percentage proportion of the Trade of the British Empire in 1885—
Total Imports .... 13·3 per cent.
„ Exports .... 18·8 „

Percentage proportion of the Trade of the United Kingdom in 1885—
Imports into United Kingdom .... 8·6 per cent.
Exports from United Kingdom .... 11·3 „

Percentage proportion of the Trade of British India with the United Kingdom in 1885—
Imports .... 70·5 per cent.
Exports .... 39·0 „

British India—Contd.

With British Possessions—
Imports... 11·4 per cent.
Exports.. 21·0   „

With Foreign Countries—
Imports... 18·1   „
Exports.. 40·0   „

Excess of Exports over Imports in 1885—
Amount £12,910,000
Per cent. .... 16·9 per cent.

The distribution of the trade in the same year was as follows :—

[000's omitted.]

British Possessions.	Imports	Exports.	Foreign Countries.	Imports.	Exports.
	£	£		£	£
Hong Kong	3,739,	9,566,	Frontier Trade..........	4,991,	4,016,
			China	1,982,	3,115,
			United States	1,437,	3,017,
Straits Settlements	1,697,	3,701,	Italy	890,	3,658,
			Persia and Gulf	832,	1,411,
			Arabia	699,	976,
Mauritius	1,106,	956,	France	656,	6,751,
			Austria	653,	2,015,
			Turkey in Asia..........	342,	425,
Australasia	980,	590,	Egypt	296,	3,386,
			Zanzibar	381,	417,
			Germany	120,	408,
Ceylon	792,	2,176,	Holland...................	12,	539,
			Belgium	267,	3,730,
.			S. America	1,	439,
All other..................	278,	1,727,	All other	219,	1,243,
Total	8,652,	18,716,	Total	13,778,	35,606,

With regard to the progress of trade in India it has been, as
already stated, continuous and very steady throughout the fifteen
years 1872-86, with an expansion in 1881-83, but the Imports have
increased in a much higher ratio than the Exports :—

	Total Value. [000's omitted.]		Percentage Difference at each Period.	
	Imports.	Exports.	Imports.	Exports.
	£	£		
1872-74........................	39,903,	59,381,	—	—
'75-77	—	—	14·8	2·9
'78-80........	—	—	13·9	9·9
'81-83......................	—	—	20·2	20·8
'84-86	—	—	11·0	6·5
Increase between 1872-74 and 1884-86			74·5	45·6

The proportions of the trade with the United Kingdom have been very similar as regards Imports, the increase in the same period having been 72·5 per cent.; but the increase as regards Exports was very different, being only 20 per cent.

With regard to shipping, its character has already been described, but may here be recapitulated. The value per ton of the cargoes in 1886 was very high, £21·4 per ton, double that of the United Kingdom. The proportion of foreign tonnage on the average of 1884-86 was low, 17 per cent.; and that of steam to sailing vessels was also low, 65 per cent.

The increase between 1877-79 and 1884-86, as shown in Table XXVI, was 26 per cent., the British showing a slight preponderance, 26·8 to 25·4 per cent. of foreign.

The proportion of foreign at the two periods was almost identical, viz., 17·6 in 1877-79 and 17·5 in 1884-86.

A table, No. XXXIV, has been prepared to show the shipping trade of India in the same form as that of the United Kingdom detailed in Table XVII. The results differ from the above owing to this latter table relating only to tonnage inwards, whereas in the former the inward and outward tonnage are thrown together. This table exhibits the following results—

1. There was a greater or less increase in British tonnage entering inwards in each period, and in each of the last three years 1884-86, except 1885.

2. Although there was a large increase of foreign tonnage in 1883-86, that increase was at the expense of British Indian and native craft, not of British. and there has been a decrease in the proportion of foreign in each of the last two years, while that of British tonnage has been on the increase.

3. The decrease both in the amount and proportion of British Indian tonnage has been continuous and large. The difference between 1886 and the average of 1877-79 has been 39 per cent. in amount, and 54 per cent. in proportion.

4. In like manner the decrease in the trade carried on in native craft has been between the same periods 32 per cent. in amount, and 71 per cent. in proportion.

5. Between the same periods British tonnage has increased by 840,000 tons, or in proportion to the whole trade from 75·2 to 79·5 per cent.; Foreign tonnage has increased 188,000 tons, or in proportion to the whole trade from 12·8 to 14·8 per cent.

TABLE XXXIV.—*Total Tonnage of Vessels (Sailing and Steamers), distinguishing British from Foreign, which entered into Ports of British India with Cargoes and in Ballast, together with the Percentage Proportion of each Class, and the rate of Increase or Decrease in each Class, in each Triennial Period from 1877 to 1886, and in each of the last three Years 1884 to 1886.*

[000's omitted.]

Periods.	TOTAL TONNAGE ENTERED WITH CARGOES AND IN BALLAST, ANNUAL AVERAGES.				
	British.	British Indian.	Native Craft.	Foreign.	Total.
1877-79	2,055,	221,	107,	349,	2,732,
'80-82	2,679,	203,	91,	472,	3,446,
'84-86*	2,761,	152,	75,	532,	3,520,
Years					
1884	2,806,	176,	83,	565,	3,632,
'85	2,581,	146,	68,	494,	3,291,
'86	2,895,	135,	72,	537,	3,640,

	PERCENTAGE PROPORTION OF EACH CLASS.				
1877-79	75·2	8·1	6·9	12·8	100
'80-82	77·7	5·9	2·7	13·7	"
'83-86*	78·6	4·3	2·1	15·0	"
Years.					
1884	77·2	4·9	2·3	15·6	"
'85	78·4	4·5	2·1	15·0	"
'86	79·5	3·7	2·0	14·8	"

	PERCENTAGE INCREASE OR DECREASE IN EACH PERIOD.				
1878-79	....	....	....	....	...
'80-82	+ 30·4	− 8·1	− 14·9	+ 35·2	+ 26·1
'83-86*	+ 3·4	− 25·1	− 17·6	+ 12·7	+ 2·1
Years.					
1884	+ 1·6	+ 15·8	+ 10·7	+ 6·2	+ 3·1
'85	− 8·0	− 17·0	− 18·1	− 12·6	− 9·4
'86	+ 12·1	− 7·5	+ 5·8	+ 8·6	+ 10·6

* Average of four years.

The shipping registered as belonging to India on 31st December 1887, was—

	Number.	Tonnage.	Average Size.
			Tons.
Sailing	101	36,692	363
Steam	71	17,012	239
Total	172	53,704	—

Of the total tonnage 43 per cent. belonged to the Bombay Presidency, 27·3 per cent. to Bengal, and 29·7 to Madras and the rest of India. Two-thirds of the steamer tonnage belonged to Bombay. The amount of shipping built in India in 1887 was insignificant: It consisted of 23 vessels, with a tonnage of 1,637, including three small steamers of 45 tons.

The Straits Settlements furnished in 1885 3·3 per cent. of the Imports and 2·1 per cent. of the Exports of the Empire, but only 1·3 and 0·8 respectively of those of the United Kingdom. More than half their trade, 56 per cent., was with Foreign Countries, one-fifth (20 per cent.) with the United Kingdom. Their Imports were 9 per cent. in excess of their Exports. The former were chiefly from Java and Dutch Possessions in Asia, United Kingdom, British India, Malay Peninsula, Hong Kong, and Siam; and the latter to the same places, but in different proportions. The average value of a ton of cargo was high, £5·4; also the proportion of foreign shipping, 35 per cent., and of steam tonnage very high, 94 per cent. From this latter fact it must be inferred that either little or no trade was carried on in native craft, or that it was not taken into account. The increase of both Imports and Exports had been continuous throughout the fifteen years. The increase of shipping has been correspondingly great in the last ten years; the percentage was double that of India. The British has increased 54, and the foreign 79 per cent. The shipping belonging to the Straits Settlements on 31st December, 1887, consisted of 385 vessels, with a tonnage of 42,343. Of these 80 were steam vessels, with a tonnage of 17,124, averaging 214 tons. Of the total tonnage 67·5 per cent. belonged to Singapore, and 32·5 to Penang.

In the case of the following Possessions, the trade of which is less than 1 per cent. of that of the Empire or of the United Kingdom, the above two general comparisons will not be noted; and to avoid repetition it must be understood that when the trade of a single year is spoken of, the year 1885 is referred to.

Ceylon.—The Import trade was almost entirely with the United Kingdom and with other British Possessions, 25 and 73 per cent. respectively; with Foreign Countries it was only 2 per cent. The Export trade was differently distributed, 58 per cent. to the United Kingdom, 23 per cent. to British Possessions, and 18 per cent. to Foreign Countries. The

K

Imports exceeded the Exports by 26 per cent. Ceylon drew nearly three-fourths of its Imports from India, and nearly one-fourth from the United Kingdom, only 3·5 per cent. from other countries. But it shipped only one-fourth to India, three-fifths to the United Kingdom, and 18 per cent. to other countries, chiefly the United States, France, Austria, and New South Wales. The Imports and Exports have both fallen off in each of the last three triads, but less in the last. Comparing the last with the first triad, the decrease in Imports has been 20 per cent., and in Exports 28 per cent. The character of its shipping has been already described.[*] The increase of tonnage has been large, 43 per cent.; of British 39, and of Foreign 66 per cent. The shipping belonging to Ceylon on 31st December, 1887, consisted of 208 sailing vessels, of 14,238 tons, and one steamer of 255 tons.

Mauritius imported one-fifth from the United Kingdom, a half from British Possessions, and more than a quarter from Foreign Countries. It exported nearly three-fourths to British Possessions, and 14 per cent. both to the United Kingdom and Foreign Countries. Its Exports exceeded its Imports by 52 per cent. Of its Import trade 37 per cent. was with India, 20 with the United Kingdom, the rest chiefly with France, New South Wales, and Madagascar. Of its Export trade 42 per cent. was with India, 14 per cent. with the United Kingdom, 23 per cent. with New South Wales, and the rest chiefly with the United States, Cape of Good Hope, Madagascar, and France. The imports fell off in each triad except 1881-83. The Exports showed a small increase in each, except the last. The Imports decreased less than 1 per cent. in the fifteen years; the Exports increased 11 per cent. The average value of the cargoes was among the highest, £8·5 per ton. The proportion of foreign shipping was very high, 45 per cent. Sailing and steam vessels were equally divided. The increase of tonnage during the last ten years has been very small for British vessels, only 9 per cent., and for foreign 48 per cent. The shipping belonging to Mauritius on 31st December, 1887, consisted of 77 sailing vessels, with a tonnage of 6,936, and 3 steamers of 92 tons. Two sailing vessels of 36 tons were built there in the year 1887.

Australia. The Statistical Abstracts of the United Kingdom do not exhibit the trade of the several Australian colonies

* P. 108.

separately. They as well as New Zealand and Fiji are included under the head of Australia. According to this arrangement the trade with Australia furnished in 1885 6·3 per cent. of the Imports, and 10·3 per cent. of the Exports of the United Kingdom.

New South Wales furnished 4·1 per cent. of the Imports, and 3·5 of the Exports of the Empire. Of the Imports more than a half, 51·5 per cent., were drawn from the United Kingdom, nearly four-tenths, 38 per cent., from British Possessions, and only a tenth, 10 per cent., from Foreign Countries. Its Exports to the United Kingdom and British Possessions were 44 per cent. to each, and to Foreign Countries 12 per cent. Its Imports, £23·4 millions, exceeded its Exports, £16·5 millions, by 42 per cent. These figures include its overland trade. The distribution of the trade in 1885 was :—

[000's omitted.]

	Imports.	Exports.
In trade with—	£	£
United Kingdom	11,985,	7,293,
Australasia	8,505,	6,838,
United States	1,008,	985,
India and Asia (chiefly Hong Kong)	551,	432,
Europe	969,	584,
Other countries	447,	409,
Total	23,465,	16,541,

The Import trade from Europe was almost entirely from Germany, France, and Belgium: the Export trade to Belgium and France.

Of the trade with Australasia, 26 per cent. of the Imports, and 47 per cent. of the Exports, were carried overland.

The progress of the Import trade of New South Wales has been continuous, but by most unequal bounds, and the same of the Export trade, except that there was a decrease in the last triad.

	Total Value.		Percentage Difference at each Period.	
	Imports.	Exports.	Imports.	Exports.
	£	£	Per cent.	Per cent.
1872-74	9·962	8,759*	....	....
'75-77	13,923	13,267	+ 39·7	not comparable
'78-80	....	....	+ 2·7	+ 4·4
'81-83	....	....	+ 39·0	+ 26·6
'84-86	....	....	+ 12·8	− 4·4

* Overland traffic not included.

The total increase between the first and last triad of Imports was 125 per cent.; the Exports are not comparable.

The average value of the cargoes was among the highest, £8·6 per ton, the proportion of foreign tonnage very small, 11 per cent., and the proportion of steam tonnage moderate, 70 per cent. The increase of tonnage during the last ten years has been large, that of foreign preponderating, viz., 77 and 108 per cent. The shipping belonging to New South Wales on 31st December, 1887, consisted of :—

643 sailing vessels, with a tonnage of 75,974, averaging 118 tons.
485 steam   „   „   52,660   „   108 „

Total....1,128   128,634

Of the total tonnage 112,272 tons belonged to Sydney, and 16,362 to Newcastle. The ships built in the several Australian Colonies are not distinguished in the returns. The total number of sailing vessels built in Australia and New Zealand in 1887 was 37, of 3,322 tons, of which 7, of 1,974 tons, were of iron; and the number of steamers was 27, of 1,397 tons, of which 4, of 656 tons, were of iron. *Queensland* furnished 1·1 per cent. both of the Imports and Exports of the Empire. Its trade was almost exclusively with the United Kingdom, Australasia, Hong Kong, and the United States. Its total foreign trade was only 3 per cent. of Imports and 0·3 per cent. of Exports. Its Imports exceeded its Exports by more than a fifth, 22 per cent. The progress of its Imports and Exports has been continuous, and by rapid strides, except in 1878-80, when there was a decrease in both. The increase of Imports between the first and last triad was 144 per cent. The Exports are not comparable, as the overland trade was not included in the first triad.

As regards shipping, the average value of cargoes was less than half of the amount in New South Wales, only £3·4 per ton, affording evidence of a smaller trade with countries beyond Australia. The proportion of foreign tonnage is less than 1 per cent. (0·7). The steamer tonnage is not distinguished in the returns. The tonnage of British vessels which entered and cleared between 1877-79 and 1884-86 increased more than threefold. The shipping belonging to Queensland consisted on 31st December, 1887, of 108 sailing vessels, of 9,225 tons, and 82 steamers, of 4,920 tons.

Victoria furnished 3·1 per cent. of the Imports and 3·3 per cent. of the Exports of the Empire. Of its Imports nearly one half, 48 per cent., were drawn from the United Kingdom, 35 per cent. from British Possessions, and 17 from foreign countries. Of its Exports more than half, 52 per cent., were shipped to the United Kingdom, 42 per cent. to British Possessions, and 6 to foreign countries. There is this difference between Victoria and New South Wales with regard to their trade with foreign countries, Victoria imported 60 per cent. more from such countries than New South Wales, but exported exactly one half less to them. The Imports of Victoria exceeded its Exports by 16 per cent.

The progress of both the Import and Export trade of Victoria shows to a disadvantage compared with that of New South Wales. A short table will best exhibit the contrast.

Percentage Difference at each Period.

	Imports.		Exports.	
	New South Wales.	Victoria.	New South Wales.	Victoria.
1872-74.........	....	....	....	....
'75-77.........	+ 30·7	+ 3·3	....	− 1·1
'78-80.........	+ 2·7	− 6·1	+ 4·4	− 1·7
'81-83.........	+ 30·0	+ 16·3	+ 26·6	+ 12·7
'84-86.........	+ 12·8	+ 4·8	− 4·4	− 11·1

In Victoria the difference between the first and last triad was for Imports an increase of 18 per cent., and for Exports a decrease of 3 per cent. The corresponding increase in New South Wales for Imports was 12·5 per cent. The increase in Exports for the same period cannot be stated, but between 1875-77 and 1884-86 it was 26 per cent. It would be interesting, but out of place, to speculate upon the causes of these great differences.

The distribution of the trade in 1885 was as follows :—

[000's omitted.]

	Imports.	Exports.
	£	£
In trade with—		
United Kingdom	8,946,	8,159,
Australasia	5,679,	5,655,
United States	747,	159,
India and Asia (chiefly Mauritius and Hong Kong).....................	1,045,	821,
China	602,	nil
Europe.....................................	773,	683,
Other countries	252,	74,
Total.....................	18,044,	15,551,

The European trade was chiefly with Norway and Sweden, Germany and France, for Imports—and with France and Belgium for Exports.

The average value of the cargoes was among the highest, £8·1 per ton; the proportion of foreign tonnage was small, 13 per cent. and that of steam tonnage moderately large, 78. The increase of British tonnage between 1877-79 and 1884-86 was 68 per cent., but that of foreign tonnage was threefold, 192. Its proportion to British tonnage had increased from 7·5 to 12·6 per cent.

The shipping belonging to Victoria on 31st December, 1887, consisted of—

	260 sailing vessels,	of 47,610 tons.	averaging	183 tons.
	115 steam ,,	29,223 ,,	,,	254 ,,
Total............	375	76,833		

Of these all but 2,089 tons were registered at Melbourne.

South Australia contributes 0·9 per cent. to the Imports, and 1·1 per cent. to the Exports of the Empire. Its Import and Export trade is carried on chiefly with the United Kingdom, 53 and 61 per cent. respectively, and with other parts of Australia; with Foreign Countries only 8 and 2 per cent., which is equally divided as regards Imports between the United States and Europe. The Exports exceeded the Imports by 2·4 per cent.

The progress of the Imports was continuous and large in the first three triads, but there was a considerable decrease in the last. The Exports showed a decrease only in 1881-83. The increase between the first and last triad was very near 50 per cent. for Imports and 30 per cent. for Exports.

As regards shipping the value of the cargoes was half-way between Queensland and New South Wales, viz., £5·9; the proportion of foreign tonnage was larger than in any other of the Australian Colonies, 16·6 per cent. The steamer tonnage was not distinguished. British tonnage had increased 90 per cent. between 1877-79 and 1884-86, but foreign tonnage had increased nearly fourfold in the same period. The shipping belonging to South Australia on 31st December, 1887, consisted of 230 sailing vessels, of 27,084 tons, and 96 steam vessels, of 11,810 tons, registered at Adelaide and Darwin.

Western Australia had little trade except with the United

Kingdom, South Australia, and Victoria; 87 per cent. of its Imports and 80 per cent. of its Exports were confined to those countries. Its trade with Foreign Countries was only 1 per cent. for Imports and 5 per cent. for Exports.

The Imports exceeded the Exports by 30 per cent. The progress of Imports had been large and increasing, except in 1878-80. That of Exports has been continuous, but in diminishing proportions, until the last triad, when there was a small decrease. The increase between the first and last triad has been 117 per cent. for Imports, and 64 for Exports.

The value of the cargoes was lower than in Queensland, only £2·8 per ton, being apparently the consequence of its large trade with the neighbouring Colonies, and the influence of a high proportion of the steamer tonnage, 80 per cent., upon the small amount of trade. The foreign tonnage was only 3 per cent. British tonnage increased threefold between 1877-79 and 1884-86; foreign tonnage increased only 78 per cent. The shipping belonging to Western Australia on 31st December, 1887, consisted of 106 sailing vessels, of 6,436 tons, and 8 steam vessels, of 737 tons.

Tasmania received 37 per cent. of its Imports from the United Kingdom, and 61 per cent. from British Possessions, of which two-thirds were from Victoria, and the rest chiefly from New South Wales, Mauritius, and New Zealand. Of its Exports 86 per cent. were shipped to Australasia, almost the whole to New South Wales and Victoria. Only 14 per cent. was sent to the United Kingdom. The Imports exceeded the Exports by 33 per cent.

The progress of the Imports has been continuous but unequal, having been very large, 25 per cent., in 1881-83, and only 5 per cent. in the last triad. In the whole period the increase has been 63 per cent. Exports increased largely up to the last triad, when they fell off heavily. Their increase during the whole period was 50 per cent.

The value of the cargoes was half-way between Queensland and South Australia, viz., £4·5. The proportion of foreign tonnage was only 1 per cent. Steamer tonnage was high, 86 per cent. British tonnage had nearly doubled between 1877-79 and 1884-86. The shipping belonging to Tasmania on 31st December, 1887, consisted of 170 sailing vessels, of 11,537 tons, and 33 steamers, of 5,378 tons. Of the total tonnage, 13,442 was registered at Hobart, the remainder at Launceston.

New Zealand contributed 1·3 per cent. to the Imports, and 1·4 per cent. to the Exports of the whole Empire. Its trade was chiefly with the United Kingdom, 70 per cent. of Imports, and 72 of Exports. Of the remainder about 8 per cent. was with foreign countries. The distribution in 1885 was as follows :—

[000's omitted.]

	Imports.	Exports.
	£	£
United Kingdom	5,227,	4,907,
Australasia, chiefly New South Wales and Victoria	1,285,	1,391,
United States	401,	405,
India	129,	—
Mauritius	139,	2,
China	129,	7,
Europe	20,	1,
Other countries	150,	107,
Total	7,480,	6,820,

The Imports exceeded the Exports by 10 per cent. The progressive increase of the Import trade has been diminishing, until in the last triad it was changed into a decrease. The increase of Exports has been continuous, but fluctuating in amount. The increase between the first and last triad was for Imports 11, and for Exports 28 per cent. As regards shipping, the value of the cargoes was £13·5, above that of the United Kingdom, and second only to that of India. The proportion of foreign tonnage was small, only 9 per cent. The steamer tonnage was not distinguished. The increase of tonnage between 1877-79 and 1884-86 has been small, and in striking contrast to the other Australasian Colonies. Of British shipping there has been an increase of 26 per cent ; of foreign shipping there has been a decrease of 33 per cent. The shipping belonging to New Zealand on 31st December, 1887, consisted of :—

388 sailing vessels, of 54,451 tons, averaging 140 tons,
168 steam   „   39,516   „   „   235 „

Total.... 556   93,967

Of the total tonnage, 22,156 was registered at Auckland, 31,419 at Littleton, 28,610 at Dunedin, and 3,771 at Wellington and other ports.

Fiji. These islands were only annexed in 1874. The record of their trade commences therefore in 1875. Their trade was chiefly carried on with New South Wales, Victoria, and New Zealand. The Imports and Exports from and to British Possessions were respectively 87 and 79 per cent. The same from and to the United Kingdom were only 9 and 7. Imports from foreign countries amounted only to 4 per cent., but Exports thereto reached 13 per cent., chiefly to Portugal and Germany. The Exports exceeded the Imports by 10 per cent.

The Imports increased greatly in 1878-80, and still more in the succeeding triad, but decreased in 1884-86. The Exports have increased largely throughout the twelve years.

The value of cargoes was moderately high, £4·9, a little above that in Tasmania; the proportion of foreign shipping was low, 10 per cent.; that of steam tonnage low, 65, the same as in India. The increase of British tonnage between 1877-79 and 1884-86 has been threefold. There has been a decrease of 27 per cent. in foreign tonnage. The shipping belonging to Fiji on 31st December, 1887, consisted of 14 sailing vessels, of 1,004 tons, and 1 steam vessel of 19 tons.

Cape of Good Hope contributed 0·8 to the Imports and 1·3 to the Exports of the Empire. In the Statistical Abstract Natal is included with it. The two Colonies contributed to the trade of the United Kingdom 1·2 of the Imports and 1·5 of the Exports. The trade of the Cape Colony was chiefly with the United Kingdom, viz., 78 per cent. of Imports and 94 per cent. of Exports. Its Imports from British Possessions were 14 per cent., and Exports to them only 1 per cent. Its foreign trade amounted to 9 and 4 per cent. of Imports and Exports respectively. After the United Kingdom the chief Imports were from Natal, South Australia, Brazil, and the United States. The Exports to any single country except the United Kingdom were insignificant. The Exports exceeded the Imports by 24 per cent. The progress of the Import trade has been very unequal, a small decrease in 1875-77, a large increase in the next triad; an increase to half the extent in the third, and a very great decrease, 45 per cent., in the last. Between 1872-74 and 1881-83 Imports had increased 50 per cent.; between the former period and 1884-86 they had decreased 18 per cent. Exports exhibited corresponding inequalities in the same periods,

but in different proportions. Between 1872-74 and
1881-83 they had increased 4 per cent.; between the
former period and 1884-86 they had decreased 12 per
cent. As regards shipping the average value of cargoes
was moderate, £5·0 per ton; the proportion of foreign
tonnage was small, 14 per cent., and that of steamer
tonnage moderately high, 78. The increase of British
tonnage has been moderate; that of foreign tonnage has
been only one-third of the amount, 33 and 11 per cent.
respectively. The shipping belonging to the Cape of
Good Hope and Natal on 31st December, 1887, consisted
of 29 sailing vessels, of 2,873 tons, and 17 steam vessels,
of 605 tons; 2 sailing vessels of 58 tons were built there
in 1887.

Natal resembles the Cape of Good Hope in the character of its
trade. It drew 81 per cent. of its Imports from the
United Kingdom, and sent thither 79 per cent. of its
Exports. It shipped however a considerable amount to
the Cape. Its foreign trade was of small amount, 7 and
4 per cent. respectively. Its Imports exceeded its Exports
by 72 per cent. Its Imports increased very largely, 80 per
cent., in 1878-80, but have fallen off in both of the
following triads. The Exports have increased moderately
except in 1878-80, when they decreased by less than 1 per
cent. These opposite changes may be ascribed to the
effects of the war in Zululand during that period. The
average value of cargoes was higher than at the Cape,
viz., £5·8 per ton; the proportion of foreign tonnage was
very small, only 8 per cent.; the steamer tonnage was not
distinguished. The increase of British tonnage in the
last ten years has been moderate, 42 per cent.; that of
foreign tonnage still less, 14 per cent.

St. Helena drew half of its Imports from the United
Kingdom, and 38 per cent. from foreign countries,
almost exclusively from the United States. Its Exports
were insignificant. The Whale Fisheries contributed
largely to its trade, and supplied the bulk of the Exports,
or rather transhipments. Its Imports were four times
the amount of its Exports.

The triad 1875-77 showed a large increase both of
Import and Exports; since then they have been rapidly
decreasing at each period; the decrease in the whole
period has been 22 per cent. of Imports, and 37 per cent.
of Exports.

The average value of cargoes was only £0·7 per ton;

the proportion of foreign tonnage was 10 per cent., that of steamer tonnage 70 per cent.

The amount of British tonnage has remained almost stationary; that of foreign vessels has decreased by 45 per cent.

West Coast of Africa. Of the four Colonies comprised under this head, three resembled one another in many respects. Gambia differed most from the others—and the differences in the others were sufficient to call for a separate notice of each.

Lagos, as well as the Gold Coast and Sierra Leone, had little trade with British Possessions. It drew 54 per cent. of its Imports from the United Kingdom, and 46 from foreign countries. It shipped 32 per cent. of its Exports to the former, and 68 per cent. to the latter. Germany was its chief market for both Imports and Exports, to which were added France and French Possessions in Africa for Exports. The latter exceeded the Imports by 13 per cent. The trade inwards and outwards was flourishing in 1875-77, fell off in the next six years, and revived in 1884-86. Between the first and last triad the Imports increased 47, and the Exports 36 per cent.

The average value of cargoes was £2·0 per ton; the proportion of foreign tonnage was low, 18 per cent., that of steamer tonnage very high, 95 per cent. It was similarly high in the other three Settlements. The increase of tonnage has been moderate—of British double that of foreign.

Gold Coast carried on a larger proportion of its trade with the United Kingdom than Lagos, viz., 63 per cent. of Imports and 48 per cent. of Exports. Its chief foreign trade was with the United States, but it exported largely to Germany. Its Exports exceeded its Imports by 6 per cent. There has been a continuous increase in Imports except in 1878-80, and in Exports except in 1881-83. The increase between the first and last triads has been 75 per cent. for Imports, and 18 per cent. for Exports.

The average value per ton was less than in Lagos, only £1·3 a ton; the proportion of foreign tonnage about the same, 16 per cent., and that of steamer tonnage 97 per cent. The increase of tonnage, both British and Foreign, has been excessively large, so much so, that it can only be accounted for by some great change such as the establishment of a line of steamers visiting the port.

Sierra Leone drew a larger proportion of its Imports from the

United Kingdom than either of its sister colonies, viz., 70 per cent. The balance was drawn chiefly from the United States, Germany, France, and West African ports. Of the Exports 37 per cent. were shipped to the United Kingdom, 56 per cent. to the same foreign countries, excepting Germany, and 6 per cent. to the Gambia. The Exports exceeded the Imports by 1 per cent. The Imports have decreased at each period except in 1878-80. The Exports decreased in 1875-77 and 1884-86. On the whole period the Exports decreased 14 per cent., and the Exports 25 per cent. The average value of the cargoes was the same as on the Gold Coast, £1·3 per ton; the proportion of foreign tonnage was rather less, 11 per cent., as also that of steamer tonnage, 94 per cent. The increase of British tonnage was 33 per cent.; foreign tonnage decreased 11 per cent.

Gambia. The smaller trade of this Settlement differed materially from that of the other three. It drew a fourth of its Imports from Sierra Leone, only 38 per cent. from the United Kingdom, and 35 per cent. from West African ports, the United States, and France. It exported 8 per cent. to the United Kingdom, and 88 per cent. to foreign countries, of which the greater portion went to France, and the remainder to West African ports, Madeira, the United States, and Italy, with a trifle to Sierra Leone and Gibraltar. The Imports exceeded the Exports by 11 per cent.; the Imports showed a large increase in 1878-80, and a decrease in each of the other triads. The Exports also showed a large increase in 1878-80, with a small increase in the next triad, and a decrease in the other two. The increase of Imports between 1872-74 and 1881-83 was 46 per cent.. but between the former period and 1884-86 was only 3 per cent. In like manner the increase of Exports in the first corresponding period was 44 per cent., while there was a decrease in the latter of 4 per cent.

The average value of cargoes was only £1·1 per ton, the proportion of foreign tonnage large, 29 per cent., explained by the large trade with France; and that of steamer tonnage also large, 90 per cent. The increase of tonnage has been very small. Although the increase of foreign has slightly exceeded that of the British, the proportion of foreign to British has decreased.

The shipping belonging on 31st December, 1887, to ports in West Africa, viz., Bathurst, Freetown, and

Lagos, consisted of 133 sailing vessels, of 2,543 tons, and six steam vessels, of 244 tons.

Canada contributed 3·7 per cent. to the Imports, and 3·9 per cent. to the Exports of the Empire. The Statistical Abstracts do not separate Canada from the "North "American Colonies," which include Newfoundland and Bermuda. These combined contributed 2·8 per cent. to the Imports, and 3·1 per cent. to the Exports of the United Kingdom.

Canada drew 40 per cent. of its Imports from the United Kingdom, only 2 per cent. from British Posses-sions, and 57 per cent. from Foreign Countries. Its Exports to the United Kingdom amounted to 47 per cent., 4 per cent. to British Possessions, and 49 per cent. to Foreign Countries. The Imports from the United States amounted to about 80 per cent., and the Exports thereto to about 90 per cent. of the whole Foreign Trade.

The distribution of the trade will be best seen in the following abstract :—

[000's omitted.]

	Imports.	Exports.
	£	£
United Kingdom	8,626,	8,724,
„ States	9,823,	8,282,
British West Indies and British Guiana	314,	362,
Other British Colonies	98,	104,
China and Japan	520,	6,
Germany	442,	55,
France	403,	63,
Spanish Possessions in West Indies	352,	167,
Brazil	252,	65,
Argentine Republic	—	146,
Other countries in Europe	406,	130,
„ elsewhere	162,	487,
Total	21,398,	18,591,

The total Imports exceeded the Exports by 15 per cent. The Imports have shown a decrease at each period except 1881-83, when there was a large increase, and the Exports differed only by showing a trifling increase in 1878-80. There was consequently a decrease on the whole period of 10 per cent. in Imports, and an increase of only 1·5 per cent. in the Exports.

As regards shipping, the average value of cargoes was £4·9 per ton ; the proportion of foreign tonnage was large, 40 per cent., and that of steam vessels exceptionally small,

59 per cent. The increase of British tonnage has been moderate, 19 per cent.; that of foreign tonnage has been much greater, 33 per cent., but the proportion of foreign to British tonnage has only increased from 35 to 40 per cent. The shipping belonging to Canada on 31st December, 1887, consisted of—

5,755 sailing vessels, of 982,196 tons, averaging 170 tons.
1,194 steam   „   108,814 „   „   99 „
──────   ──────────
6,949   1,091.010

The distribution of this among the several Provinces was as follows :—

	Sailing Vessels.		Steam Vessels.	
	Number.	Tons.	Number.	Tons.
Canada	1,201	133.482	321	37,007
„ inland only	978	129,103	601	51,117
	2,179	262,585	922	88,124
Nova Scotia	2,426	469,193	76	4,698
New Brunswick	883	220,772	79	5,955
Prince Edward's Island ...	211	26,955	14	2,076
British Columbia	56	2,691	63	7,961
Total	5,755	982,196	1,194	108,814

One hundred and ninety-nine sailing vessels, of 21,148 tons, and 85 steam vessels, of 2,674 tons, of which 2, of 283 tons, were of iron, were built in British North America in the year 1887.

Newfoundland. Its Import trade was nearly equally divided between the United Kingdom, Canada, and the United States. The remainder was almost confined to the British West Indies, Spain, and Portugal. Its Exports were differently distributed, viz., 36 to the United Kingdom, 10 per cent. to Canada and the British West Indies, and 54 per cent. to Foreign Countries, chiefly Portugal and Brazil, with smaller quantities to the United States, Spain, and Italy. The Imports exceeded the Exports by 41 per cent.

The progress of both Imports and Exports has been very unsteady : on the whole period the former have not increased by 1 per cent., and the latter have decreased by 17 per cent.

The average value of cargoes was £3·7 per ton, the proportion of foreign tonnage was only 3 per cent.; that

of steamer tonnage was also very small, 54 per cent.
The increase of British tonnage has been smaller even
than in Canada, 16 per cent., and there was a decrease of
70 per cent. in foreign tonnage. The shipping belonging
to Newfoundland on 31st December, 1887, consisted of
2,026 sailing vessels, of 86,047 tons, and of 26 steam
vessels, of 5.079 tons.

Bermuda drew 61 per cent. of its Imports from foreign countries,
chiefly from the United States, to which country it sent
the greater part of its Exports. The remainder of its
Imports were from the United Kingdom and British West
Indies; the amount of its Exports to the United Kingdom
was insignificant. The Imports were nearly three times
as large as the Exports. The progress of both has been
unsteady. Imports on the whole period have increased
3, and Exports 17 per cent. The average value of cargoes
was £1·2; the proportion of foreign tonnage 15 per cent.,
and of steamer tonnage 78 per cent. British tonnage has
increased 51 per cent., foreign has decreased 15 per cent.,
hence the proportion of foreign to British tonnage has
decreased from 25 to 15 per cent. The shipping belonging to Bermuda on 31st December, 1887, consisted of
23 sailing vessels, of 3,673 tons.

British Honduras carried on its trade exclusively with the
United Kingdom and foreign countries: in Imports in
the proportion of 43 and 57 per cent., and in Exports in
the proportion of 58 to 42 per cent. respectively. Its
chief foreign trade was with the United States, Central
America, and Mexico. It imported also from Germany
and France. The Imports exceeded the Exports by 4 per
cent. In 1875-77 there was a decrease in both Imports
and Exports : in the subsequent triads there was an
increase in both, but least in the latest. The average
value of cargoes was £2·6 the ton; the proportion of
foreign tonnage was exceptionally large, 56 per cent., and
that of steamer tonnage moderate, 75 per cent. The
increase of British tonnage was large, 92 per cent., but
that of foreign tonnage was nearly threefold, 259 per
cent. Hence the proportion of foreign to British has
increased from 39 to 56 per cent. The shipping belonging to Honduras on 31st December, 1887, consisted of
166 sailing vessels, of 3,937 tons, and 3 steam vessels, of
246 tons; 4 vessels of 37 tons were built in the colony in
1887.

Bahamas. Both Import and Export trade was carried on

chiefly with foreign countries, mainly the United States,
viz., 77 and 87 per cent. respectively. The trade with
British Possessions did not amount to 2 per cent. The
Imports exceeded the Exports by 30 per cent. The
progress of the Import trade has been irregular, and shows
a small decrease in the last triad. The Exports show an
increase in the last three triads. On the whole period
Imports have decreased by 1 per cent ; Exports have
increased by 7 per cent. The value of cargoes averaged
£1·6 a ton ; the proportion of foreign tonnage was higher
than in any other British Possession, except the neighbouring colony of the Turks Islands, viz., 72 per cent.,
and that of steamer tonnage was moderate, 68 per cent.
Tonnage has increased but slowly, foreign in a larger
proportion than British. The shipping belonging to the
Bahamas on 31st December, 1887, consisted of 557 sailing
vessels, of 23,886 tons, and 17 steam vessels, of 4,210 tons.

Turks Islands exhibited the smallest amount of trade among
the British Possessions, except Montserrat and the Virgin
Islands. Four-fifths of their trade was carried on with
foreign countries, chiefly the United States. They exported nothing to the United Kingdom.

The Exports exceeded the Imports by 10 per cent.
They, as well as the Imports, have considerably increased
in the last two triads; their increase in the whole period
has been : of Imports 16, and Exports 18 per cent. The
average value of cargoes was as low as £0·3 per ton ; the
proportion of foreign tonnage was 74 per cent., of steamer
tonnage 62 per cent., both low. There has been a large
increase of both British and foreign tonnage—133 and
169 per cent. respectively—the proportion of foreign
to British remains nearly the same.

Jamaica imported more than a half, 53 per cent., from the
United Kingdom, to which it exported 38 per cent. It
exported 55 per cent. to foreign countries, and 38 per
cent. to the United Kingdom. Its trade with the other
British West Indies, Mauritius, the East Indies, and
Australasia, amounted to 14 per cent. of the Imports,
and 7 per cent of the Exports. The former exceeded the
latter by 5 per cent. Imports showed a decrease in each
triad except the last, when there was an insignificant
increase of 0·5 per cent. Exports have been irregular;
in the last triad there was an equally insignificant
decrease of 0·6 per cent. On the whole period the
Imports have decreased largely, 14 per cent. ; the Ex-

ports have slightly increased, 2 per cent. The average
value of cargoes is about the same as that of Honduras
or Western Australia, £2·8 per ton; the proportion of
foreign tonnage is low, 24 per cent., differing in this
respect from its neighbour Honduras; and that of
steamer tonnage is higher, 79 per cent. The increase
of British and foreign tonnage has been moderate,
greater in the former, viz., 31 and 21 per cent. respectively. The shipping belonging to Jamaica on 31st
December, 1887, consisted of 66 sailing vessels of 3,439
tons, and 1 large steamer of 758 tons.

St. Lucia drew about an equal proportion of its Imports from
the United Kingdom and foreign countries, chiefly the
United States and France, and 13 per cent. from the
British West Indies, chiefly Barbados. It exported 53
per cent. to the United Kingdom, and 45 per cent. to
foreign countries, chiefly the United States, France, and
French West Indies. The Exports exceeded the Imports
by 29 per cent. The Imports showed a decrease in each
triad except 1881-83; the Exports no change, or an
increase, except in the last triad, in which there was a
heavy decrease, 38 per cent. The average value of
cargoes was very small, £0·5; the proportion of foreign
tonnage small, 12 per cent., and of steamer tonnage very
large, 94 per cent. The increase of British tonnage was
very large, 258 per cent.; that of foreign small, 17 per
cent. The above figures indicate some peculiarity in the
recent shipping trade of this island, or some change in
the form of making the returns, possibly the latter.
Perhaps the explanation may be found in the insertion
or omission of the passenger steamers periodically calling
at the island.

The shipping belonging to the smaller West India
Islands is not distinguished in the returns. The total
number of sailing ships on 31st December, 1887, was
337, of 19,091 tons, and 6 steam vessels, of 247 tons.
The shipping built in the same islands in 1887 consisted
of 35 sailing ships, of 664 tons.

St. Vincent received nine-tenths of its Imports in nearly equal
proportions from the United Kingdom and British West
Indies, probably chiefly Barbados, the returns not distinguishing the islands, with 12 per cent. from foreign
countries, chiefly from the United States. It exported
39 per cent. to the United Kingdom, and 54 per cent. to
foreign countries, chiefly the United States. The

L

Exports exceeded the Imports by 28 per cent. The Imports showed little variation, a small decrease until the last triad, when they fell off heavily, 26 per cent. The Exports showed a decrease at each period, heaviest at the last. Thus the Imports have fallen off 33, and the Exports 50 per cent. The average value of cargoes is very low, £0·4; also the proportion of foreign tonnage, 6 per cent., and that of steamer tonnage high, 91 per cent. A comparison of the increase of tonnage is vitiated by the remark applied to the corresponding comparison in St. Lucia.

Barbados drew 35 per cent. of its Imports from the United Kingdom, 22 per cent. from British Possessions, chiefly North America, India, British West Indies, and Guiana, and 43 per cent. from foreign countries. It exported 34 per cent. to the United Kingdom, 27 per cent. to British Possessions, chiefly British North America, West Indies, and British Guiana, and 39 per cent. to foreign countries, almost exclusively to the United States. The Exports exceeded the Imports by 12 per cent. The Imports have remained nearly stationary, except in the last triad, when they fell off 15 per cent. The Exports were also stationary in the six years 1878-83, but fell off 12 per cent. in 1884-86. The average value of cargoes was £1·7 per ton, the same as in Ceylon, and much higher than in any other of the Windward or Leeward Islands; the proportion of foreign tonnage was small, 10 per cent. There was no return of the steamer tonnage; British tonnage had increased largely, 146 per cent.; foreign tonnage remained the same.

Grenada imported little, 13 per cent., from foreign countries, chiefly the United States; 46 per cent. from the United Kingdom, and 41 per cent. from British Possessions, chiefly Barbados and Trinidad. It exported almost all its produce, 89 per cent., to the United Kingdom; the remainder to France, Trinidad, and Barbados. The Exports exceeded the Imports by 29 per cent. The changes in the Imports have not been great, but variable. In the Exports there was a large increase in 1881-83, and no falling off in 1884-86. On the whole period there has been an increase of Imports of 10 per cent., and on Exports of 27 per cent., exhibiting in these respects a striking contrast to the neighbouring Island of St. Vincent. The average value of cargoes was £1·0 a ton; the proportion of foreign tonnage was only 2 per cent.; that of steamer tonnage was high, 92 per cent. There has been a large increase of British tonnage, 104 per cent., and a large decrease of foreign tonnage, 74 per cent.

Tobago had the smallest trade among the Windward Islands. It imported 53 per cent. from the United Kingdom, and 46 per cent. from Barbados. It exported 69 per cent. to the United Kingdom, 16 per cent. to Barbados, and 15 per cent. to the United States and French West Indies. Its Exports exceeded its Imports by 22 per cent. Its Imports have fluctuated greatly: in the last triad they fell off 45 per cent. Its Exports have fallen off in increasing proportions in the last three triads: the fall in 1884-86 was 44 per cent. On the whole period the decrease of both Imports and Exports was 43 per cent.

The average value of cargoes was £0·4; the proportion of foreign tonnage only 1 per cent., while that of steamer tonnage was 91 per cent. The figures do not appear to admit of a comparison of the increase of tonnage.

Virgin Islands had the smallest trade among the Leeward Islands, or among the whole of the British Possessions. Their trade, amounting to a very few thousand pounds annually, was carried on exclusively with the United States. Their Imports exceeded their Exports by 20 per cent. Imports showed an increase and Exports a decrease. The average value of cargoes was £0·7 a ton. The proportion of foreign tonnage was 3 per cent. There was no steamer tonnage.

St. Kitts and Nevis imported 42 per cent. from the United Kingdom, 12 per cent. from Canada, the British West Indies and British Guiana, and 46 per cent. from foreign countries, chiefly the United States. They exported 27 per cent. to the United Kingdom, 5 per cent. to Canada and the West Indies, and 68 per cent. to foreign countries, chiefly to the United States, with a small quantity to the French West Indies and Italy. The Exports exceeded the Imports by 30 per cent. The Imports and Exports both showed a decrease in the first and last triads, and an increase in the two intermediate periods. On the whole period the Imports decreased 9 per cent., and the Exports 6 per cent. The average value of cargoes was £0·8 per ton; the proportion of foreign tonnage was very small, 5 per cent.; that of steamer tonnage was large, 87 per cent. The excessive apparent increase of tonnage must be referred to the cause suggested under the review of St. Lucia.

Antigua imported equal quantities from the United Kingdom and foreign countries, chiefly the United States, with 14 per cent. from British North America and West Indies. It exported 17 per cent. to the United Kingdom, 16 per cent. to Canada and the West Indies. and 67 per cent. to foreign countries, chiefly the United States. Its Exports exceeded its Imports by 10 per cent. Its Imports have been nearly stationary, except in the last triad, when they fell off 14 per cent. Its Imports increased largely in 1875-80, but fell off slightly in the next triad, and heavily in the last, 26 per cent. On the whole period the Imports fell off 14 per cent., and the Exports increased 15 per cent. In the three intermediate triads the increase was very much greater.

The average value of cargoes was £0·7 per ton; the proportion of foreign tonnage was very small, 5 per cent., and that of steamer tonnage large, 88 per cent. The increase of British tonnage was considerable, 34 per cent., and three times that of foreign tonnage, the proportion of foreign to British tonnage having greatly decreased.

Montserrat imported a third from the United Kingdom, 55 per cent. from Canada and other West Indian Islands, chiefly Antigua, St. Kitts, and Barbadoes, and 12 per cent. from foreign countries, chiefly the United States. It exported 22 per cent. to the United Kingdom, 8 per cent. to British Possessions, and 70 per cent. to foreign countries, chiefly the United States. The Imports exceeded the Exports by 25 per cent. The Imports showed a slight increase until the last triad, when they fell heavily, 21 per cent. The fall of Exports in the same triad was still heavier, 34 per cent. The average value of cargoes did not exceed £0·1, which is explained by the proportion of steamer tonnage being 96 per cent. The proportion of foreign tonnage was 1 per cent. The enormous increase of British tonnage can only be accounted for by the visits of passenger steamers.

Dominica imported about equal quantities from the United Kingdom and foreign countries, chiefly the United States and French West Indies, and 23 per cent. from the West Indies, chiefly Barbados. It exported 25 per cent. to the United Kingdom, 3 per cent. to Barbados, and 72 per cent. to the United States and French West Indies. The Exports exceeded the Imports by 4 per cent. The Imports were nearly stationary until the last triad, when they fell off 23 per cent.; the Exports have fallen off in each of the last two triads 18 per cent. On the whole period the decrease in Imports has been 16 per cent., and of Exports 28 per cent.

The character of the shipping resembled closely that of Montserrat. The average value of cargoes was only £0·3; the proportion of foreign tonnage 1 per cent., and of steamer tonnage 96 per cent. The growth of British tonnage is subject to the same remark as in previous comparisons. Foreign tonnage has largely decreased.

Trinidad imported 29 per cent. from the United Kingdom, 11 per cent. from British Possessions, viz., Canada, West Indies, Guiana, and the East Indies ; and 60 per cent. from foreign countries, chiefly from Venezuela, France, and other European countries. Gold constituted the principal portion of the Imports from Venezuela. Trinidad exported 53 per cent. to the United Kingdom, only 2 per cent. to the West Indies and British Guiana, and 45 per cent. to foreign countries, of which more than half was to the United States, and the remainder chiefly to Venezuela and France. The Exports exceeded the Imports by 0·2 per cent. There has been a continuous but diminishing increase both of Imports and Exports, amounting to 100 per cent. for the former, and 66 per cent. for Exports.

The average value of cargoes was moderately large, £4·2 per ton, approaching that of Canada or Tasmania. The proportion of foreign tonnage was high, 33 per cent.; that of steamer tonnage moderate, 76 per cent. The increase of British tonnage was 65 per cent.; that of foreign 47 per cent. The shipping belonging to Trinidad on 31st December, 1887, consisted of 85 sailing vessels, of 2,696 tons, and one steamer of 65 tons.

British Guiana imported 49 per cent. from the United Kingdom, 23 per cent. from British Possessions, of which more than half was from the East Indies, the rest from Canada and the West Indies ; and 28 per cent. from foreign countries, chiefly from the United States. It exported 72 per cent. to the United Kingdom, 5 per cent. to the West Indies and Canada, and 23 per cent. chiefly to the United States and Foreign West Indies, with a small quantity to Portugal and Holland. The Exports exceeded the Imports by 22 per cent. The Imports showed a small increase in the six years 1875-80, and a heavy falling off, 20 per cent., in the last triad ; the Exports showed an increase in 1881-83, and a still heavier falling off, 33 per

cent., in the last triad. On the whole period the Imports
had decreased 13 per cent., and the Exports 20 per cent.
If the comparison had been with the years 1881-83, both
Imports and Exports would have shown an increase.

The average value of cargoes was £5·2 per ton, which
was high, above that of Canada or the Cape of Good
Hope; the proportion of foreign tonnage was also high,
35 per cent., and that of steamer tonnage exceptionally
low, 44, which may seem to explain the high average
value of the cargoes. The total increase of tonnage was
small, 21 per cent. The returns for the earlier triad did
not distinguish foreign from British tonnage. The
shipping belonging to the Colony on 31st December, 1887,
consisted of 133 sailing vessels, of 5,566 tons, and 9 steam
vessels, of 849 tons. One sailing vessel of 18 tons was
built in the Colony in 1887.

Falkland Islands.   Their trade was almost exclusively with the
United Kingdom, 83 per cent. of Imports and 98 per cent.
of Exports. The remaining Imports, 17 per cent., came
from Chile and Uruguay. The 2 per cent. of Exports
were sent to Chile. The Exports exceeded the Imports
by 2 per cent. The progress of both Imports and Exports
has been continuous and rapid. On the whole period
Imports have increased 117 per cent., and Exports 158 per
cent. The average value of cargoes was £3·1 a ton; the
proportion of foreign tonnage was exceptionally large,
65 per cent.; that of steamer tonnage exceptionally small,
56 per cent. British tonnage has scarcely increased;
foreign tonnage has increased eight fold. The shipping
belonging to the Colony on 31st December, 1887, consisted of 7 sailing vessels, of 805 tons.

In concluding these separate reports, the caution must be
reiterated that there are no means of showing, or ascertaining,
how far the recorded amounts of value of Imports and Exports of
each Possession are affected by changes in the prices of commodities during the period under observation. Each however has
the means at hand of calculating this by the method explained and
applied to the trade of the United Kingdom in the early part of
this review.

Recapitulation.

It may be a convenience to the reader to sum up briefly the contents of this treatise, for such it has become.

The first part, which was published in March last, deals with the Tariffs of each part of the British Empire, their character, and financial results.

The second, published at the same time, exhibits the maritime trade of each part of the Empire, in the year 1885.

The third, contained in this volume, displays the maritime trade of the United Kingdom for a series of years from 1854 to 1887, and carries back the export trade to 1834.

The fourth, and last, part furnishes a similar review of the maritime trade of the whole Empire, and of each part of it, for the fifteen years from 1872 to 1886.

The following concise summary applies only to the last two parts; a more detailed one is prefixed to this volume.

The first chapter treats of the different methods of ascertaining the volume of trade, and the changes in the aggregates of value of Imports and Exports, from which may be deduced fluctuations in prices. It discusses the methods of Mr. Giffen and Mr. Bourne, suggests new methods, and advocates the monthly official publication of the results of their application to the Import and Export Trades of the country. In a series of curves the annual fluctuations in the Quantities, Value and Prices of Imports and Exports, are shown separately. The great and increasing amount of Coal exported, and its preponderance in the Returns of Tonnage outwards, are pointed out.

Dealing in the second chapter with Imports and Exports, the proportions in which each principal article contributes to the composition of the aggregates are shown;—also their average prices; a comparison of prices at different periods; a comparison of changes in the prices of raw materials with those of goods manufactured from them; the proportions between Imports and Exports and the Quantities of Goods re-exported and transhipped, and the countries to and from which they are conveyed.

The results of this examination are exhibited graphically in a Diagram, and to this are attached Tables of the character of the trade, and of the principal events, political and economical, which influenced, or resulted from, the trade of each year.

Dealing in the third chapter with Shipping, the increase of Tonnage inwards and outwards in the fifteen years from 1872 to 1886 is shown; the nationality of the shipping;—the amount of Passenger traffic, and of the Coasting trade; the Tonnage of vessels, sailing and steam, belonging to, and built in, the United Kingdom

—their size and the materials of which they were built, and the number of vessels struck off the Register.

In the fourth chapter the shipping belonging to the United Kingdom and employed in its trade is compared with that of other maritime countries, and some information is given as to the amount of British Shipping employed in the carrying trade of other countries.

The fourth part exhibits the Trade of the British Empire from 1872 to 1886.

The first chapter deals with the Imports and Exports of the whole Empire, of each British Possession, and of the same in groups.

The second gives a similar view of the shipping of the whole, and of each part.

The third furnishes a summary of the maritime trade of each British Possession, from India to the Falkland Islands,—and of its progress during the fifteen years 1872-86.

It would be impossible within a reasonable space to point out even the most prominent results exhibited in the preceding pages, but it may be permitted to direct attention to the suggestion for supplying to the public, monthly and with the least possible delay, the information which it seems easy to afford with regard to the monthly fluctuations in the volume and prices of Imports and Exports, and to the expediency of taking steps to obtain similar information from the several British Possessions. It is also desirable to point out to each Colonial Government, that it is in their own as well as in the imperial interest that the greatest possible amount of uniformity, accuracy and completeness should be introduced into their annual returns, so that each part of the British Dominions may be fairly and adequately represented in future similar reviews of the Empire, of which, it may be hoped, the present one is only a precursor. Possibly the British Government, if it were furnished annually by each British Possession with such an epitome of its trade as is contained in the summaries at pp. 123—50 of this volume, might publish it in the Board of Trade Journal, and thus keep the mercantile community throughout the Empire acquainted up to the latest date with the commercial movements of each part of the Dominions.

153

APPENDIX A.

CORRECTIONS AND ADDITIONS TO PARTS I AND II.

˙In consequence of the following Circular Despatch from Her Majesty's Secretary for the Colonies, replies have, up to the present date, been received from fifteen colonies, viz., Hong Kong, Ceylon, Mauritius, Western Australia, Tasmania, New Zealand, Cape of Good Hope, Natal, Lagos, Gold Coast, Gambia, Bahamas, Jamaica, Barbados, and British Guiana. The substance of these has been embodied in the annexed notes :—

" *Circular.*   " *Downing Street,*
    " SIR,   *3rd April,* 1888.
        " I have the honor to transmit to you a copy of a " ' Synopsis of the Tariffs and Trade of the British Empire,' " compiled by Sir R. Rawson, K.C.M.G., C.B., President of the " Statistical Society, for the Commercial Sub-committee of the " Imperial Federation League.

    " Sir R. Rawson has suggested that it would be a great " assistance to the Imperial Federation League, which has incurred " heavy expense in printing the volume, if your Government " would supplement, explain, or correct, as may appear desirable, " any of the statements contained in the remarks or the tables. " The information so collected could be embodied in an Appendix " to the second part of the work upon which Sir Rawson " W. Rawson is now employed.

                        (Signed)   " KNUTSFORD."

P. 9, line 7. After the word " duties" *read* " on enumerated articles."

„ 11 „ 13. Natal. The additional charge of 2½ per cent. is not levied on the value of the goods, but on the amount of duty. It is only a warehouse charge, levied on goods taken out of a bonded warehouse.

„ 15 „ 12. Mauritius. The Governor remarks : The accounts are recorded in rupees valued at 2s. each ; but for the last two years the average value for bills at sight has

P. 15, line 12. Mauritius been 1s. 4d. Hence all values and
—Contd.   duties relating to Mauritius in the
   synopsis should be reduced by one-
   third. The same remark applies to
   the Returns published by the Board
   of Trade.

„ 15, note. Ceylon. Dele note.

„ 16, line 4. Barbados. The old wine gallon is used ; one-fifth
   therefore must be added to the duty.

„ 21 „ 16. Cape of Good Hope. If Government articles and
   specie be excluded, for 21·50 *read*
   23·23.

„ 23 „ 34. Mauritius. The increase of duties is only apparent,
   being caused by an amalgamation of
   the old quay dues of $\frac{3}{4}$ per cent. with
   the old customs duties of $6\frac{1}{2}$ per cent.

„ 28, under head Cocoa. For 2/3¼ Barbados *read* 2/4.

„ „ „ Meat. For 15/0 Jamaica *read* 8/5.

„ 29 „ Cigars, &c. In Jamaica cigarettes pay 1/0 per
   lb. as manufactured tobacco.

„ „ „ Cider. For 0/2¾ Barbados *read* 0/2 Tnrk's
   Islands.

„ „ „ Wines, sparkling. For Barbados read Virgin
   Islands.

„ „ „ Gunpowder. For 20/10 Honduras *read* 100/0
   Jamaica.

„ „ „ „ For 0/6 New Zealand *read* 1/0
   Jamaica.

„ 34, line 11. Ceylon. The duties on cinchona, cocoa, coffee,
   and tea, which in 1885 yielded
   £5.745, are levied to meet the medi-
   cal wants of the planting districts,
   and are not included in the general
   revenue.

„ 35 „ 14. For Victoria *read* Western Australia.

„ 36 ., 22. Ceylon. In 1885 drawbacks amounted to £1,129.

„ „ „ „ Jamaica. In 1885 drawbacks amounting to £590
   were allowed on re-exports valued at
   £4,000. The total value of re-exports
   in that year, chiefly entered as supplies to shipping, was £24,567.

„ „ „ „ „ The cost of collection was estimated at
   5·58 per cent.

„ „ „ „ Ceylon. It was 4·5 per cent. on the gross
   revenue in 1885.

P. 3G line 29.   Jamaica.   To the table in this page may be added Jamaica, with the following figures: Duties, Specific, £187,418; *Ad val.*, £77,913; Total, £365,601; Percentage proportion, 70·7; 29·3.

„ „ „ „   Ceylon.   Add to same table for Ceylon: Specific Duties, £224,071; *Ad. val.*, £39,792; Total, £263,863; Percentage proportion, 84·9; 15·1.

„ 37 „ 1.   Jamaica.   To the table in this page add Jamaica, £732,532; £640,631; £115,270; £1,487,834; 49·2; 43·1; 7·7.

„ 41 „ 12.   „   It depends on the port of shipment.

„ „ „ „   It has been suggested that often all the manifests are improperly made out for the last port to which the vessel is destined.

„ 42 „ 11.   Cape of Good Hope.   For £69,069 *read* £69,064.

„ 43 „ 6.   Jamaica.   Transhipments are not included, and there is no transit trade.

„ 44 „ 24.   Cape of Good Hope.   Goods in transit are excluded from returns of Exports.

„ „ „ 37.   Natal.   It is pointed out that the trade with inland foreign States absorbs quite one-half of the Imports. This would apply to other Possessions similarly situated, and would affect all comparisons made between the value of Imports and amount of Customs Duties and the population in such possessions.

„ 45 „ 7.   Gold Coast.   Entries for consumption are recorded.

„ „ „ 22.   Natal.   Bullion and Specie are not included in the Imports. Gold raised in the colony is included in the Exports.

„ „ „ 44.   For £162,288 *read* £162,298.

„ 53 „ 17.   Jamaica.   Import duties are charged on Value at port of shipment.

„ „ „ „   Mauritius.   Since 1882 the duties have been charged on the declared first cost at the port of shipment, but for statistical record to this have been added cost of freight charges and exchange.

„ „ „ „   Natal.   10 per cent. is by law added to the invoice value of Imports in levying the duties, which is very much less than the amount of freight and charges.

Table 1.	Ceylon.	For Customs Duties £267,280, *read* £269,608.
	Natal.	As to additional duty of $2\frac{1}{2}$ per cent., see note above on p. 11.
	Tasmania.	Unenumerated articles are charged 10 per cent.
	Western Australia.	Collection of Customs duties, for £134,116 *read* £134,842.
	Cape of Good Hope.	If Government articles and specie be excluded, *read* in Column of Customs Duties and those following for £1,073,372, £1,040,098; for 32·3, 31·3; for 17·1, 16·3; for 21·50, 23·23; for 22·35, 24·07.
Tables II, III, and IV.		Cape of Good Hope. Changes corresponding to the above. See also note above, Natal, p. 44.
Table V.	Gold Coast.	The tariff duties on malt liquor and spirits are levied on the old wine gallon.
	Lagos.	Lead pays 1/2 per lb.
	Ceylon.	Tin and zinc pay $0/11\frac{1}{4}$ per cwt.
	Natal.	As regards additional duty of $2\frac{1}{2}$ per cent., see note above, Natal, p. 11.
	Barbados.	Cocoa, prepared, and chocolate pay 8%. In consequence of the difference between the old and Imperial gallons liquors pay the following duties:—

Malt liquor, in wood, per imp. gal. $0,4\frac{1}{2}$.

  ,, in bottle per doz. 2,6

Spirits, rum and gin, per imp. gal. 6/0

  ,, other ,, 9/0

Wine, sparkling, in bots., per doz. 5 0

  ,, all others per imp gal. 1/1

	Jamaica.	Biscuits, sweet, charged as confectionery, pay $12\frac{1}{2}$%.

Cocoa, prepared, and chocolate, pay $12\frac{1}{2}$%.

Coffee and rum, foreign, are prohibited for consumption.

Molasses are free.

Cigarettes are charged 1/0 per lb. as manufactured tobacco.

Salt pays 1/0 per 100 lbs.

Copper and other metals $12\frac{1}{2}$%.

Table V. Tasmania. Unenumerated articles pay 10% *ad val.*
Pickles, for pints *read* quarts.
Cape of Good Hope. Wheat flour pays 3/11 per cwt.
Copper pays 15 %.
Copper and iron ores, if Foreign, pay
15 %.
Tin in blocks pays 15 %.
Tasmania. Linen Piece Goods, Caoutchouc wares,
and Gutta Percha pay 10%.
Gold Coast. Cartridges, not filled, pay 1/0 per 100.
Ceylon. Blasting Powder pays 15/0 per 100 lbs.
Barbados. Arms, guns, pay 10/0 each.
Gunpowder pays 0/3 per lb., charged
for storing in Government magazine.
Cement pays 1/3 per barrel.
Starch pays 1/1½ per cwt.
Jamaica. Shingles, Cypress, pay 6/0 per 1,000 ;
other kinds 4/0.
Cape of Good Hope. Hoop iron pays 15 %.
Sewing Machines pay ,,
Silver and plated wares 15 %.
Table VI. Ceylon. For £3,070,751 *read* £3,071,751.
For 4,889, 0·41, 0·16, *read* 10,508, 0·90,
0·34. See note above at p. 34.
Table VIII. Ceylon. For 3,102, 75, 1,956, 73·3, 1·8, 58·3,
read 3,056, 121, 1,955, 72·2, 2·8, 58·2.
Tasmania. For 1,124, 1,317, 14·3, 85·7, *read* 1,123,
1,314, 14·5, 85·5.
Cape of Good Hope. The year ends 31st December.
Table VIIIA. Ceylon. For 3,010, 3,885, 689, 7,586, 39·7, 51·3,
9·1, *read* 3,013, 3,871, 736, 7,620,
39·5, 50·8, 9·7.
Near the bottom. Total of British Empire, for
£1,048,342 *read* £1,046,342.
Table XI. Ceylon. Imports from China, for £1,756 *read*
£2,171.
Total Exports, for £25,412 *read*
£25,891.
Some other trifling changes need not be
specified.
Table XII. Cape of Good Hope. Column of Imports :
United Kingdom, for £3,878,071 *read*
£3,377,537.
After Sandwich Bay *read* Foreign Possessions.

Table XII. Cape of Good Hope—*Contd.*   Portuguese Territories,
for £1,919 *read* £2,403; Native
States, for £1,988 *read* £1,088.
Sweden, *read* £24,653.
Column of Exports:
Opposite Italy insert 15; countries not
distinguished *read* 192.
Jamaica.   Column of Imports.   Those from
Foreign States not distinguished are
chiefly from Colon.
Table XIV. Gold Coast. Goods   entered   for   consumption,
£449,947.

The Governor of the Bahamas reports the following changes made
since the publication of the first part :—
Tobacco raw, Salt, Steam Launches,
Half Barrels, &c. used for packing,
Staves, Hoops, and Heads for making
Barrels, exempted from duty.
Hemp, hitherto free, charged with
20 % *ad val.*
Bounty of ½*d.* per lb. on exportation
of Sisal Fibre, or Hemp, in quantities
of not less than one ton avoirdupois.

The Governor of New Zealand sends, with the Trade Statistics
for the year 1887, a copy of an entirely new tariff, dated 8th July,
1888. An analysis of this tariff in the same form as that employed
in Table I of the former Part for the preceding tariff shows—

187 articles enumerated exempt from duty.
All articles unenumerated exempt from duty; also such articles
as may from time to time be specified by the Commissioner
of Customs, which are suited only for, and are to be used
wholly in the fabrication of goods within the Colony.
242 articles charged.
326 rates of duty, of which—
143 specific.
183 *ad valorem*, viz., at 5 per cent. 3
„   10   „   1
„   15   „   49
„   20   „   110
„   25   „   20

In addition to a Customs Duty of 3 6 per lb., Tobacco pays an
Excise Duty of 1/0 per lb., and Cigars and Cigarettes, in addition
to 7/6 per lb., pay an Excise Duty of 1/6 per lb.

APPENDIX B.—*Note to Statement at pp.* 52 *and* 53.

The following is a collocation of the annual aggregates of the prices of the chief articles of Import and Export, as stated in Tables X and XI, in each year from 1854 to 1886, showing by a difference of type as well as by the figures whether the aggregates indicate a rising or a falling market, and how far the fluctuations agree with those indicated in Table I :—

Years.	Imports.		Exports.	
	Average Value per Ton. As in Table I.	Aggregate of Value of Imports, as in Table X. Food and Raw Materials.	Aggregate Value of Exports as in Table XI.	Average Value per Ton, as in Table I.
	£	£	£	£
1854	19·3	49.097	22.9c8	14·7
'55	20·4	48,308	21,851	14·0
'56	20·9	48,106	22,190	14·4
'57	21·5	48,879	22,574	14·1
'58	18·6	45,165	21,157	14·1
'59	19·7	47,464	21,353	15·2
1860	20·9	49.107	21,228	15·2
'61	20·5	46,609	20,728	14·1
'62	21·0	47,706	21,567	14·2
'63	22·3	46,979	24.003	16·5
'64	24·3	46,811	26.070	17·4
'65	22·3	46,631	25,086	17·0
'66	22·2	47,828	25,741	17·1
'67	20·6	48.406	24,786	15·2
'68	21·2	48,766	23.567	14·7
'69	20·4	47,420	23,434	14·9
1870	20·3	46,449	22,988	14·6
'71	20·1	45,271	23,311	14·9
'72	19·8	45,944	29,424	16·3
'73	19·7	45,501	32,852	16·2
'74	19·4	44,181	29,087	15·1
'75	19·6	43,578	25,997	13·8
'76	17·8	43,562	23,613	11·9
'77	17·8	44,901	22,307	11·9
'78	17·3	41,926	21,216	11·4
'79	17·2	39,792	19,534	10·9
1880	17·1	41,595	20,597	11·1
'81	17·1	40,518	18,379	11·3
'82	16·6	40,436	18,753	11·1
'83	16·2	40,020	19,169	10·4
'84	15·8	37,641	18,034	10·1
'85	14·4	35,006	17,981	9·3
'86	14·1	32,474	17,488	9·2

Bearing in mind that when two consecutive years exhibit the same average or aggregate they are placed in the same category of ascent or descent, and that the slightest difference in the amount may change the category, it is remarkable to what extent the aggregates, heterogeneous as they are, agree with the averages derived from so different a source, especially in the first half of the period, before the disturbing influences of the years 1872-74.

This agreement is further shown in the following comparison of the fluctuations of an annual standard for Exports calculated from the above averages, taking the aggregate of the first year 1854 as equivalent to the average value of a ton of Exports in that year, as shown in Table I :—

Years.	Average Value per Ton as in Table I.	Annual Fluctuations in Prices, Calculated on above Aggregates.	Years.	Average Value per Ton as in Table I.	Annual Fluctuations in Prices, Calculated on above Aggregates.
1854	14·7	14·7	1870	14·6	14·7
'55	14·0	14·0	'71	14·9	14·9
'56	14·4	14·2	'72	16·3	18·9
'57	14·1	14·1	'73	16·2	21·2
'58	14·1	13·5	'74	15·1	18·7
'59	15·2	13·6	'75	13·8	16·7
			'76	11·9	15·1
1860	15·2	13·6	'77	11·9	14·3
'61	14·1	13·3	'78	11·4	13·6
62	14·2	13·8	'79	10·9	12·5
'63	14·5	15·4	1880	11·1	13·1
,64	17·4	16·7	'81	11·3	11·7
65	17·0	16·1	'82	11·1	11·9
'66	17·1	16·5	'83	10·4	12·2
'67	15·2	15·9	'84	10·1	12·5
'68	14·7	15·1	'85	9·3	11·4
'69	14·9	15·0	'86	9·2	11·1

It will be seen how, with the exception of the years 1859-60, for which doubtless an explanation may be found, the two columns run in close agreement up to the year 1872, when that abnormal rise in prices took place, and caused a disturbance in the former equilibrium of these arbitrary aggregates, from which they have not yet recovered. But the error may be detected and measured by a reference to the recorded facts of the amount of tonnage and value of Exports in these years; because if the average arbitrary price in 1886 remained as high as £11·1, the recorded tonnage would not have been sufficient to have taken away the recorded value, estimated on the same relative basis as before the year 1872.

This incongruity arises from the very great influence of the export of coal, which has been since ascertained and described at pp. 33—39.

(For sources of information, see Explanatory Notes, etc.)

Explanatory Notes to Appendix D.

Item.
1. Furnished by Secretary to Central Chamber of Agriculture.
2. From Government Gazette.
3. Same as No. 1.

4. ⎧ Quantities taken from Appendix No. 9 to First Report of
5. ⎨ Royal Commission on Depression of Trade and Industry,
   ⎩ 1885. Continued from Annual Statistical Abstracts of
   the United Kingdom.

Prices from Annual Statistical Abstracts.

6. ⎱
7. ⎰ Quantities and value from Annual Statistical Abstracts.

8. ⎱ Imports and consumption from same as Nos. 4 and 5,
8A. ⎰ Appendix No. 11.

Price and value from Annual Statistical Abstracts.

9. ⎱
9A. ⎰ Same as Nos. 4 and 5, Appendix No. 14, and annual abstracts.

10.	,,	15	,,
11.	,,	2	,,
12.	,,	26	,,
13.	,,	27	,,
14.	,,	28	,,
15.	,,	33	,,
16.	,,	32	,,
17.	,,	30	,,
18.	,,	40	,,
19.	,,	41.	
20.	,,	42.	

21. For years 1876 to 1881, from Mr. Giffen's paper on the
Use of Import and Export Statistics, in "Journal of
"Royal Statistical Society," June, 1882.
For subsequent years, compiled from half-yearly returns in
the "Statist."

22. Furnished by Mr. H. C. Burdett; compiled from his annual
volumes of "Official Intelligence."

Generally—Figures for 1887, where not otherwise stated, have
been obtained from official sources.

LONDON :

HARRISON AND SONS, PRINTERS IN ORDINARY TO HER MAJESTY,

ST. MARTIN'S LANE.

www.ingramcontent.com/pod-product-compliance
Lightning Source LLC
Chambersburg PA
CBHW020534270326
41927CB00006B/571